Kitchen & Bath Products

Materials ◆ Equipment ◆ Surfaces

Ellen Cheever, CMKBD, ASID

Professional Resource Library

About The National Kitchen & Bath Association

As the only non-profit trade association dedicated exclusively to the kitchen and bath industry, the National Kitchen & Bath Association (NKBA) is the leading source of information and education for all professionals in the field.

NKBA's mission is to enhance member success and excellence by promoting professionalism and ethical business practices, and by providing leadership and direction for the kitchen and bath industry.

A non-profit trade association with more than 25,000 members in North America and overseas, it has provided valuable resources for industry professionals for more than forty years. Its members are the finest professionals in the kitchen and bath industry.

NKBA has pioneered innovative industry research, developed effective business management tools, and set groundbreaking standards for safe, functional and comfortable design of kitchens and baths.

NKBA provides a unique, one-stop resource for professional reference materials, seminars and workshops, distance learning opportunities, marketing assistance, design competitions, consumer referrals, job and internship opportunities and opportunities for volunteer leadership activities.

Recognized as the kitchen and bath industry's education and information leader, NKBA provides development opportunities and continuing education for all levels of professionals. More than 100 courses, as well as a certification program with three internationally recognized levels, help kitchen and bath professionals raise the bar for excellence.

For students entering the industry, NKBA offers Supported and Endorsed Programs, which provide NKBA-approved curriculum at more than 47 learning institutions throughout North America.

NKBA helps members and other industry professionals stay on the cutting-edge of an ever-changing field through the Association's Kitchen/Bath Industry Show, one of the largest trade shows in the country.

NKBA offers membership in four different categories: Industry, Associate, Student and Honorary. Industry memberships are broken into eleven different industry segments. For more information, visit NKBA at www.nkba.org.

THANK YOU TO OUR SPONSORS

The National Kitchen & Bath Association recognizes with gratitude the following companies who generously helped to fund the creation of this industry resource.

PATRONS

www.americanwoodmark.com

www.kohler.com

BENEFACTORS

www.monogram.com

www.subzero.com   www.wolfappliance.com

CONTRIBUTOR

www.groheamerica.com

SUPPORTERS

www.nyloft.net

www.showhouse.moen.com

TOTO®

www.totousa.com

DONORS

Rev-A-Shelf | Viking Range Corp. | Whirlpool Corp.

This book is intended for professional use by residential kitchen and bath designers. The procedures and advice herein have been shown to be appropriate for the applications described; however, no warranty (expressed or implied) is intended or given. Moreover, the user of this book is cautioned to be familiar with and to adhere to all manufacturers' planning, installation and use/care instructions. In addition, the user is urged to become familiar with and adhere to all applicable local, state and federal building codes, licensing and legislation requirements governing the user's ability to perform all tasks associated with design and installation standards, and to collaborate with licensed practitioners who offer professional services in the technical areas of mechanical, electrical and load bearing design as required for regulatory approval, as well as health and safety regulations.

Information about this book and other association programs
and publications may be obtained from the
National Kitchen & Bath Association
687 Willow Grove Street, Hackettstown, New Jersey 07840
Phone (800) 843-6522
www.nkba.org

ISBN 1-887127-54-2

First Edition 2006

Illustrations by: Jerry Germer, Paula Philport and Jim Grinestaff

Top cover photo courtesy Tom Trzcinski, CMKBD – Pittsburgh, Pennsylvania
Bottom cover photo courtesy Americh

Published on behalf of NKBA by Fry Communications, Irvine, California

Peer Reviewers

Timothy Aden, CMKBD	Jim Krengel, CMKBD
Julia Beamish, Ph.D, CKE	Chris LaSpada, CPA
Leonard V. Casey	Elaine Lockard
Ellen Cheever, CMKBD, ASID	Phyllis Markussen, Ed.D, CKE, CBE
Hank Darlington	Chris J Murphy, CKD, CBD, CKBI
Dee David, CKD, CBD	David Newton, CMKBD
Peggy Deras, CKD, CID	Roberta Null, Ph.D
Kimball Derrick, CKD	Michael J Palkowitsch, CMKBD
Tim DiGuardi	Paul Pankow, CKBI
Kathleen Donohue, CMKBD	Jack Parks
Gretchen L. Edwards, CMKBD	Kathleen R. Parrott, Ph.D, CKE
JoAnn Emmel, Ph.D	Al Pattison,CMKBD
Jerry Germer	Les Petrie, CMKBD
Pietro A. Giorgi, Sr., CMKBD	Becky Sue Rajala, CKD
Tom Giorgi	Betty L. Ravnik, CKD, CBD
Jerome Hankins, CKD	Robert Schaefer
Spencer Hinkle, CKD	Klaudia Spivey, CMKBD
Max Isley, CMKBD	Kelly Stewart, CMKBD
Mark Karas, CMKBD	Thomas Trzcinski, CMKBD
Martha Kerr, CMKBD	Stephanie Witt, CMKBD

TABLE OF CONTENTS

Kitchen & Bath Products

Introduction

A key ingredient in any successful new kitchen or bathroom project is the right match between the client's dreams, the project budget and the materials, equipment and surfaces specified by the design professional.

This book is a comprehensive reference source describing typical materials, equipment and surfaces used in all facets of residential kitchen and bath design. Its focus is on basic knowledge for new members of our industry as well as seasoned professionals who want to expand their knowledge into new areas (for example, the kitchen designer who is exploring the options available for residential bath design).

The broad areas of the industry's discipline are divided into cabinets (Chapter 1), appliances (Chapter 2), fixture materials (Chapter 3), fixture design and planning (Chapter 4), fitting materials and engineering (Chapter 5), bathroom fitting design and engineering (Chapter 6), and surfacing materials (Chapter 7).

Kitchen & Bath Products

CHAPTER 1: The Storage Systems: The Kitchen and Bathroom Cabinet Industry Today

At one time, virtually all kitchen cabinets were custom built by local cabinet shops or mills for each house. Today, a great majority of kitchen cabinet systems are produced in highly sophisticated manufacturing facilities, both here in North America and internationally. As a kitchen specialist, you may work for a retail organization representing specific cabinet manufacturers, for a cabinet manufacturer or distributor, or actually fabricate the cabinets in your own woodworking shop or milling facility.

Regardless of the type of business you are affiliated with in North America, cabinet specifiers work with three broad categories. Within each of these sources, the quality levels, production costs, retail selling price, delivery schedules and reliability factors vary. In the United States, stock, semi-custom and custom cabinet definitions are outlined below. (In the international community, the United States definition of semi-custom is considered custom.)

Stock

Stock cabinet manufacturers offer a full range of cabinets in specified sizes. The cabinets are made in quantity and are then shipped to a distributor's or manufacturer's warehouse so they are available for quick delivery. Because the cabinets are produced in quantity, the assembly lines cannot be stopped for special units. Therefore, the cabinet manufacturer's catalog generally reflects the entire product offering. Stock manufacturers use market research so that they offer the most popular finishes and door styles.

This type of manufacturing method provides the specifier good value because of the economies of manufacturing. The biggest advantages of stock cabinetry are its availability, specified quality level and consistency of service from these large, stable manufacturers. Stock cabinets offer an excellent product for a project faced with budget or time constraints. Because styles and special sizes are limited, you should investigate the breadth of the line before designing with the product. However, the designer need not forego creative cabinet design with this type of cabinet. Once familiar with

CABINET TYPES

the line, consider adapting specific case types to usage ideas appropriate for the project you are working on. For example, use wall cabinets as shallow base units by adding a toe-kick.

Stock cabinets do vary in quality levels. Some lines use doors of mismatched or lower-quality woods. They may use thin laminates or actual paper products to simulate wood on finished sides. The parts of the case may be glued together with no mechanical fasteners, which is not as durable a method of case construction as combining both glue and mechanical fasteners. Make sure you carefully compare the construction of the stock cabinets you are considering for the project you are designing. For example, one line may be just right for a laundry room application, while a sturdier product may be required for the adjacent kitchen.

Semi-Custom

Semi-custom cabinets are produced by both stock and custom manufacturers. This type of product is produced on an assembly line basis, but the offerings include more interior fittings in the form of accessories and some custom cabinet size possibilities. Typically, a wider finish and style palette will be offered as well.

This product combines the advantage of an assembly line process with the ability to create limited custom cabinet sizes. Traditionally, more door styles and finishes are also available in a semi-custom product.

Semi-custom cabinets come in a wide variety of quality and price levels. Because they may be high on style but limited in their size offering, review the manufacturer's catalog carefully before beginning the design process.

For international cabinet producers who focus on a finely engineered specific style—used to define their cabinet branding—extensive customization is neither recommended nor offered. Therefore, the manufacturing definition of semi-custom defines their highest level of product offering.

Custom

Custom cabinet manufacturers make one kitchen at a time. The cabinets are not produced until the kitchen has been designed and all details are finalized. Custom cabinets may be made by a local fabricator or in a large manufacturing facility. Generally, they publish a specifications manual listing a range of specific cabinet sizes, but special sizes are available for a perfect fit. One-of-a-kind, hand-made specialty pieces, such as mantel hoods, wood turned posts, curved/angled cabinetry elements and free-standing furniture pieces are also available.

These totally custom "built-to-order" cabinets are considered "furniture grade" cabinet systems. These manufacturers generally offer the latest in functional hardware, technology, construction methods and case materials, and the most extensive array of accessories available. These companies offer new, trendsetting styles and finishes to the market. These cabinets are also the most expensive and take the longest to get. Much like custom furniture, an eight to twenty-week delivery time is to be expected.

DEFINITIONS OF KITCHENS

- Custom-made, English "Bespoke" or "One-off" Kitchen: A set of cabinets made specifically for one client or one project.

- Fitted Kitchen: A set of cabinets sized and scribed to the room, allowing the cabinetry to become part of the woodwork of the house.

- Unfitted Kitchen: A set of cabinets, which are not scribed to the walls, ceiling or floor of the room. Although they are secured to the wall for stability, they appear more like furniture than casework.

CABINET MANUFACTURING SYSTEMS

As you consider cabinet options, one of the first decisions you must make is whether you will represent a cabinet featuring frame construction or one featuring frameless construction. Your product offering may be manufactured in North America, or may be imported from another part of the world.

Because the cabinet industry is an international one, there are two common methods of sizing cabinets: the English imperial system, based on inches, and the international metric standard. Since both dimensioning systems are used by cabinet companies, the typical United States cabinet company dimensions in inches and the corresponding typical Canadian cabinet company dimensions in centimeters are listed. An exact translation is called a "hard conversion." The resulting converted inches or centimeters is a useless set of numbers. Therefore, actual sizing is listed on the following page. Designers must be aware that the two measuring systems are not exactly the same sizing.

As you consider representing a cabinet line make sure you find out how the cabinet is sized: *are the cabinets sized on an imperial system; are they sized in a metric system; or, are they a hybrid of the two?* This is important as there may be slight differences in cabinet case sizing that will affect the cabinet's fit with adjacent appliances and other pieces of equipment.

MATHEMATICAL CONVERSIONS
(Courtesy of Niagara Artcraft Woodwork Co. Ltd.)

- To convert inches to centimeters you must multiply the inches by 2.54 e.g., 23-5/8" (23.63") x 2.54 = 60 cm

- To convert centimeters to inches you must divide the centimeters by 2.54 e.g., 60 cm ÷ 2.54 = 23.63" (23-5/8")

| From Centimeters to Inches | | | From Inches to Centimeters | | |
mm	cm	inches	inches	mm	cm
2.5	0.25	1/8"	1/16"	1.59	0.16
5.0	0.50	3/16"	1/8"	3.18	0.32
7.5	0.75	5/16"	1/4"	6.35	0.64
10.0	1.00	3/8"	3/8"	9.53	0.95
12.5	1.25	1/2"	1/2"	12.70	1.27
15.0	1.50	5/8"	5/8"	15.88	1.59
17.5	1.75	11/16"	3/4"	19.05	1.91
20.0	2.00	3/4"	7/8"	22.23	2.22
22.5	2.25	7/8"	1"	25.40	2.54
25.0	2.50	1"	3"	76.20	7.62
50.0	5.00	2"	6"	152.40	15.24
100.0	10.00	4"	9"	228.60	22.86
150.0	15.00	5-7/8"	12"	304.80	30.48
200.0	20.00	7-7/8"	15"	381.00	38.10
250.0	25.00	9-7/8"	18"	457.20	45.72
300.0	30.00	11-13/16"	21"	533.40	53.34
350.0	35.00	13-3/4"	24"	609.60	60.96
400.0	40.00	15-3/4"	27"	685.80	68.58
450.0	45.00	17-11/16"	30"	762.00	76.20

From Centimeters to Inches			From Inches to Centimeters		
mm	cm	inches	inches	mm	cm
500.0	50.00	19-11/16"	33"	838.20	83.82
550.0	55.00	21-5/8"	36"	914.40	91.44
600.0	60.00	23-5/8"	39"	990.60	99.06
650.0	65.00	25-9/16	42"	1066.80	106.68
700.0	70.00	27-9/16"	45"	1143.00	114.30
750.0	75.00	29-1/2"	48"	1220.00	122.00
762.0	76.20	30"	51"	1295.40	129.54
800.0	80.00	31-1/2"	54"	1371.60	137.16
850.0	85.00	33-1/2"	57"	1447.80	144.78
900.0	90.00	35-7/16"	60"	1524.00	152.40
915.0	91.50	36"	72"	1828.80	182.88
950.0	95.00	37-3/8"	84"	2133.60	213.36
1000.0	100.00	39-3/8"	96"	2438.40	243.84
1050.0	105.00	41-5/16"	108"	2743.20	274.32
1100.0	110.00	43-5/16"	120"	3048.00	304.80
1150.0	115.00	45-1/4"			
1200.0	120.00	47-1/4"			
1220.0	122.00	48"			
1250.0	125.00	49-3/16"			
1300.0	130.00	51-3/16"			
1350.0	135.00	53-1/8"			
1400.0	140.00	55-1/8"			
1450.0	145.00	57-1/16"			
1500.0	150.00	59-1/16"			
1800.0	180.00	70-7/8"			
2130.0	213.00	83-7/8"			
2154.0	215.40	87-1/8"			
2410.0	241.00	94-7/8"			
2440.0	244.00	96-1/16"			

Figure 1.1 *The Storage Systems: Typical Imperial Cabinet Dimensions*

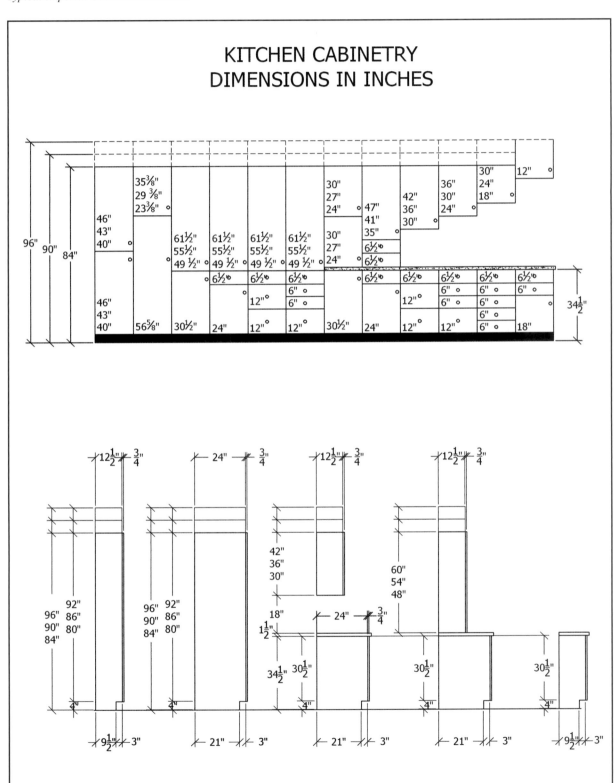

VANITY CABINETRY
DIMENSIONS IN INCHES

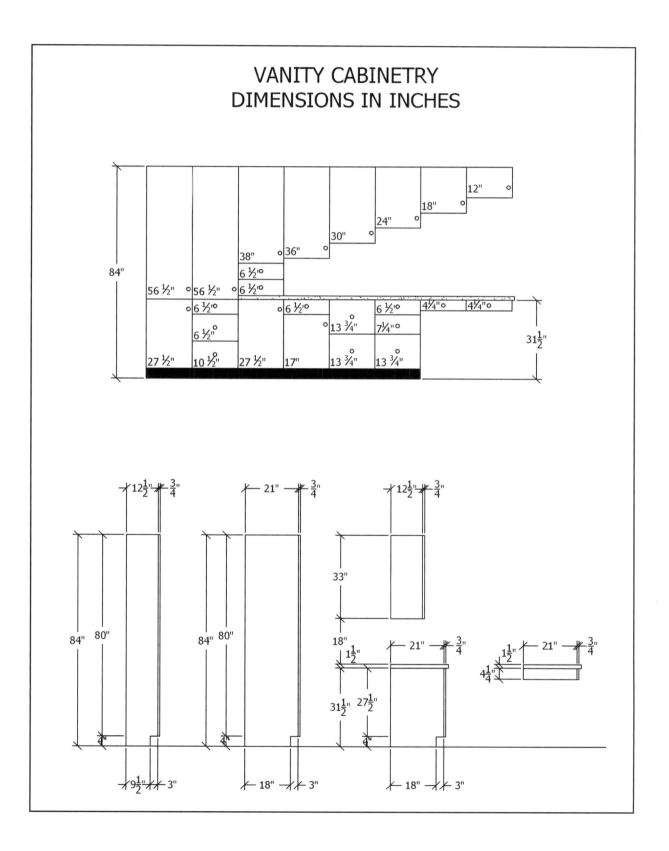

DESK CABINETRY
DIMENSIONS IN INCHES

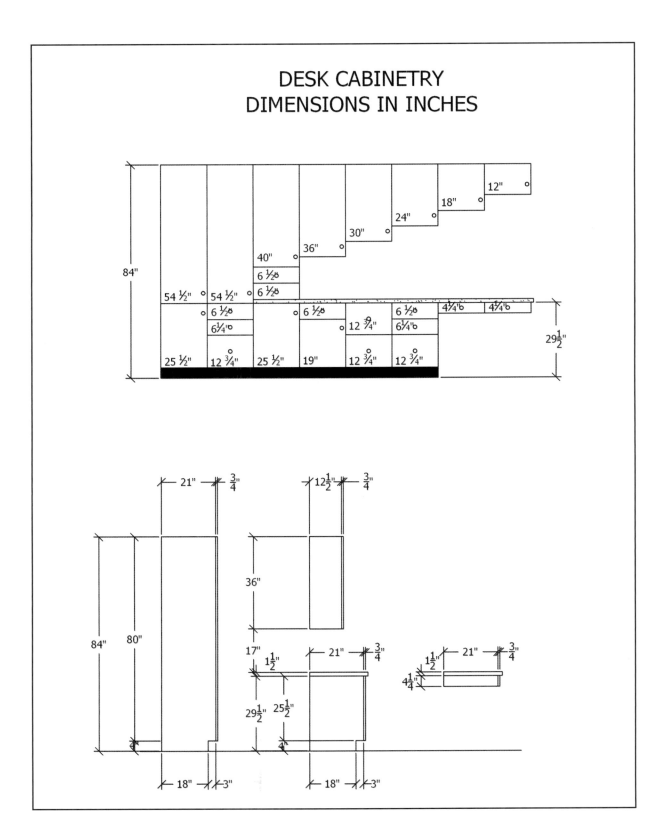

Figure 1.2 *The Storage Systems: Typical Metric Cabinet Dimensions*

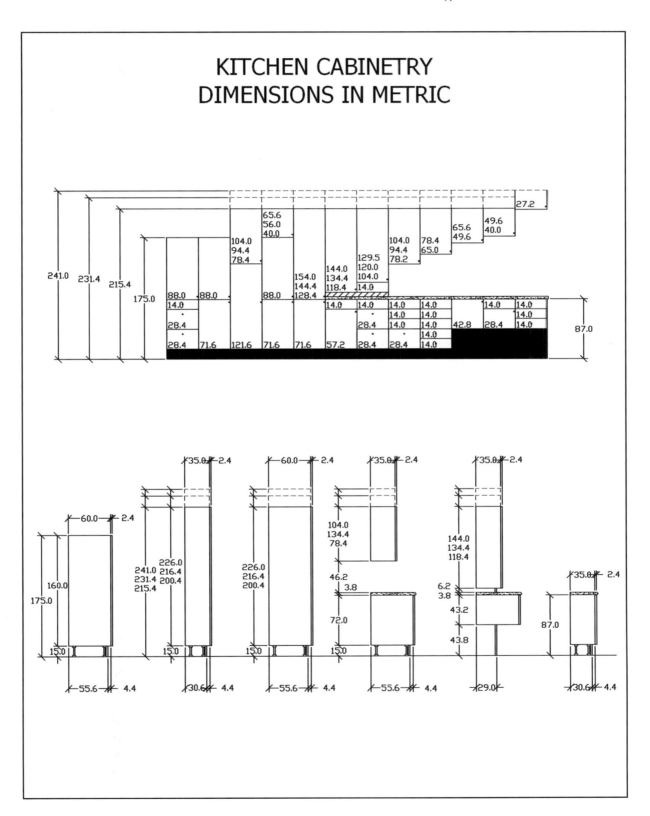

KITCHEN CABINETRY
DIMENSIONS IN METRIC

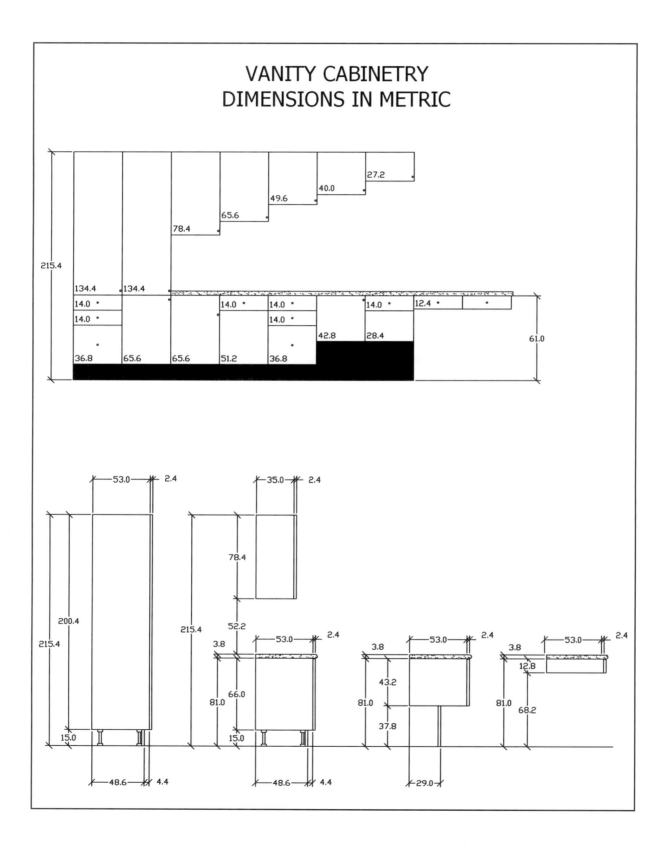

VANITY CABINETRY
DIMENSIONS IN METRIC

DESK CABINETRY
DIMENSIONS IN METRIC

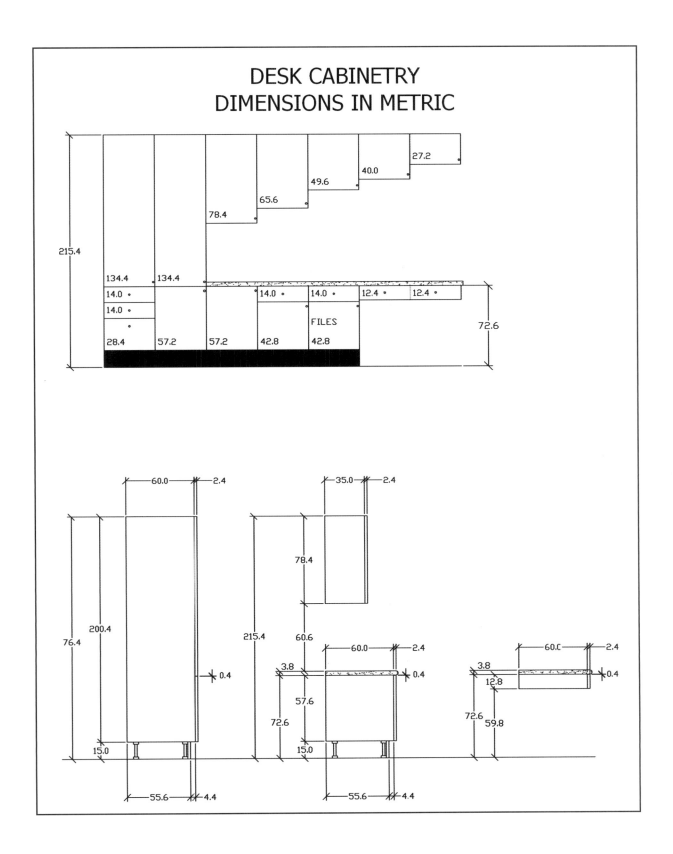

DEFINITIONS

- **Dowel**: A short, round wooden stick with ends cut flat. In cabinet construction, they are chiefly used to reinforce the corners.

- **Lap Joint**: A joint made by overlapping two ends or edges and fastening them together.

- **Mortise-and-Tenon**: Slot cut into a board, plank or timber, usually edgewise. The mortise receives a projecting part, or tenon, of another board, plank or timber to form a joint. Many years ago, mortise-and-tenon joints were used in house building. Today, they are mainly used in assembling cabinets.

- **Mullion/Muntin**: A vertical post or other upright that divides a window or other opening into two or more panes. Sometimes only ornamental.

- **Rail**: A cross member of a panel door, or a frame cabinet face.

- **Stile**: Vertical flanking members on a panel door or a frame cabinet face in which the horizontal top and bottom rails are secured to.

Typical Imperial Cabinet Widths	Imperial Conversion	Typical Metric Cabinet Widths
6"	5-7/8"	15 cm
9"	11-3/4"	30 cm
12"	15-3/4"	40 cm
15"	17-3/4"	45 cm
18"	19-3/4"	50 cm
21"	23-5/8"	60 cm
24"	25-5/8"	65 cm
27"	27-5/8"	70 cm
30"	31-1/2"	80 cm
33"	35-1/2"	90 cm
36"	37-3/8"	95 cm
39"	39-1/2"	100 cm
42"	41-1/2"	105 cm
45"	43-1/4"	110 cm
48"	45-1/4"	115 cm
51"	47-1/4"	120 cm

Frame Construction

In frame cabinet construction, component parts make up the sides, back, top and bottom of the cabinet. These parts are then joined together and attached to the face frame, which is the primary support for the cabinet. Doors and drawers are then fit in one of three ways: flush with the frame (called "inset"), partially overlaying the frame (called 1/4 overlap or lip), or completely overlaying the frame.

Frame cabinets are easy to install because they do not have the minimal door clearance tolerances found in the frameless method of cabinet construction, and may offer extended stiles to facilitate scribing on the jobsite. However, this method of construction has less interior storage space because the interior size of drawers or roll-out accessories is smaller than the overall width of the cabinet.

- 1-1/4" to 1-1/2" front frames are usually made of hardwood, 1/2" to 3/4" thick. Some cabinet manufacturers offer 1" thick framing. Rails, stiles and mullions are doweled (or mortise-and-tenon) as well as glued and stapled for rigidity. Lap joints and screws are also used.

- End panels typically consist of 1/4" to 3/4" plywood, particleboard or engineered board which is dadoed into the back of the stiles and then glued, stapled or nailed in place. They are secured square in each corner with a plastic, metal or fall-off scrap material gusset. Some manufacturers provide a full top to increase stability.

- Backs are generally 1/8" hardboard to 3/4" plywood or particleboard.

- Bottoms and tops are 3- or 5-ply plywood or particleboard. They are 1/4" to 1/2" and are dadoed into the sides of the cabinet.

- Shelves are lumber, plywood or particleboard, 1/2" to 3/4" in specification, with square or rounded front edges. Plywood and particleboard shelves are generally banded with hardwood or with a PVC wood-grained edging.

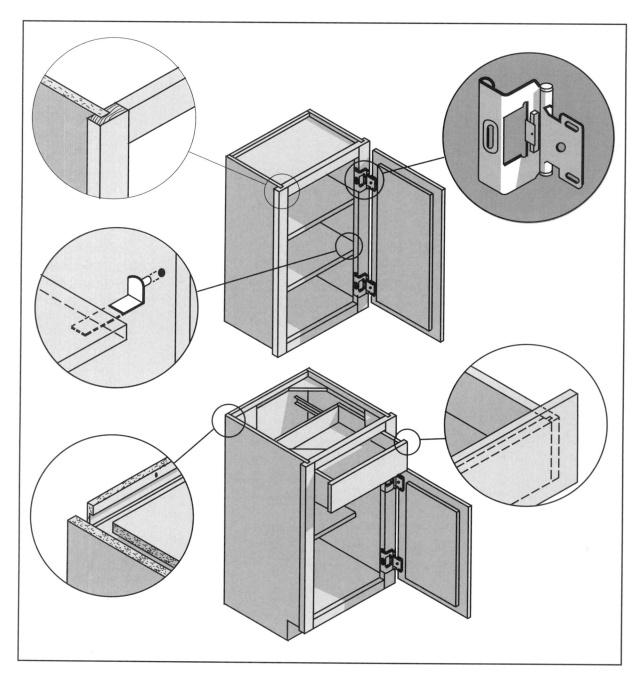

Figure 1.3 *The Storage Systems: Typical Framed Cabinet Component Parts*
Framed cabinets are fitted together with various forms of wood joinery and without special hardware fittings. Door hinges attach to face frame and generally do not have multiple adjustments.

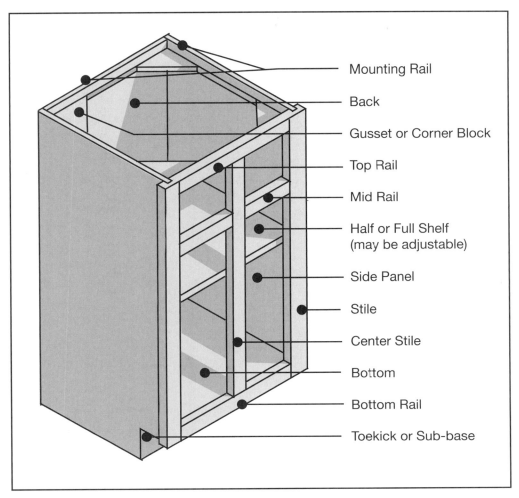

Mounting Rail

Back

Gusset or Corner Block

Top Rail

Mid Rail

Half or Full Shelf
(may be adjustable)

Side Panel

Stile

Center Stile

Bottom

Bottom Rail

Toekick or Sub-base

Figure 1.4 *The Storage Systems: Framed Cabinet Construction Details*

Frameless Construction

This second major category of case construction is called "frameless." While both types of cabinetry are built in the United States, the majority of cabinetry built in Canada and imported from Europe are frameless. With this method of construction, because of their thickness, these case parts form a box that does not need a front frame for stability or squareness. Doors and drawers cover the entire face of the cabinet.

- 5/8" to 3/4" (19 mm) particleboard, plywood or engineered wood sides are connected to the back, top and bottom with either a mechanical fastening system or a dowel method of construction.

- Backs are 1/4", 1/2" or 3/4" (5 mm, 13 mm or 19 mm).

- Tops are both 1/2" or 3/4" (13 mm or 19 mm).

- The sides are drilled for adjustable shelf clip holes or dadoed for fixed shelves.

- The doors are bored for adjustable, fully concealed, self-closing hinges.

- All exposed edges are generally banded.

You will hear these cabinets sometimes referred to as "32 mm" or "System 32" cabinets. The term 32 refers to the basic metric sizing of all these cabinets: all the holes, hinge fittings, cabinet joints and mountings are set 32 mm apart. This spacing is based on the boring equipment that is used in the manufacturing process.

The major advantages of frameless construction are total accessibility to case interior and the clean, simple design statement made by the finished product. Some concerns exist regarding the stability of this type of construction: the tendency for frameless cases to "rack" and the additional planning expertise required to insure proper clearance between these full overlay doors and adjacent cabinets and appliances of the plan. The fit and finish of the cabinets to adjacent walls and the overhead ceiling also requires knowledge about the use of scribe trim molding and fillers.

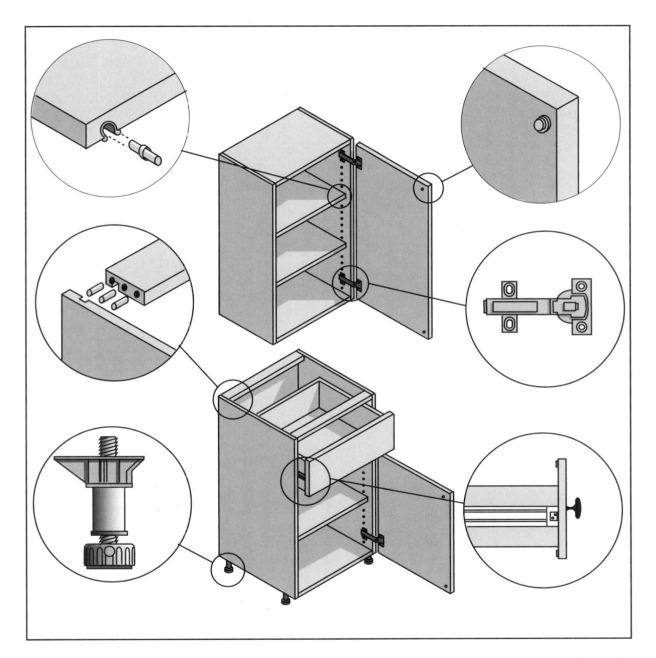

Figure 1.5 *The Storage Systems: Typical Frameless Cabinet Component Parts*

Typical frameless cabinet construction is oriented to hardware and production. Pins and dowels, which might be wood or metal, are made to fit specific holes, all of which are drilled when the cabinet is manufactured. Hinges are completely concealed. Leveling legs may be used instead of an attached subbase.

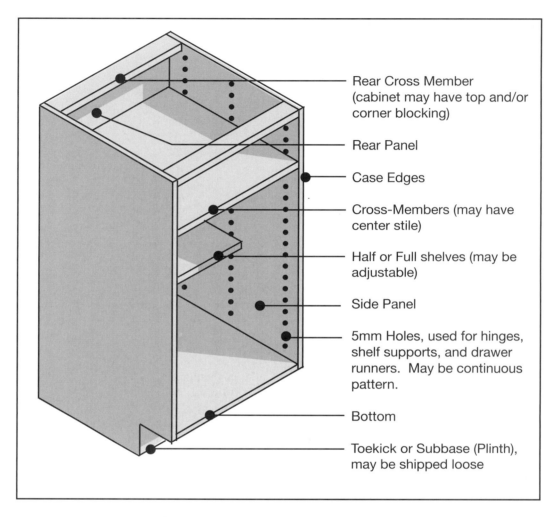

Rear Cross Member (cabinet may have top and/or corner blocking)

Rear Panel

Case Edges

Cross-Members (may have center stile)

Half or Full shelves (may be adjustable)

Side Panel

5mm Holes, used for hinges, shelf supports, and drawer runners. May be continuous pattern.

Bottom

Toekick or Subbase (Plinth), may be shipped loose

Figure 1.6 *The Storage Systems: Typical Frameless Cabinet Construction Details*

Hybrid Frame/Face Frame Construction

Some manufacturers have created a hybrid cabinet construction system allowing them to utilize the engineering method of frameless construction for the case, while creating the look of hand-crafted joinery by adding a non-functional face frame to the front exterior of the cabinet.

In this method of construction, the width of the face frame (less the thickness of the side material) extends beyond the case side, resulting in a void space between each cabinet.

**CABINET COMPONENT
SYSTEMS**

Drawer/Roll-Out Component Systems

DRAWER/ROLL-OUT CONFIGURATIONS

All kitchens include a combination of cabinetry featuring fixed or adjustable shelving combined with single drawers above doors or banks of drawers which may be in two-, three- or four-drawer configurations. Most manufacturers also offer some type of roll-out shelf system, which is actually a drawer mounted on top of a shelf or to the inside vertical partitions of the cabinet.

The advantage of drawer storage or roll-out storage is clear: the items stored within the cabinetry become much easier to see, retrieve and replace.

There are four major types of drawer construction systems used within the cabinetry industry:

Butt Joint Drawer System. A butt joint drawer system secures the individual pieces of component parts together without an interlocking joint. Once thought to be a less durable form of construction, butt joint drawers today, which utilize better adhesives and which capture the bottom of the drawer in channels machined into sides, front and back of the drawer, can be considered as durable as a classic dovetail joint.

Dovetail Drawer System. A four-sided wood drawer box engineered with dovetail joints is offered by many manufacturers. A hallmark of craftsmanship in fine woodworking for centuries, the dovetail joint is considered by many to be the preferred method of joining two pieces of wood together. The name comes from the protruding portion of the joint, reminding one of a "dove's tail." Because of the interlocking nature of this joint, it readily accommodates the natural expansion and contraction of the wood over the life of the drawer without affecting the structural integrity of the joint.

Metal Drawer System. Drawer slide manufacturers offer a totally integrated drawer system featuring a stainless steel, aluminum extruded, or other metal-type three-side drawer system which typically has a shaped profiled top edge and bottom edge. The drawer bottom repeats the material selected for the case interior. These three-sided drawer component systems then connect directly to the drawerhead and usually incorporate the drawer guide system into their construction.

Figure 1.7 *The Storage Systems: Cabinet Joinery Methods*
Cabinet joinery methods can include all of the details below. In nearly all cases, the joints are held together with staples or brads to allow glue time to cure. It is glue that locks the joints. Rabbet and dado cuts are used in case construction. Dovetail joints and dowels provide more drawer strength.

Miter Framed Drawer System. A four-sided miter framed low-pressure melamine drawer system, or a boxed melamine drawer system is considered an entry-level drawer. This type of interior normally matches the case interior. Miter framed drawer systems score the core material of the drawer—then the sections of the drawer are folded together to form the box.

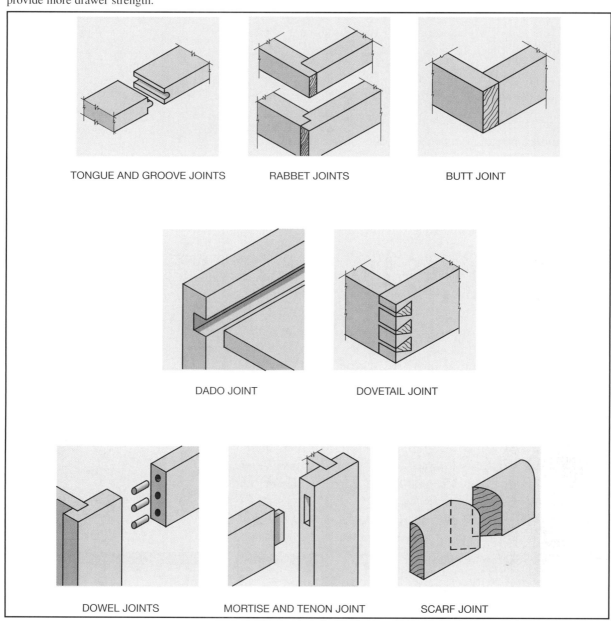

TONGUE AND GROOVE JOINTS   RABBET JOINTS   BUTT JOINT

DADO JOINT   DOVETAIL JOINT

DOWEL JOINTS   MORTISE AND TENON JOINT   SCARF JOINT

Special Purpose Component Storage Systems

Both cabinet manufacturers and accessory manufacturers also offer special purpose interior accessory programs that feature formed plastic, coated steel or stainless steel units. For example, a recycling center may include two large plastic trash receptacles that slip into openings in a roll-out shelf, or sit in a roll-out attached to the drawer. Spice shelves and canned-good storage systems may be available in wire or chrome offerings. Corner swing-out shelves may form plastic half-moon sections, or a system designed from wire.

In addition to plastic, coated-wire and chrome-wire systems, many custom manufacturers offer a full complement of wood accessory component systems, which maximizes the customization of a cabinet order specifically designed per client.

All types of drawer systems have coordinating storage inserts to separate and conveniently store cutlery, serving pieces, silverware, spices and knives. These storage systems may be formed plastic, wire or custom-made wood, sized to the specific drawer being constructed. The inserts may be designed as compartments storing a quantity of items or may be individually sized and shaped for specific kitchen utensils and cooking paraphernalia.

Figure 1.8 The Storage Systems: Examples of Cabinet Storage Systems (Courtesy of Merilat Industries Inc.)

Mixer

Pantry

Wine Storage

Tray Storage

Sink Front Storage

Spice and Condiment Storage

Figure 1.9 *The Storage Systems: Examples of Cabinet Storage Systems*
(Wine storage courtesy of American Woodmark, tray storage courtesy of Decorá Cabinets, sink front and spice and condiment storage courtesy of Rev-A-Shelf.)

CABINET MECHANICAL/ FUNCTIONAL HARDWARE

Cabinet Door Hinging

FRAME CABINETRY

Traditional frame cabinets use a surface-mounted hinge that attaches to the inside edge of the frame and the outside edge of the door. The relationship of the door to the frame determines the type of hinging specified.

Square Edge. For inset door styling, hinges have an exposed barrel with or without decorative finials at the top and bottom. Some hinge manufacturers offer a custom-designed European styled hinge, which fits on the inside of the framed case, and does not have any exposed mechanical elements on the exterior: oftentimes called a "concealed inset hinge."

Profile (Shaped) Edge. For framed cabinetry offering an overlay door configuration (the door may lay completely against the face of the cabinet, or be notched around the cabinet opening) similar hinges are designed that are shaped to fit the door profile. These hinges come in a variety of quality levels and a multitude of finishes.

FRAMELESS CABINETRY

Frameless cabinetry uses totally concealed hinges on the inside of the cabinet: one hinge end is inserted in the door back and the other into the side of the cabinet. Most of these hinges are "de-mountable," which means they easily snap on and off during installation. They are typically adjustable in three directions (up and down, in and out, and left and right), allowing the installer to maintain correct reveal dimensions between the doors and drawers, critical in this type of cabinetry.

Hinges designed for full overlay cabinetry may be considered "low-profile"—which means they do not protrude into the cabinet space more than 1" (2.50 cm) and are typically 110°, 120° or 125° openings. The larger the opening, the easier it is to access the interior of the cabinet. Some oversized hinges are available, which allow the door to open a full 170°. The client and designer need to compare and evaluate the advantages of the increased opening against the disadvantages with the overall size of the hinge.

SPECIAL PURPOSE

All of the hinges described above are designed for 3/4" (oftentimes called 4/4) door thicknesses. Some manufacturers offer full 1" thick doors (called 5/4 doors) which require special hinging considerations.

In addition to the two cabinet hinging systems just described, there are many special purpose hinging systems offered by cabinet manufacturers. These include retractable door systems to conceal televisions, home office equipment or a microwave. Doors tilt up or swing down. Several systems allow doors to slide left to right as well.

Although frame cabinetry hinge sizing is relatively similar, some manufacturers offer oversized hinges that add greatly to the aesthetics of Old World rooms or very largely proportioned spaces.

Interior Shelf Adjustability

Usually cabinet systems—whether frame or frameless—offer full depth adjustable shelves in wall cabinets. Base cabinet shelves may be one-half the depth of the cabinet, three-quarters the depth of the cabinet or full depth. Some custom manufacturers make these shelves adjustable, as well, while most stock and semi-custom producers fix the lower shelf in-place.

What the shelf is made of, what the banding material is, and whether all four edges are banded impact how flexible it is for the homeowner over the years to turn the shelf if an edge is damaged during use. The core material also dramatically affects the deflection rate of the shelf and, therefore, how wide a cabinet can be without a center stile. To keep the box rigid, many manufacturers will not build a cabinet wider than 30" without a center stile. Other manufacturers have engineered their cases to allow the designer to specify a cabinet as wide as 42" to 48" with no center stile and with a shelf, engineered so the cook can stock the shelves with evenly distributed weight without noticeable deflection.

Whatever the limits on the overall shelf length, adjustable shelf systems come in a variety of sizes, shapes and configurations; however, they all typically serve the same function.

- A metal strip, or a series of holes, run vertically along the side of the cabinet. If a drilling pattern is used, it will have punched holes 2 mm or 5 mm in diameter. These holes may be clustered around typical shelf locations, or may run the length of the cabinet, offering total flexibility.

- The shelf pin will normally be metal and will be as simple as a pin that recesses into the hole on the side of the cabinet and fits in a shaped opening on the underside of the shelf—to as elaborate as a locking system which secures the shelf in-place.

The most typical shelf pin requires a 5 mm hole, is metal and has a J-shape with an extension, which is the portion secured into the cabinet sides (oftentimes, this piece is threaded to increase shelf stability). Shelf pins used for glass shelves may be the same design with the addition of a small bumper to insure the glass does not slip or slide out of place.

Drawer Guide (Slide) Systems

Other than small decorative antique drawers which have a wood slide system, all manufacturers in the kitchen industry today offer well-engineered drawer guide systems (some manufacturers call them "slide" systems).

SIDE-MOUNTED SYSTEMS

Epoxy-coated, side-mounted guide systems that have a slant at the back of the track so the drawer guide self-closes once it is within 1" or so of the cabinet face are available in entry-level products. The guides allow the door to extend three-quarters of the way into the kitchen, or can be specified in a full extension configuration.

Some heavy-duty side-mounted metal drawer guides are also available for general purpose use or for special purpose applications such as heavy double trash bins, file drawers or other cabinetry which will be required to carry extra weight.

A third type of side-mounted drawer guide system features a sophisticated rack-and-pinion system designed to carry a very large drawer which will be loaded with heavy cooking pots and pans.

UNDER-MOUNTED SYSTEMS

Under-mounted guide systems come in both "three-quarter extension" and "full extension." These drawer guide systems are engineered to provide a self-closing—or soft-close—feature, be easy to remove and replace by the users over the years, and include some type of adjustability so the drawerhead can be slightly realigned against the case. These drawer guide systems also have a high load bearing capacity, and enclose the track system to simplify maintenance over the life of the drawer guide.

CABINET SIZES

Each manufacturer publishes a paper or electronic catalog of their product range. Following is a general discussion of the most widely used cabinet sizes and types.

Kitchen Cabinetry Units

BASE UNITS AND SPECIAL PURPOSE BASE UNITS

Base cabinets, which are set on the floor, are 21" deep in many systems built internationally. Most North American cabinets are 24" deep, front to back, and 34-1/2" to 34-3/4" high including the subbase (which is also called the toe kick or plinth). This raised portion underneath the cabinet is generally 4" to 4-1/2" high in domestic cabinetry and 6" high in international cabinetry.

The common base cabinet has a single drawer over a single door which has either a half shelf or a full shelf in the middle, and a full shelf at the bottom of the cabinet.

North American single door base cabinets are generally available in 3" increments, starting with 9", 12", 15", 18", 21" and 24". The 9" wide cabinet generally will not have a drawer and may not be available in heavily detailed door styles. Double door cabinets are usually available in widths from 24" to 48"; however, some manufacturers do not provide 39" wide or 45" wide units. Others stop the line at 42" wide.

International metric sizing is based on centimeters, with typical sizes being 10 cm, 15 cm, 20 cm, etc.

Typical Metric Cabinet Sizing			
Depths			
35.0 cm + Door (2.5)	14-3/4"		
53.0 cm	21-15/16"		
60.0 cm	24-9/16"		

Widths			
15.0 cm	5-7/8"	60.0 cm	23-5/8"
25.0 cm	9-13/16"	70.0 cm	27-9/16"
30.0 cm	11-13/16"	76.2 cm	30"
35.0 cm	13-3/4"	80.0 cm	31-1/2"
40.0 cm	15-3/4"	85.0 cm	33-1/2"
45.0 cm	17-11/16"	90.0 cm	35-7/16"
50.0 cm	19-11/16"	91.5 cm	36"
55.0 cm	21-5/8"	100.0 cm	39-3/8"

Heights (Including Subbase/Toe Height/Leg Dimensions – 15 cm = 5-7/8")			
27.2 cm	10-11/16"	104.0 cm	40-15/16"
40.0 cm	15-3/4"	118.4 cm	46-5/8"
49.6 cm	19-1/2"	134.4 cm	52-15/16"
65.6 cm	25-3/16"	144.0 cm	56-11/16"
78.4 cm	30-7/8"	175.0 cm	68-7/8"
87.0 cm	34-1/4"	215.4 cm	84-13/16"
94.4 cm	37-13/16"	231.4 cm	91-1/8"
		241.0 cm	94-7/8"

(Courtesy of Niagara Artcraft Woodwork Co. Ltd.)

Figure 1.10 *The Storage Systems: A Base Cabinet with Half Shelf and Roll-out Shelves*

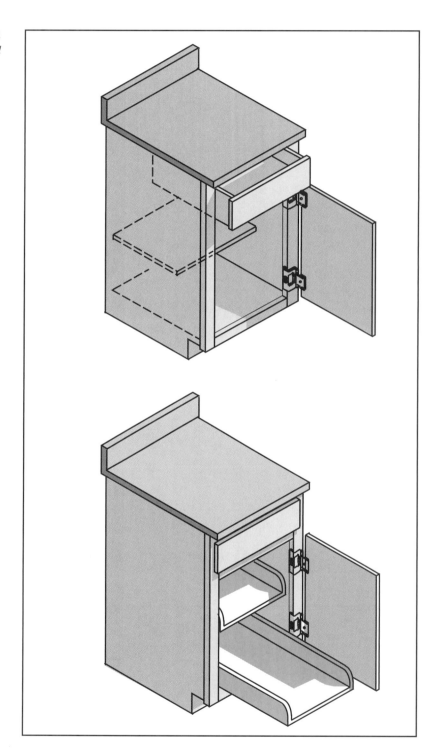

SPECIAL PURPOSE BASE CABINETS

In addition to the standard base cabinet, special purpose base cabinets are available for specific needs. At the end of this section, you will find a listing of typical cabinets which discusses each one of these types of cabinets.

Generally, the categories of base cabinets you can choose from are:

- **Drawer Cabinets.** A cabinet that features two, three, four or five drawers. Two-drawer units are used frequently today to create a recycling unit. Three- and four-drawer units are typically seen near the primary sink for flatware and kitchen linen storage. Wide, two- or three-drawer units are often used below a cooking surface to conveniently store pots, pans, lids and utensils used at the cooking surface. Try to avoid drawer units smaller than 15" wide because the interior drawer space will be too small to be functional.

- **Corner Cabinets.** A variety of corner cabinets are available:

  "Lazy Susan" Base Cabinet: Generally requires between 33" and 36" of space on each wall. A round shelf swings out into the room and past the door opening. The door may be bifold or may actually swing through the cabinet interior. The wider the door, the more functional the circular shelf.

  "Blind" Cabinet: A cabinet that has a shelf, pull-out or swing-out apparatus to provide accessibility into the corner. They generally require 42" to 48" of wall space. Although available in 36" and 39", avoid any unit less than 42" wide to insure reasonable access.

  "Pie-Cut" Cabinet: A corner cabinet that requires 36" on each wall (much like a Lazy Susan) and features stationary shelving as opposed to a rotating shelf. Maximum shelf space is provided. One type of pie-cut unit may be rounded with a curved door.

- **Recycling Center.** Specialized cabinets which are designed to hold bins to facilitate the separation and recycling of refuse.

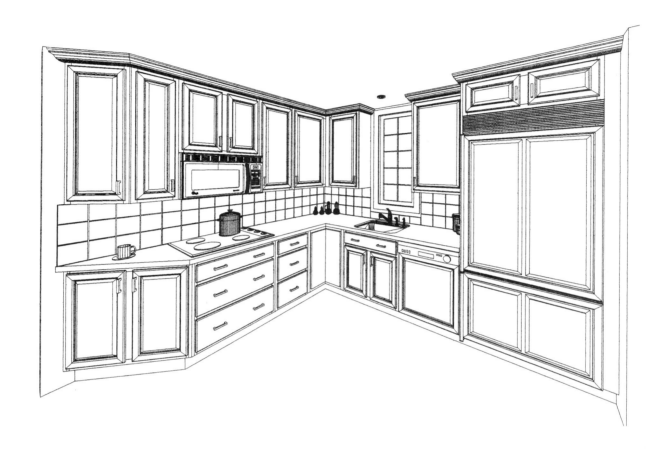

Figure 1.11 *The Storage Systems: An Example of a Corner Cabinet Solution in a Kitchen*

This kitchen utilizes many standard base cabinet types: a cabinet with full height doors has been used on an angle to the far left. This angled cabinet extends the counter space, while maintaining clear walkway access to the doorway. Wide drawers are below the cooktop, with typical sized units adjacent. A Lazy Susan in the corner features two doors that rotate into the opening.

- **Sink/Cooktop Cabinet**. These are base cabinets with a voided top drawer, or a tilt-down front which houses a plastic or stainless steel container. The tilt-down is designed to utilize the top drawer space that would otherwise be lost once the cooktop or sink is installed. The drawer area can also be replaced with a special cut-out to receive a farmhouse sink or a front-controlled cooktop. These cabinets may be pulled away from the wall with decorative columns or turnings finishing each side, creating a focal point within the room. This type of cabinet configuration is called a "bump-out."

Figure 1.12 *The Storage Systems: The Sink Area in a Kitchen*
A special cabinet houses a sink with a front apron, called an "apron" sink. (Courtesy of Wm Ohs Inc.)

Figure 1.13 *The Storage Systems: A Sink Area in a Kitchen*
An open cabinet decorative storage area is above the sink. (Courtesy of Christopher Peacock Cabinetry)

WALL UNITS AND SPECIAL PURPOSE WALL UNITS

Wall cabinets, which are fixed to the walls with screws, are generally 12" deep. They come in a variety of heights ranging from 30" to 36" to 42". Some manufacturers offer sizes to 48". The 30" high wall units are designed to be installed in a room with 96" high ceilings with an extended, flush or recessed soffit (drop) above them. "Soffit" is an industry word identifying a boxed-in area above the cabinets. The proper construction term would be a "bulk head," made up of fascia (the front panel) and the soffit (the underside). However, it is typical in the industry to call the entire structure a soffit.

The 36" high units are designed to be installed in a 96" high room with a 6" trim connecting the cabinets to the ceiling. The 36" high units are also used in a 108" high ceiling to provide better balance between the cabinet spacing and the architectural envelope of the room. The 42" high wall units are designed to extend all the way up to a ceiling in a 96" high room, or to be used with an extended, flush or recessed soffit in 108" or 120" high ceilings.

See page 27 for typical metric cabinet sizing.

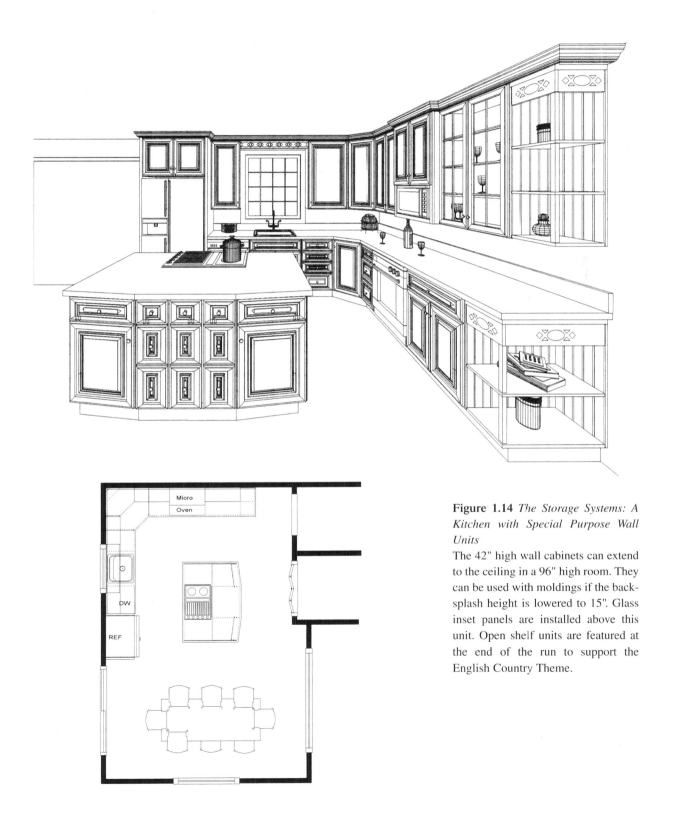

Figure 1.14 *The Storage Systems: A Kitchen with Special Purpose Wall Units*

The 42" high wall cabinets can extend to the ceiling in a 96" high room. They can be used with moldings if the back-splash height is lowered to 15". Glass inset panels are installed above this unit. Open shelf units are featured at the end of the run to support the English Country Theme.

Figure 1.15 *The Storage Systems: A Kitchen with Special Purpose Wall Units*

In a room with a 108" to 120" high ceiling, the 42" wall cabinets may be used with the molding or soffit to finish the space between the cabinets and the ceiling. The proportional relationship between the doors and the height of the soffit is critical. In this room with 9' ceilings, the massive hood area balances the long, slender doors.

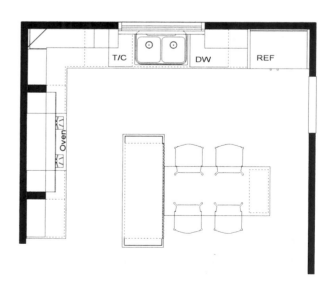

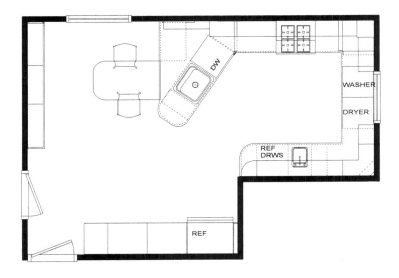

Figure 1.16 *The Storage Systems: Combining Cabinet Heights in a Kitchen*

Cabinet heights can be combined. In this example, 42" high units are featured in the working portion of the kitchen. A custom tall cabinet in the breakfast nook finishes off at 84", leaving an open soffit above for display.

For use above microwave ovens, hoods, refrigerators or other tall obstructions, wall cabinets are also available 12", 15", 18" and 24" high. Some of these sizes are often available 24" deep to provide an accessible wall cabinet above a refrigerator. Wall cabinets are generally installed from 15" to 18" off the finished counter surface. This clearance is typically required so small hand appliances can fit under the wall cabinet.

As a standard, wall cabinets feature two adjustable interior shelves in a 30" high unit. The 36" and 42" high units will generally include three shelves. To maximize the accessibility of wall cabinets, always specify wall units without a center stile. Many manufacturers install this vertical support member in wall cabinets wider than 30", which blocks access. If available, specify a manufacturer that provides an open space the entire width of the cabinet.

SPECIAL PURPOSE WALL CABINETS

- **Appliance Garage**. A cabinet with a roll-up door, called a "tambour" unit, that extends to the countertop. Sometimes referred to as a small appliance garage. Appliance garages can also be featured with regular cabinet doors.

- **Corner Cabinet**. Much like base units, blind corner units and pie-cut cabinets are available. An angled, diagonal corner wall unit is also frequently specified. These units typically require 24" of wall space. The blind unit requires 27" to 30" to insure a reasonable cabinet opening.

- **Glass Door Cabinet**. Full glass panels, or glass sheets that are framed in the door material are popular. The cabinet interior should be finished to match the exterior. Glass may be clear, frosted, etched. They may also feature decorative, stained or leaded glass patterns.

- **Microwave/Television Cabinet**. Deeper wall cabinets with special retractable swing-up doors (horizontal or vertical) are manufactured for television and microwave appliances.

should be finished to match the exterior. Glass may be clear, frosted, etched. They may also feature decorative, stained or leaded glass patterns.

- **Microwave/Television Cabinet**. Deeper wall cabinets with special retractable swing-up doors (horizontal or vertical) are manufactured for television and microwave appliances.

- **Open Shelf Unit**. Open shelf units can be attractively mixed with enclosed cabinets to provide design relief to the overall room by introducing a display of the client's collectibles.

- **Peninsula Cabinet**. A wall cabinet that is accessible from two sides and is installed above a cabinet that juts out into the center of the room.

- **Special Interior Accessories**. Include door-mounted spice racks, interior step shelving, swing-out can goods or spice shelf units. Some manufacturers also offer wall cabinets that have built-in integral fluorescent or low-voltage halogen lighting systems, which provide optimum task lighting above the work surface.

TALL UNITS AND SPECIAL PURPOSE TALL UNITS

Tall cabinets are used for a variety of purposes in kitchen planning. They come in two size categories:

Mid-height	48" to 72"
Full-height	84" to 96"

They may be used as a tall closet with no shelves to house cleaning equipment, as a food storage cabinet with specialized swing-out shelves, and as a replacement for standard base or wall units with adjustable shelves and/or roll-outs.

Tall units are typically specified in 12", 18", 21" or 24" depths for kitchen use. These units are often available in 18", 24", 30" or 36" widths.

Mid-height units feature single height doors. Full-height configurations include a tall door approximately 65" high below a smaller door. This door size is specified to minimize warpage problems.

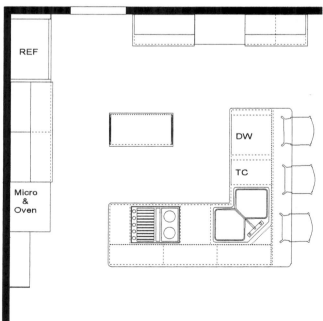

Figure 1.17 *The Storage Systems: A Kitchen with Special Purpose Tall Units*

Tall units are generally best located at the end of a run of cabinets. Oftentimes, an oven cabinet will be placed at the end of a counter, with a refrigerator at the opposite end, as seen in the left hand view of this kitchen. Tall units may be a bit awkward if placed in the center of a run unless perfectly balanced on each side, as seen in this same example to the far right.

SPECIAL PURPOSE TALL CABINETS

- **Built-in Oven Unit.** Cabinets that house double ovens or combination appliance stacks generally have one drawer below the oven. Single oven cabinets have two or three drawers below the appliances. Many manufacturers provide a "universal" oven case, which has three drawers that are designed to be eliminated at the jobsite if necessary, to accommodate a double oven.

- **Built-in Refrigerator Unit.** Some manufacturers offer a three-sided tall enclosure with a 24" deep upper cabinet to surround a refrigerator.

Bathroom Cabinetry Units

VANITY BASE UNITS

Some vanity base unit systems are designed to "float" off the floor and are installed 6" to 18" up the wall. Base cabinets, which are set on the floor, are 21" deep (front to back) and 30" to 34-1/2" high including a subbase, or "toe kick," that is 4" high.

Cabinetry designed for bathroom storage include special purpose base cabinets for linen storage, built-in hampers and specially divided drawer or pull-out storage for grooming aids and cosmetics. Suspended drawers are also available to be used in a sit-down area sometimes planned for a grooming/make-up counter. For children's bathrooms, a stepstool is available which is concealed in the base cabinet toe kick area, or hidden in a low drawer.

WALL UNITS

Wall cabinets were traditionally designed for kitchen usage. However, creative designers adapt various wall unit sizes for interesting and functional bathroom applications. Specialized cabinets designed to be placed over the water closet (toilet) and extending down to the vanity countertop are offered in some lines in 6" to 8" deep bathroom units.

TALL UNITS

Tall cabinets provide excellent storage in a bathroom space when countertop requirements have been met. Tall cabinets are attractively used to separate double lavatories, or to flank lavatory or toilet areas. Tall cabinets to be used as linen or utility cabinets are 84", 90" or 96" high. Some units offer concealed drop-down counters, providing a seated space in a small bathroom.

Figure 1.18 *The Storage Systems: A Gallery of Bathroom Cabinetry Ideas* A dressing area in a vanity section includes full-sized drawers for clothing storage. Note the framed mirror above this area. (Courtesy of Brookhaven)

Figure 1.19 *The Storage Systems: A Gallery of Bathroom Cabinetry Ideas* This vanity solution separates the "his and her" area with a large storage unit. In the second example, a tall unit is placed to the side of a dressing area. (Courtesy of American Woodmark Corporation)

Figure 1.20 *The Storage Systems: A Gallery of Bathroom Cabinetry Ideas* In this bathroom plan, a dressing area to the left is finished with a tall cabinet detailed to include drawers below the upper door for grooming aids. The single vanity is flanked left and right with raised drawer cabinets. (Courtesy of Wellborn Cabinet Inc.)

Figure 1.21 *The Storage Systems: A Gallery of Bathroom Cabinetry Ideas* A Contemporary bathroom with an angled lavatory cabinet and bump-out cabinet. Note the entire elevation floats off the floor. (Courtesy of Dura Supreme Cabinetry)

Figure 1.22 *The Storage Systems: A Gallery of Bathroom Cabinetry Ideas* In this Contemporary bath, two furniture pieces provide counter space for the above-counter lavatories. Additional storage is built in to the wall between the two units. (Courtesy of Anthony Binns, CKD, CBD – Toronto, Ontario)

Fitted Furniture Cabinetry For Other Rooms of the Home

The kitchen and bathroom specialist is often asked to extend his or her expertise into other rooms of the home which would benefit from custom designed built-in cabinetry: home offices, media centers, entertaining counter/bar areas, children's bedroom storage, laundry rooms, hobby centers and garage work spaces are just a few of the rooms you may be asked to design.

Just as a kitchen or bathroom requires specialized training, so too do these auxiliary spaces. Utilize your knowledge of cabinetry construction and size flexibility, while developing a specialized questionnaire to clearly understand what the client hopes to accomplish in these other areas.

CABINET CORE MATERIALS (CASE AND DOOR COMPONENT PARTS)

In both frameless and frame construction, the cabinet core material determines the cabinet stability. Following is an overview of cabinet materials currently used by both large manufacturing facilities and smaller custom cabinet shops. Some of these materials are used for both cabinet component parts and as door substrates.

Particleboard

Today, with the advent of new technology and improved resin and glue methods, the best interior surface for many cabinet applications is an engineered substrate that has been covered with either a high- or low-pressure decorative laminate. Such an engineered substrate is generically called particleboard.

Particleboard was originally a by-product of the western lumber and plywood mills which utilized sawdust, shavings and other fall-off from the industry. Because some type of particleboard is the most widely used core material for cabinet construction today, its usage is so great it is made from trees harvested specifically for particleboard production.

Particleboard obtained its name based on its composition of particles of wood fall-off bonded together with resin under pressure. The size and species of the particles in this type of engineered substrate generally vary depending on the designed end use. Many times, a multi-layered process is used to develop the stability and screw holding capacity of the core material.

For example, underlayment is a form of particleboard that has a low-density and low-resin content. Therefore, it is not recommended for a laminate substrate because it has lower dimensional stability, structural strength and moisture resistance.

Most particleboard used in the kitchen and bath industry is rated under three classifications: M1, M2 and M3. M3 is the best quality board for laminating partially because of its superior screw holding capability and internal bond strength; however, M2 board is also widely used. These high-quality engineered substrates usually fall in the range of 40- to 45-pound density. This density rating is the weight of the board per square inch. Better particleboard materials are rated as "45 lb. commercial grade."

One of the most frequently used types of substrate material is medium-density fiber board identified as MDF. This board is made of even finer fibers than normal particleboard. Its density adds superior screw holding power, a very tight clean edge, and an extremely smooth surface. The MDF edge can be shaped to a profile and painted, resulting in an acceptable finished edge for many surfaces. Medium density fiber board is a popular substrate for painted and veneered doors.

A limited number of manufacturers offer a fire-rated particleboard for use in commercial applications requiring fire resistant capability. This board is produced under a similar process as the normal core materials. The primary difference is that salts are added in the manufacturing process.

This board is more difficult to cut and machine than normal particleboard, is limited in sizes available, and few distributors stock the item. Additionally, the salts in the board make it susceptible to moisture. Storage conditions are therefore a prime consideration, as well as a balanced glue system that will be compatible with the board during fabrication.

Plywood

Some designers and consumers consider a "solid wood" cabinet to be better than one made from man-made materials. Therefore, plywood is often used as a core material in cabinet construction. It provides good strength and superior screw holding ability. Fire-rated plywoods are also available in limited sizes. The addition of salts is again employed, so the same concerns exist for fire-rated plywood as those listed for fire-rated particleboard. When considering a plywood interior, designers should specify that the face veneers on the plywood do not produce a grain rise, that a high grade of solid core plywood be used to avoid the presence of voids in the built-up layers of veneer, and that the finish surface of the plywood have only a limited number of "plugs." Plugs are the "football" shaped plywood sections that are used to replace knots in the veneer.

Engineered Board

Over the last decade, major inroads have been made with the introduction of engineered boards which combined the attributes of both plywood and particleboard. For example, engineered boards are available today with an industrial board core—providing stability—and then plywood layers on each side completing the overall board thickness. Such engineered board satisfies the client or architect who has specified an "all wood" case, while accommodating the manufacturing requirements of dimensional stability within the board's stock.

Straw Particleboard (Wheatboard/Agri)

Wheat straw particleboard is made from wood fibers that are bound together with resin. Wheat straw particleboard is made from wheat straw, a waste product from wheat farming. Bales of wheat straw are milled into fine particles, sorted and dried and then bound together with a formaldehyde-free resin. The particles are then hot-pressed into sheets of the desired thickness. The sheet is sanded and cut to required sizes. It is produced in industrial-grade sizes and strengths, and it can be machined in the same way as wood fiber particleboard.

One of the primary advantages of this product is the resin which binds the straw fibers together is formaldehyde-free, and is thus free of harmful emissions, both in manufacture and end-use. Other benefits include reducing depletion of forestry resources by utilizing an agricultural waste product, and the creation of a secondary source of farm income. Manufactured in the United States under the trademark Wheatboard, an industrial-grade particleboard, it is 5% to 10% lighter than its wood-pulp counterpart. The adhesive used to bind the fiber is nontoxic and emission-free once cured. The adhesive is also rated as an exterior-grade binder, making the end product more water-resistant than standard industrial-grade wood-pulp particleboards.

CABINET INTERIOR AND EXTERIOR FINISH MATERIALS/SYSTEMS

The materials used on the exposed parts of the cabinets and the finishing methods are both factors in cabinet quality and price. Cabinet manufacturers use a variety of materials for construction of cabinets. Some fine custom producers have 12 or more steps in the finish process and include hand-wiping and sanding between steps. You should learn all the details of the finishing process developed by the manufacturers you represent.

Melamine/Vinyl Surfaces

THERMALLY FUSED MELAMINE

Thermally Fused Melamine (TFM), also known as low-pressure laminate (LPL), low-pressure melamine, melamine component panels (MCP) or just melamine are melamine-impregnated papers that can be fused to a substrate by heat and pressure.

- **Advantages**. Cost effective. Good performance for most applications; availability of colors.

- **Disadvantages**. Tendency to chip and crack, which can be mitigated through the use of better substrates and proper cutting tools. Is not as impact resistant as high pressure laminates.

RESIN-IMPREGNATED FOIL

Resin-impregnated foil is an alpha-cellulose paper impregnated with either urea, acrylic or melamine resins. It is sometimes called paper or melamine paper, and in Europe it is called foil.

Generally, impregnated papers are offered in wood grains and some solid colors. The paper can be used for profiling and can be embossed to simulate real wood veneer graining. Some manufacturers consider their product to be a synthetic veneer.

Impregnated papers have a cost advantage over high-pressure laminate and composite panels. It is about equivalent of the cost of vinyl, but has a better look than vinyl.

There's a big difference between the durability of heavier and lighter weights of paper. The paper is measured in weight per square meter. Weights range from 18 gram to 30 gram papers (most imported from Japan), also known as low-basis-weight-papers, through intermediate weights (40 grams to 70 grams). Heavy weight paper has an internal impregnation that gives it some surface integrity. The heavier the weight, the more scratch and scuff resistant the paper will be. Lighter weight papers use waxes or silicon coatings to protect the surface and these will wear off under use.

A simple test to judge the quality of the paper is to attach a small piece of ordinary scotch tape for a few hours to an unobtrusive spot. When removed, the surface should be unharmed on a high quality, heavyweight paper.

- **Advantages**. Lower cost than LPLs because they are laminated on roll-laminating equipment, which is less expensive than thermo-fusing equipment; lower chip-out rate than LPLs.

- **Disadvantages**. Most paper suppliers are foreign, which means prices fluctuate sharply with the value of the dollar.

VINYL FILMS

Vinyl films of 2-4 mils are used on many inexpensive cabinets and furniture items. Vinyl films are heat-laminated using adhesives. The surface of a panel laminated with vinyl film is not very durable unless it is top-coated.

- **Advantages**. Low cost; material is more impervious to water than other materials.

- **Disadvantages**. Inferior quality of print and design.

HOT-STAMPED TRANSFER FOILS

Hot-stamped transfer foils (HSTF) are laminated by the continuous hot-roll method. They produce good printing quality and fidelity. HSTF is basically paint or ink reverse printed on a Mylar carrier foil, with an adhesive top-coat. Heat and pressure activate the top-coat and deposit the ink or paint, and the Mylar is peeled away. It is offered in wood grains and solid colors, and is used most often on edges and profiles.

It is self-seaming or self-trimming, since it only leaves the Mylar backing where heat and pressure is applied. It can be used on medium density fiberboard or wood, but not on particleboard.

- **Advantages**. The product offers cost savings over most other methods of surfacing. It can be applied to curves and profiles with contour rollers, with virtually no evidence of a seam. A wide range of colors and patterns is offered.

- **Disadvantages**. Hot-stamped foils have very little stain, scuff or wear resistance due to the extreme thinness of the material. It cannot fill a gap or defect, since it is almost without mass. It does not give as good an appearance on flat panels as papers or even vinyls.

Laminate Surfaces

HIGH-PRESSURE LAMINATES

High-pressure laminates (HPL) are produced in sheets in many decorative colors and in thicknesses typically from 0.030" to 0.050". These products have been around a long time. In fact, they were, for years, the only laminates available. The most common uses of HPLs are for kitchen countertops, desk tops, dining room and dinette tables, and restaurant countertops and work stations.

- **Advantages**. Best performance of any laminate for most purposes; available in a multitude of colors; readily available from several manufacturers in the United States, Canada and Europe.

- **Disadvantages**. Relatively expensive; performance features may be excessive for most applications.

CONTINUOUS HIGH-PERFORMANCE LAMINATES

Made of the same raw materials as HPLs, they have the same basic characteristics, but are thinner and slightly softer. This means durability and impact resistance are proportionately lower.

- **Advantages**. Lower cost than HPLs, but the product has many of the same performance characteristics; can buy panels prelaminated.

- **Disadvantages**. Not yet widely available; colors are limited.

EDGEBANDING CHOICES

When considering laminate cabinetry, the edgebanding material must also be evaluated. There are seven major edgebanding choices available:

- **Laminated Vinyl**. A lamination of two materials, generally vinyl to vinyl, although ABS and paper backers may be used.

  The carrier is generally a rigid PVC 0.101" to 0.030" thick and may be clear or in color. The surface is a printed or solid color lamination grade vinyl, usually reverse printed, and 0.002" to 0.008" thick.

- **PVC**. A thermoplastic edgebanding made of polyvinyl chloride, used to match vinyl, paper, paint or high-pressure laminates. PVC offers unlimited color and pattern availability, a wide range of widths (to 3.5"), thicknesses (0.016" to

0.187"), surface textures and gloss levels. The printed surfaces, as well as the solid colors, are generally top-coated with a UV-cured resin for protection.

PVC is mainly used for straight line and contour automatic edgebanding applications. Thicker versions are available preglued for hot air applications. PVC is not recommended for softform applications.

- **Polyester Laminate.** Decorative papers, often matching popular high-pressure laminates, are impregnated with polyester resin and laminated to a variety of backers. Typically produced in light and heavy weight versions, either can be preglued for heat bar or hot air application. The heavy weight version is excellent for straight line, contour and softform automatic edgebanding applications.

- **Melamine.** The term melamine edgebanding covers a broad range of paper edgebanding materials, including single-layer printed products, laminated foils and continuous melamine laminates. Largely produced in Europe, melamine is an economical, preglued, automatic edgebanding product suitable for straight line, contour and softform edgebanding applications.

- **Wood Veneers.** Wood veneers that are either rotary cut or sliced from a variety of domestic and imported hardwood species. The veneers are sliced from 1/25" to 1/15" thick and are available plain, paper or fleece-backed in varying degrees of flexibility. The backers provide stability and strength to the veneer, and minimize splintering, cracking and checking. The veneers may be finger- or butt-joined to produce continuous coil edgebanding. Veneer edging products are suitable for straight line, contour and softform applications.

- **Reconstruction Wood Strips.** A man-made veneer generally manufactured in Europe. Light colored woods are cut, dyed and reformed into logs before being resliced into sheets that approximate flat cut or quartered veneer. This produces a consistent, custom colored and grained wood veneer. These veneers can be processed into fleece or paper-backed strips or coils for straight line, contour or softform automatic edgebanding applications.

Natural Wood

Woods are universally popular and generally available to the cabinet industry in the United States and Canada. They are used in both local custom cabinet fabrication and in large national and international cabinet manufacturing facilities

Hardwood lumber is produced from deciduous trees that drop their broad leaves each year. *Softwood* lumber is produced from coniferous or evergreen species that have needles or scale-like leaves and remain green throughout the year.

Because of the differing inherent qualities and growth characteristics, the end uses of hardwoods are considerably different than softwoods. Softwoods are normally used in construction, while hardwoods are reserved for flooring, furniture and cabinets.

FROM FOREST TO CABINETS: PROTECTING THE ENVIRONMENT, WHILE CREATING BEAUTIFUL KITCHENS AND BATHROOMS

Within the global community, the United States is envied for our natural wood resources: according to the USDA Forest Service, approximately one-third of our nation's land area is forest land. Canada is also a nation rich in wood natural resources.

Within North America, about one-third of all our forests are considered hardwood forests, with 90% of them located in the Eastern United States. Hardwood trees require from 50 to 120 years to reach a harvestable size, and approximately 50% of the lumber produced is not used for kitchen, bath or other fitted room cabinetry because it contains characteristics not accepted in furniture.

In today's foresting industry, managed forest lands are far more the norm: as the industry works feverishly to grow trees fast enough to be timbered to meet the demand for hardwoods while managing forests for future yield. The term "old growth" refers to large trees that have grown in natural forests. Smaller, younger, trees are grown on farms specifically to be harvested for the furniture, cabinetry and building industry.

What does this mean to you, as the designer? First, there is great uncertainty in the hardwood industry about what impact exporting lumber will have on the wood available for domestic kitchen production in the future. Secondly, the width of planks available today and the levels of acceptability of wood characteristics are changing because more "juvenile" logs do not have the same characteristics of "old growth" logs. Thirdly, imports of veneer and wood products from other parts of the world, where forests are being harvested without concern for the environment, have led world conservationists to develop a program to "certify wood." What this means to you is you should only work with mills or cabinet manufacturers who pay close attention to sourcing of their raw materials, and who are dedicated to responsible resource management.

HARDWOOD VS. SOFTWOOD

Solid Wood Cabinet Doors vs. Veneer Cabinet Doors

Door styles are designed two ways:

- Strips of solid wood are laid up to create a solid wood center panel, and then are framed with stiles (vertical members) and rails (horizontal members), creating what is oftentimes called "5-piece solid wood doors."

- Veneers are constructed by adhering real wood, reconstituted wood, wood-looking/color laminates to engineered board substrate doors (often called slab doors).

WOOD WARPAGE

Warping is a common worry in the kitchen and bathroom industry. The relationship between the relative humidity of the atmosphere at the place of installation, and the moisture content of the wood causes changes in wood structure. If the moisture content of the wood is higher than the relative humidity, the wood will give off moisture and shrink in volume. If the wood is dryer than the relative humidity, it will take on moisture and swell.

The shrinking and swelling tendency of wood varies with the species and the direction of the grain. For minimal problems, the moisture content of the wood at the time of manufacturer and finishing should be approximately the average moisture content that it will eventually attain in use, or slightly less. The possibility of warpage is considerably reduced when the cabinet is finished at a manufacturing facility. A cabinet which must be shipped to an area of different relative humidity should be finished, with all exposed surfaces covered before it begins the journey. Unfinished casework installed in a new home without climate controls in-place and then left unfinished for some time is a recipe for disaster.

In conjunction with the inherent warpage problem in woods, the door style construction will affect its stability. A stile-and-rail door with a fixed-in-place flat panel will not be stable. A similar door with a floating center panel will withstand humidity changes much better. A solid lumber door is susceptible to a great deal of movement, while a veneered plywood will overcome the wood's natural shrinkage and swelling tendencies. Alternative products also solve the warpage problems; steel, particleboards, hardboards and laminates all relieve the cabinet of movement problems.

POPULAR SPECIES

The following discussion details popular solid woods used in cabinetry with a special note for woods selected as furniture-grade veneer for cabinetry. A full discussion about planning with veneers follows this review of wood concerns and dictionary of popular species.

General color—that is categorizing wood by its color tones—is a good way to sort through the most popular species. Some hardwoods are used in the cabinet industry for both solid wood stock and veneer parts: cherry is a good example. Other woods are very rare and are typically selected only for use as a veneer: Bird's-eye Maple is an example.

To begin the discussion about wood species, we have listed them in six possible color tones:

- **Wood that is whitish**: Ash, Bird's-eye Maple, and Sycamore.

- **Wood that is yellowish**: Birch, Lacewood, Ponderosa Pine, Primavera, Satinwood and Zebrawood.

- **Wood that is purple or crimson**: Bubinga and Purple Heart.

- **Wood that is reddish or pinkish**: African Mahogany, Beech, Cherry, Douglas Fir, Honduras Mahogany, Pearwood, Sapele and Western Red Cedar.

- **Wood that is brownish**: Alder, Brazilian Rosewood, Elm, Oak, Walnut and Teak.

- **Wood that is blackish or has gray tones**: Ebony.

A more detailed description follows of the most popular woods used in cabinetry. For more specific information about a certain wood specie, visit the Hardwood Information Center at the Hardwood Manufacturers Association's website, or other similar information/ educational websites. However, never specify a wood you have not worked with for cabinetry without first consulting your supplier about the availability of the species in your area, the appropriateness of the wood for cabinetry, as well as special handling and costs associated with unusual woods. This discussion should be part of your estimating process—before the project is presented to the client, not part of the ordering process afterward.

Alder

Principally grown in the Pacific Northwest, where it is the most abundant commercial hardwood, alder is often used in place of cherry because the coloration is somewhat similar. Red alder is a relative of birch—almost white when freshly cut, then quickly changing on exposure to air, becoming light brown with yellow or reddish tinges. Heartwood is formed only in trees of advanced age and there is no visible boundary between sap and hardwood. The wood is fairly straight grained, as well.

Designers should be aware that alder is considered a relatively soft wood of medium density that has low bending strength, shock resistance and stiffness.

Ash

Of the sixty-five species of trees and shrubs called ash, six—white, pumpkin, blue, black, green and Oregon ash—are commercially important for lumber and other wood products. White ash grows throughout almost the entire wooded area of the United States east of the Great Plains, except the Gulf and South Atlantic coasts, and in Southern Ontario and Quebec. Green ash has practically the same geographic distribution, except it also grows along the coast, follows the tributaries of the Mississippi River westward across the prairies, and extends farther northward in Canada. Black ash grows along the Great Lakes and St. Lawrence River from New England westward to Minnesota and Northeastern Iowa.

White ash shrinks moderately, but can be kiln dried rapidly and satisfactorily. Ash commonly is dried from the green condition in the kiln and requires ten to fifteen days for 1" lumber. It machines well, is better than average in nail and screw holding strength, and is intermediate for gluing. Other ash species have lower strength properties than white ash, but still compare favorably with other native hardwoods. These species also split easier, shrink more, are average in workability and perform somewhat less favorably than white ash when exposed to extreme cycles of moisture content.

The principal use of ash is in furniture, interior parts of upholstered furniture, kitchen cabinets and architectural trim and cabinetry. Ash is straight-grained, still, strong and hard. White ash is superior to other ash species in these qualities. Ash also has good bending properties, high-shock resistance, and it wears smooth in use.

Birch

Yellow birch grows in the Lake states, New England, New York, New Jersey, Pennsylvania and along the Appalachian Mountains into Southern Georgia. It reaches its best development near the Canadian border. Sweet birch grows in New England, New York, New Jersey and Pennsylvania, and extends southward along the Appalachian Mountains to Northern Georgia and Alabama. Paper birch has a transcontinental range extending throughout Canada to Alaska. In the United States, it occurs eastward from the Lake states to New York and New England.

The wood of yellow and sweet birch is relatively heavy, hard and strong, and has high-shock resistance. Although the wood is difficult to work with hand tools, it can be readily shaped by machine and ranks high in nail-withdrawal resistance. Sweet birch ranks slightly above yellow birch in most strength properties. The wood of paper birch is considerably lighter than the other two birches and ranks below them in hardness, strength and stiffness.

All birches shrink considerably during drying. Yellow birch must be seasoned carefully to prevent checking and warping. Eleven to fifteen days are required to dry 1" lumber from the green condition to 6% moisture content. Because yellow and sweet birch are difficult to glue, special veneer and adhesive treatments are usually required to obtain the best results. They are glued more easily with synthetic-resin glues than with natural glues.

Yellow birch is one of the principal furniture woods in the United States because of its good machining and finishing properties, hardness, pleasing figure and attractive color. Sweet birch lumber and veneer also are used in furniture. Both species are also used in kitchen cabinets and architectural trim, paneling and cabinetry. Much paper birch is used for specialty veneer products, such as toothpicks and tongue depressors.

Cherry

Black cherry is found principally throughout the eastern half of the United States, but grows in significant commercial quantities only in the Northern Allegheny Mountains.

Cherry wood is reddish and takes a lustrous finish. It is a prized furniture wood and brings high prices in veneer log form. It is increasingly popular in kitchen cabinets and is often used in architectural trim, paneling and cabinetry.

Black cherry is relatively easy to dry, requiring ten to fourteen days to kiln dry 1" lumber from green to 6% moisture content. It stays in-place well after seasoning and is comparatively free from checking and warping. It is easily machined, can be sawn cleanly, turns well and planes excellently with standard cutting angles. Screw-holding ability is good. Gluing also is good except when gum streaks are present. The wood has sufficient hardness to allow it to take hard use and withstand knocks without marring.

A Popular Veneer: Cherry is a popular veneer because of the repetitive cathedrals seen throughout an elevation of plain sliced cherry veneer. Special quarter-sawn cherry can be specified to create a more ribbon-like grain pattern. Typical cherry wood characteristics (for example, worm tracking) will be seen repetitively throughout an elevation of cherry veneers once laid up and sequence matched for a kitchen or bath project.

Hickory and Pecan

Typically, hickory and pecan are grouped together. However, botanically, they are slightly different: the true hickory has no fruit, and the pecan hickories are fruit-bearing. These two species grow principally in the Eastern United States in Central and Southern states.

Hickory and pecan color tones can vary widely: the sap wood of hickory is white, tinged with inconspicuous, fine brown lines, while the heartwood is pale to reddish brown. Both are coarse textured, with grain anywhere from straight to very wavy or irregular.

Mahogany

In some parts of the world, mahogany is considered an endangered species: the most notable area of concern is uncertified mahogany harvested from South American Rain Forests. African mahogany is more readily available, and is not considered an endangered species.

The wood is medium hard, pink when freshly cut, darkening to copper-red-brown with pale golden brown tones. The grain can be straight or wavy in solid woods. The texture is medium to coarse, with growth rings fairly distinct. Therefore, noticeable color variations are present in laid up solid panels.

A Popular Veneer: "Ribbon" mahogany is oftentimes requested by designers or clients. Sapele veneer can be substituted to insure a more consistent striped figure with broad alternating pink and red-brown bands. This repetitive grain appearance is possible because of clearer rings and the greater hardness of the wood. The coppery-red color resembles mahogany.

Lyptus wood, a plantation-grown hard wood from Brazil, is an environmental alternative to mahogany. Details of this eco-friendly wood will be found at the end of this section.

Maple

Commercial maples grow throughout the eastern United States and southeastern United States, with the exception of big leaf maple, which grows on the West Coast. Maple is often divided into two classes—hard maple and soft maple. Hard maple includes sugar maple and black maple. Soft maple is made up largely of silver maple and red maple with a very small proportion of boxelder.

Maple is heavy, strong, stiff and hard; has a high resistance to shock; and ranks high in nail-holding ability. The wood turns well on a lathe and is markedly resistant to abrasive wear. It takes stain satisfactorily and is capable of a high polish. The wood of soft maples is not as heavy, as hard or as strong as that of the hard maples.

Maple is a consistently popular wood for furniture and cabinetry. As much as 90% of the maple lumber produced is further manufactured into a variety of products such as furniture, kitchen cabinets, architectural woodwork and flooring.

A Popular Veneer: Plain sliced maple, quartered maple and Bird's-eye Maple are often used as veneer surfacing. Plain sliced maple will feature typical cathedral patterns. Quartered maple has a much more striped look because of the smaller size of maple trees. Bird's-eye Maple is a specialty product appreciated because of the figure created when clusters of cells within the maple explode after being frozen and then thawed in cold climate maple forests. In natural products the bird's-eye pattern is irregular, tending to cluster as opposed to being spread throughout the log.

For all maple veneers, the natural wood characteristics (mineral streaks, for example) will be repetitively seen when maple veneer "leaves" are laid up together in an overall cabinet elevation.

Oak

Oak species are found throughout the United States. Commercial stands generally grow east of the Great Plains. Oaks are grouped as white oaks or red oaks. Both red and white oak are used extensively for furniture and flooring. White Oak typically has a straighter grain than Red Oak and longer rays, therefore, it has more figures. Oak is the most popular wood for kitchen cabinets and is widely used in architectural trim, paneling and cabinetry.

Oak is hard, stiff, strong and shock resistant. It is above average in all machining properties except shaping. The wood undergoes large shrinkage while drying; seasoning must be done carefully to avoid checking and warping.

A Popular Veneer: Oak veneers are popular with straight grain cuts, typically called "quartered oak" or "rift cut oak."

Pine – Ponderosa

Ponderosa pine is the most widely distributed pine in North America, extending from British Columbia into Mexico and from the Pacific Coast to Nebraska. The wood is comparatively light in weight, soft, moderately weak in bending and moderately low in shock resistance. The grain is generally straight, but frequently shows dimpling on the tangetial surface. It resists splitting when nailed, but is only average in nail-holding ability. Ponderosa pine dries easily, either in dry kilns or by air seasoning, and is moderately low in shrinkage.

Ponderosa pine is the principal millwork species and is used for window framing, sashes, doors, molding, shelving and paneling. It is well suited for furniture, kitchen cabinets and architectural woodwork if hardness or high strength are not required.

Pine – White

Western white pine (Pinus Monticola) grows on western mountain ranges from Southern British Columbia and Southwestern Alberta to Northern Idaho, Northwestern Montana, and Eastern Oregon to the southern end of the Sierra Nevada Mountains in California. Eastern white pine (Pinus Strobus) grows from Newfoundland to Lake Winnipeg in Canada and southward through the Lake states and New England, and in the Appalachians as far south as Northern Georgia.

The wood of eastern and western white pine have similar characteristics. Both are moderately soft, straight-grained, light woods that are moderately low in shock resistance. They work easily with tools, are easy to glue and hold paint very well. They do not split readily when nailed, but have only medium nail-holding ability. They are fairly easy to dry, shrink moderately and stay in-place well when properly dried. The occurrence of "wet pockets" or "wetwood" in some lumber may require special attention during drying.

Eastern white pine is more commonly used for furniture, although some western white pine is used. Western white pine is often used for Colonial period furniture reproductions.

Walnut

From ancient Greece through modern European history walnut has been a favored wood by cabinetmakers. Walnut is a tough hardwood of medium density.

The sap wood of walnut is creamy white, while the heartwood is brown to a dark chocolate brown, occasionally with purple, darker streaks. The wood develops a rich patina that grows more lustrous with age. It is usually supplied steamed to darken the sap wood. It is generally straight grained, but has wavy or curly grain and burled figure patterns.

Walnut is one of the few American wood species planted on tree farms as well as naturally regenerated. American walnuts are darker in color than those from other parts of the world. All walnuts have lively color variations due to dark brown, dark gray and black streaks following the ring pattern in the wood. Tones can be pinkish-brown with blackish-brown streaks as well.

Specialty Veneers

Designers may be asked to specify exotic veneers. Working with unique veneers is a specialty. Designers should partner with experienced experts before specifying unusual woods. Popular veneers are as follows:

Special Cuts of American Popular Wood Species

- **Anegre:** Anegre has a beautiful repetitive figured pattern that makes it a popular natural material to use. Laminate-looking Anegre woods are also very popular.

- **Bubinga:** Bubinga is an unusual wood with a distinctive figure.

- **Lacewood:** A highly figured decorative veneer.

- **Pearwood:** International manufacturers use natural Pearwood. Simulated laminate Pearwood is also used.

- **Wenge:** A very dark, distinctly textured wood that is used by international manufacturers as well.

Planning Tips When Working with Veneers

With a renewed interest in fine veneers comes new responsibilities for the designer. Veneers allow the designer to work with a product that produces unlimited visual effects. Each specie offers its own interplay of color, grain, figure and texture. Each log within a specie possesses an unrepeatable character produced by the individual circumstances of its growth.

Additionally, in its natural state, veneers provide an impressive palette of colors—tans, browns, reds, violets, blondes and pinks. Besides color, grain patterns are naturally distinct from species to species and from log to log. The log's basic grain structure, created by the annual growth rings, produces different grain patterns depending on the direction the veneer is sliced in relationship to the log's growth rings. For example, veneers cut at a tangent to the ring (flat cut) produce narrow heart and cathedral grain patterns. Veneers cut through the radius (quarter cut) produce straight comb and ribbon striped grain patterns.

Figure adds yet another variable. Curly, fiddle-back, mottle, pommelé, bird's-eye, burl and crotch figures add unique texture and may be evident in varying emphasis in a given log.

Because of the wide variety of species available, and the highly individual characteristic of each log, a designer must partner with an expert who can assist in selecting—not settling on—the best wood for the job.

DESIGN CONSIDERATIONS

- In entry-level stock products the drawer head and doors are cut in mass, therefore, there is no grain matching on the veneer between drawers and doors installed on the case. This may not be considered a detriment in that the grain pattern on the drawer of inexpensive veneer cabinets runs horizontally, while the grain runs vertically for the door.

- In Level 1 grain matching projects, the designer may specify grain matching within each unit: this means the door and drawer grain runs in the same direction and is cut from the same panel. Such a specification is more costly because it does not allow for "yield maximization" when the veneer panels are cut from large 4' x 8' sheets of panel stock.

- In Level 2 grain matching projects, grain is matched throughout each elevation: each entire run of cabinet needs to then be cut from sequential panels from the same log. This type of project requires a close collaboration as the designer presents his/her full set of finished plans to the wood supplier for sourcing and estimating before the final contract is signed.

- In Level 3 grain matching projects, each door has balanced veneer figures. This effort is called "blueprint matching." It is the customized manufacture of panels and doors of various sizes in which entire rooms are matched in sequence with door and cabinet components by using balanced or center balanced matched panels.

- Of special note: whenever grain matching is planned, three special planning requirements exist:

  1. The consumer must understand and accept that any damage to the veneer on the jobsite must be repaired by a finishing expert because the sequence matched veneer pattern cannot be interrupted by a replacement piece.

  2. All appliance panels, accent pieces and custom end panels must be cut from the same stock as the door panels are cut.

  3. Solid wood accents from the same wood species (if available) are best avoided because the grain pattern, figure and color will not match the veneers used.

VENEER SPECIFICATIONS

Whenever a grain matching specification is planned:

- Veneer specialists first focus on the amount of veneer needed for a project. Before material selection begins, the following requirements must be considered:

  1. Ceiling Height: Determines length of panels required. (Architectural panels are generally 8' to 12' in height.)

2. Key Elevations: Determines the need for any accent veneers (burl, etc.) in featured areas.

3. Net Square Footage: Determines panel surface area. Generally, it takes 3 square feet of veneer to yield 1 square foot of finished paneling.

4. Panel Width: Panels with widths to 48" are standard, widths up to 60" can be produced.

5. Architectural Panels: Architectural panels are generally 3/4" thick. The thickness of the veneer is often determined by the rarity of the wood and where the product is milled. This is critical: a very thin (1/8," 3.3 mm thick) exotic Pearwood panel from Europe cannot be hand sanded during the finishing process because of the fear of "sand through."

- Next, the actual flitch(es) which will best fit the specifications must be identified. This is done by inspecting veneer samples.

APPROVING A FLITCH SAMPLE

Normally, three leaves (sheets) are drawn from evenly spaced positions within a flitch to give a broad picture of how the grain pattern progresses through the flitch and what character marks develop. The sample is identified with the sheet and flitch number, along with a note identifying the total square footage of the flitch available. Placed side-by-side, these samples show the designer and client what is happening to the grain and character of the wood throughout the flitch from outside of the tree to the center.

Typically, younger wood on the outside will be narrower and will show fewer defects than those found in the center. Such a flitch sample must be approved by the client and the log reserved for the project for upscale custom work.

Only after the extensive selection process has been completed will manufacturing begin.

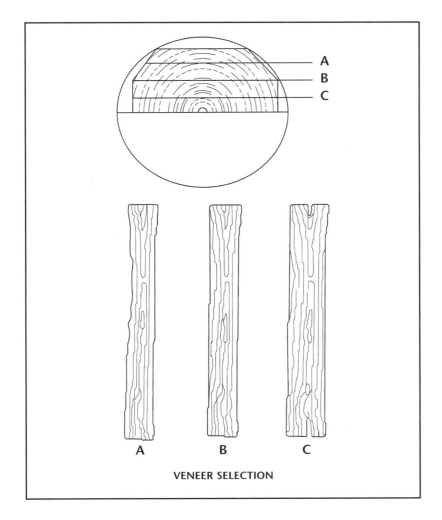

A
B
C

A   B   C

VENEER SELECTION

Figure 1.23 *Approving the Veneer Flitch* (Courtesy of Dooge Veneers Inc.)

VENEER CUTTING METHODS

The way veneer is cut is an important factor in producing a variety of visual effects. A mill could conceivably take a single panel, cut it in four/five different ways, and end up with four/five distinct-looking pieces of veneer.

Figure 1.24 *Veneer Cutting Methods* (Courtesy of Dooge Veneers Inc.)

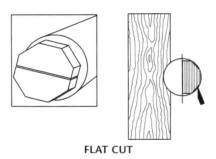

FLAT CUT

• Flat Cut (Plain Slicing): A log is cut in half length-wise, then placed on the slicer where the knife cuts individual leaves of veneer parallel to the original cut. Flat cutting produces a cathedral or loop grain effect in the center of the leaf and straighter grain along the edges.

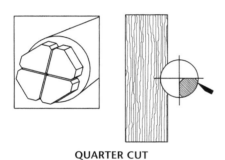

QUARTER CUT

• Quarter Cut: A quartered section of log is placed on the slicer and the knife cuts individual leaves of veneer at a 90 degree angle to the growth rings. Quarter cutting produces a striped effect—straight in some species and varied in others.

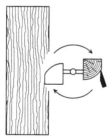

RIFT CUT

• Rift Cut: Oak is the only species that is rift cut. Oak produces cells that form a pattern of medullary rays which radiate from the center of the log. To avoid the bold, flake effect of cutting oak on the true quarter, a quartered section of log is placed on a rotary slicer and veneer is cut at an angle, about 15% off the quartered position. Rift cutting produces a rift or comb grain effect.

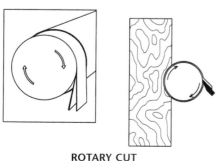

ROTARY CUT

• Rotary Cut: A full log is placed in the lathe and turned against a razor-sharp blade which peels a continuous sheet of veneer along the annular growth rings. Rotary cut veneer is exceptionally wide and produces bold, variegated grain markings.

VENEER MATCHING TECHNIQUES

Veneer is bundled and stored in the exact sequence in which it was sliced from the log. Before it is laid up for practical use, the designer or mill worker must select one of many methods of matching the individual leaves. Each method produces a unique visual effect and should be selected based on the type of veneer used, the visual effect desired and the intended application.

• Typically seen in the cabinet industry: Book and Slip Match

• Special matches used in accent wood areas: Book and Butt Match, Diamond and Reverse Match.

BOOK MATCH

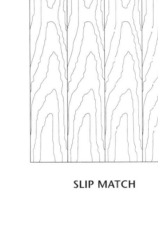

SLIP MATCH

Figure 1.25 *Veneer Matching Techniques* (Courtesy of Dooge Veneers Inc.)

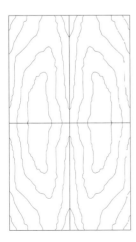

BOOK & BUTT MATCH

DIAMOND MATCH

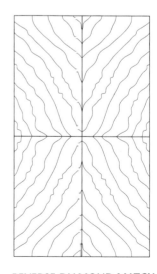

REVERSE DIAMOND MATCH

An Alternative to Veneers: "Super Natural" Woods

Anyone who has worked with veneers knows how temperamental they can be. Color variations, grain irregularities and imperfections can result in low yield and too many dissimilarities in the final product to satisfy the client.

Still, demand for veneers is growing. Sourcing raw natural veneers for projects that require minimum levels of surface structure consistency presents a continuing challenge. Therefore, designers are forced to either reconsider the species they want to work with, or to dramatically increase budgets to accommodate the cost of quality raw veneers.

A third option is to consider engineered or reconstituted veneers. Many are emerging "green" wood products. Here are five popular choices currently being used in the cabinet industry.

- **Bamboo**. Bamboo is a renewable grass product. Manufacturers harvest this renewable wood source by cutting it and leaving a 4' stump that will regenerate in five years. It is the quick growing nature of bamboo that makes it such an important "green" product—it has a much lower environmental impact than environmentally-managed wood forests.

  Bamboo is 30% harder than oak, and generally comparable in price to oak. The natural color of bamboo is light and resembles maple. It also comes in a caramel or carbonized version that is a deeper brown. An advantage of this darker finish: because the color goes all the way through, it can be sanded and refinished. If scratched, the darker color will remain whereas most wood receives a topical stain so the lighter wood underneath is exposed when scratched.

- **Bleaching**. The bleaching process neutralizes variations of color in the woods, removing color differences that could be considered unacceptable in the final product. The dying process then penetrates the entire thickness of the veneer—it can even be repaired by sanding if scratched—and improves the appearance of the wood grain.

- **Lyptus**. Lyptus is a premium plantation-grown hardwood from Brazil that has excellent workability, machining properties, density and finish possibilities. It is considered a wise environmental choice and an alternate to mahogany because it is produced in a sustainable way by environmentally responsible plantations. Because it grows fast in cool climates it can be harvested in 14 to 16 years. It is highly valued because it preserves natural habitat eco systems. It is available in two commercial grades:

1. Standard Grade: A clear face grade free of knots, holes, gum pockets and stains, it contains all colors in the wood's natural continuum from pink and red. However, no two pieces are allowed with sharp contrasts within the piece, therefore providing a more evenly finished face elevation.

2. Striped Grade: It has a clear face free of knots, holes and gum pockets, and contains pieces with sharp color contrast within the piece, presenting a dramatic contrast between sap wood and heartwood which gives a striped effect.

- **Dyed Veneers**. Natural veneers have been bleached and then dyed either back to natural or to fantasy colors.

- **New Wood**. Reconstituted veneers are real woods that have been reglued, resliced and dyed to mimic more valuable woods. Reconstituted woods take consistency to another level. They are created by gluing together natural veneers in special presses, and reslicing to get certain predetermined effects: either faithful reproductions of natural veneers or off-the-wall geometric effects. These reconstituted and recut veneers demonstrate a responsible use of limited natural resources, and are beginning to be seen in the kitchen cabinetry industry as well.

Finishing Systems

Although most cabinet manufacturers supply prefinished casework, designers should have a working knowledge of wood coloring and wood finishing.

VARIATIONS IN COLOR

The designer must understand why wood parts finish differently and various wood species require special finishing considerations. For example, there can be different absorption rates present within one piece of wood. This defect is associated with random variation in porosity, such as the tissue around knots in pine.

The variation can be caused by how the tree grows or caused by a bundle of fibers growing in a wavy fashion within the tree and at angles to the vertical access. When the log is cut, some bundles of fiber are cut parallel to the main direction of growth and some are cut at an angle, exposing the fiber end with its open water conducting channels or pores. Such open surface inevitably will assume darker hues than surfaces composed of near parallel bundles of fiber, producing a "blotchy" effect when stain is applied. A similar variation in color caused by differing wood fibers occurs when veneer panels are rounded or solid wood molding are curved.

Additionally, some natural wood colors (in the presence of oxygen and light) will change to darker finishes. For example, cherry will become much redder during the life of the furniture piece. When this darkening occurs in lacquered veneers it is often viewed—erroneously—as the fault of the finish.

ENHANCING NATURAL WOOD TONES

The natural color of the wood can be enhanced by simply adding a coat of oil. The approximate color resulting from a transparent finish can be determined with a "wet test." Simply moisten an area of the unfinished wood with clean water. The more porous woods will show a greater change in color than woods with closed grains.

STAINING WOODS

Stains are employed to bring out the full beauty of the grain, or to emphasize the color of the woods.

Woods with no color that must be stained are: basswood, poplar, gumwood and white pine.

Light-colored woods that may be finished in their natural color or stained include: ash, beech, birch, cherry, elm, oak, maple, chestnut and mahogany.

Stain is not usually used on veneers or wood with natural beauty and rich color, such as butternut, mahogany, rosewood, teak and walnut. These woods, which have a natural beauty of pattern and color, should receive a clear finish which will magnify their beauty.

It must be remembered that a stain is not a finish, and that a finishing coat must be applied over it, except in the case of varnish stains, penetrating wood-sealer finishes and lacquer containing stain.

TYPES OF STAIN

- **Water Stain**. Powder, best applied with spray equipment. Will raise grain of wood. No preliminary sealer coat required.

- **NGR Stain (Non-grain Raising)**. Stains in which powders are dissolved in a solvent other than water to minimize the problem of grain raising. Best applied with spray equipment, which carries mixture into the pores of the wood and later evaporates.

- **Spirit Stain**. Powders soluble in alcohol which are very quick drying. Best applied with spray equipment. Can result in a slight muddiness in the finish.

- **Pigmented Wiping Stain**. Effective in staining a cabinet made from different woods. Pigments are in suspension in a penetrating resin vehicle. While all stains are wiped, wiping is the most important step in the application of this type of stain.

- **Varnish Stain**. Not often used for fine wood finishes, these stains fill, color and add a gloss to the surface, all in one coat. When a product is made from less expensive grades of lumber, varnish stains may be successful because they give a uniform coloring to woods streaked with very soft and porous parts.

COLORING WOODS

Paint, colored lacquer and tinted varnish will provide a painted appearance on cabinetry. Painting will conceal the wood grain on tightly grained wood species. During painting, an undercoat primer with no gloss is applied, then followed by a finish coat of high gloss, semi-gloss or satin. The lacquer will give a colored finish, yet retain the beauty of the wood grain.

Pickled finishes (white pigment rubbed into woods to enhance the grain) give wood cabinets the look of an antique scrubbed surface. Pickling is most dramatic on woods with large pores such as oak and ash, although it works well on others too.

Additionally, paint dragging—white or off-white paint left in cabinet joints and within distressed sections—heightens this "Old World" antique look. This appealing vintage effect works beautifully in many kitchens and bathrooms.

SEALING WOODS

A sealer coat should be applied to a wood surface after a stain has been used, unless otherwise directed. The sealer coat is normally a thin coat of the material used for the coloring. The purpose of the sealer is to keep the stain from bleeding into succeeding coats, by sealing the pores and to smooth it for the final finish.

TOP COATING (FINISHING) WOOD

The finish coat will give a high gloss, stain-rubbed or polish-rubbed finish. The most common clear finishes are lacquer, oil, penetrating wood sealer, shellac and varnish.

- **Lacquer Finish**. A finish which has generally replaced varnish and shellac. Spray equipment is required for proper application. The lacquer offers a hard, durable, water-resistant surface. It is mirror-smooth and transparent, enhances the colors over which it is laid, and brings out the beauty of the wood grain.

- **Oil Finish**. A most satisfactory finish on hard or close-grained woods. When this finish is properly applied, the wood is impervious to water, heat, scratches and most stains.

- **Penetrating Wood Sealer Finish and Penetrating Resin-oil Finish**. These finishes withstand stains, water marks, minor burns and scratches. These sealer finishes are of two general types: one which contains wax and one which contains varnish. The finish coating wax will give a soft sheen rather than a high gloss. Thin, medium and heavy consistencies are available.

- **Polyurethane Finish**. In addition to the conventional varnishes, there are several other synthetic clear coatings which make excellent finishes for furniture. Of these finishes, the clear, oil-modified urethanes are the most popular. They are highly resistant to abrasion, scratching, water, chemicals, grease, solvents, food stains, alcohol and oils. They form a coating on the surface without penetrating. They can be applied over bare wood, sealer, or a varnish finish. Do not apply a polyurethane finish over shellac or lacquer finish, unless it has been specifically formulated for polyurethane finishes.

- **Varnish**. Available in all gloss finishes. Will provide a finish that is resistant to water, alcohol and other liquids. Most varnishes today are made of synthetic resins which dry fairly rapidly to form a hard surface coating that is exceptionally resistant to rough wear.

- **Wax Finish**. A simple, effective way of finishing wood. Generally, the wax is applied over a dried and sanded sealer coat of shellac, varnish or oil.

VINTAGE FINISHES

In addition to a wide array of wood stains and fashionable colors for cabinetry, many consumers request cabinetry with hand-applied finishes creating an antique look. These finishes are reminiscent of a room that has developed the patina of a cherished, but well-worn furniture piece. Generically, they may be called "Vintage" multi-step or layered finishes.

To create these finishes, there are three broad categories of special effects employed.

- **Glazing**. Glazing is the application of a colored material after the base coat of stain or paint has been applied. There are four broad categories of glazing.

  1. *Patting Glazing*: Applied on white wood edging after wear, before finish, with "pat-pat-pat/sponge" rhythm.

  2. *Burnished Glazing*: Glazing applied over all surfaces and wiped off, leaving residue in all crevices and shaped elements. Also identified as a "penetrating glaze": laying color into the pores of the wood, allowing it to make a contribution to the finished color of the wood.

  3. *Striated Glazing*: A faux finish technique where the consistency of the glazing is such that it appears to be stripes of paint left from brush strokes in both a horizontal and vertical direction.

  4. *Dry Glazing*: Almost chalk-like consistency of material, applied after burnishing with a glancing stroke: appears on lead raised edges. Identified as "defining glazing."

- **Physical Distressing**. A person damages the wood finish to create the look of aged, beaten furniture. A variety of distressing systems are available, the techniques include: dents, relief cuts, chisel cuts, peck marks, and worm tracking. Such distressing can mimic natural wear, or be taken to an extreme level to create a rugged, worn look. Distressing is limited to wood; it is not applicable to veneers.

- **Special Effects**. Special effects are the application of specialized materials to recreate the sense of an aged wood surface. Typically, there are three broad categories that many manufacturers employ:

1. *Crackle*: Crackle is a random look reminiscent of common finish deterioration seen in porcelain (a very small crackle application), or weather deterioration of a furniture finish caused when the finish dries and cracks because of exposure to heat.

2. *Spatter/Cowtailing*: Spatter can be large and watery, small pinpoint black or light/dark brown lacquer which is sprayed across the finish in a random fine pattern to add depth to the finish. Small wisps of accent paints, sometimes called "cowtailing," may also be applied.

3. *Wear-thru*: Wear appears on the edge of the doors, the raise of moldings and other areas where a finish would naturally have been worn off through the continual opening and closing of doors over years of use. Wear also appears on the door, drawer and cabinet face frame.

Figure 1.26 *A Close-up Example of Cabinetry Featuring Physical Distressing and Wear-thru* (Courtesy of Dura Supreme Cabinetry)

TYPICAL DOOR STYLES

The door and drawer fronts are the most visible part of the cabinets, so they determine the style of the cabinets and usually set the design theme for the entire space. While a single cabinetmaker might have dozens of door styles, they generally fall into several broad categories.

SQUARE

| RAISED | RAISED BEADED | RECESSED SQUARE | RECESSED BEADED |

CURVED

| ARCH | RAISED CATHEDRAL | RECESSED CATHEDRAL |

FLAT

COLOR   WOOD

Figure 1.27 *Typical Door Designs* Cabinet door styles fall into broad categories based on their basic shape. Additional variations are created by adding special treatments such as beading, moldings, or beadboard. (First and third rows, courtesy of Wood-Mode Inc. Second row, courtesy of Shenandoah Cabinetry)

Flat Doors: Veneer and Laminates

These are flat shaped pieces of lumber, plywood or engineered board substrate. If a veneer is used, the designer should verify what grade of veneer is specified and how the door panels will be laid out permitting grain consistency per cabinet, per elevation or not at all.

This type of door style may have the edges finished in a PVC edge tape designed to blend with the doors, a finger-jointed wood veneer edge tape, or a solid wood edging.

Figure 1.28 *The Storage Systems: A Kitchen Featuring a Full Overlay Flat Door*
Sequence-matched panels add to the visual interest in this room. (Courtesy of Ellen Cheever, CMKBD – Wilmington, Delaware)

Flat Doors With A Wood Frame

Laminate or wood doors may be of a slab configuration with a wood, thick PVC edging or metal frame around the doors and drawers. This can provide a very high-tech, Contemporary look, or can have a Transitional sense if laminate and wood are combined.

Figure 1.29 *The Storage Systems: A Contemporary Kitchen Featuring a Framed Panel Door*
Cabinets with cherry wood doors mix with glass in this soft contemporary kitchen. (Courtesy of Robert Schwartz–New York, New York)

Flat Doors With A Continuous Pull/C-Channel/J-Channel Integral Pull

A wood or laminate slab door can have a metal or wood continuous strip of routed or shaped hardware that acts as the pull on the cabinet. This hardware may be placed at both the top of drawers and the top of doors to create two horizontal lines through the space. Alternatively, the hardware may be at the top of the doors and the bottom of the drawers so one wider strip is featured.

Figure 1.30 *The Storage Systems: A Kitchen Featuring a Framed Panel Door* The door style helps to create a charming Old World feel in this space. (Courtesy of Plain & Fancy Custom Cabinetry)

Figure 1.31 *The Storage Systems: A Transitional Kitchen Featuring a Framed Panel Door*
The combination of doors with framed wood panels and framed glass panels creates a transitional style room. (Courtesy of Plain & Fancy Custom Cabinetry)

Figure 1.32 *The Storage Systems: Bathroom Featuring a Full Overlay Door*
Vertical spice drawers and pulled base cabinets provide visual dimension and extra storage in this bath with square raised panel full overlay doors. (Courtesy American Woodmark)

Figure 1.33 *The Storage Systems: Bathroom with Curved Cabinet Doors* Curves of cabinet doors are echoed in the curved toe kick with ball feet in this transitional vanity with two drawer banks. (Courtesy MasterBath by RSI)

Figure 1.34 *The Storage Systems: A Traditional Kitchen with Miter Framed Cabinet Doors*
A feeling of elegance is created by the detailing on these flat panel doors. (Courtesy of Yorktowne Cabinetry)

Miter Framed Doors With Raised/Flat Panels

Doors that have a frame made up of two horizontal rails and two vertical stiles which are joined by a miter in each corner, with a panel floating in between. The door may have a flat or a raised center panel. The center panel may be made up of solid wood strips laid up as one panel, or a veneer center panel. When this look is created by routing a one-piece door, it is a false raised panel door. If the panel is flat, it is a recessed panel door. If the center section is raised, it is called a raised panel door. A raised or recessed panel door with an arch that is formed into the top and/or bottom rail is called a cathedral door. These doors are typically seen in Traditional settings.

Mortise-and-Tenon Doors With Raised/Flat Panels

Doors having a frame made of two horizontal members (called "rails") and two vertical members (called "stiles") which have a square joined corner and a panel floating in the center are mortise-and-tenon doors.

The door may have a flat or raised center panel. The center panel may be made up of solid wood strips laid up as one panel, or a veneer center panel. This door style is typically seen in Traditional and Old World settings. It can also be used in Transitional Rooms.

Specialty Doors

There are a wide variety of special materials used for accent doors in kitchen and bathroom cabinetry. Several of the most popular are detailed below.

MDF CARVED OR SHAPED DOORS

MDF material is shaped to emulate a mortise-and-tenon raised or flat panel door. This type of base material is typically used under a painted surface and in a Thermo Foil finishing system.

STAINLESS STEEL

Accent doors that feature a stainless steel pan are popular in both European and North American kitchens. The stainless steel pan receives a second pan of stainless steel (called a "double pan" door), or has a laminate, wood or melamine panel to match the case interior.

Figure 1.35 *The Storage Systems: An Example of Stainless Steel Accent Doors*
A kitchen combines stainless steel and Wenge wood to create a contemporary room. (Courtesy of Downsview Kitchens)

SPECIALTY CENTER PANELS

Miter framed doors and mortise-and-tenon doors may feature center panels of contrasting veneers, wood, wire, lattice, glass, rattan or other specialty materials. These types of doors are typically called "frame-only" doors.

Figure 1.36 *The Storage Systems: A Traditional Kitchen Featuring Rattan and Lattice Panel Inserts*
The dark finish is offset by the change in texture of the inset panels. (Courtesy of Plato Woodwork Inc.)

Figure 1.37 *The Storage Systems: An Example of Special Center Panels* Decorative "frame-only" glass doors add to the Old World nature of this kitchen. (Courtesy of Donald Gustason, CKD – Minneapolis, Minnesota)

SPECIALTY GLASS DOORS

Many manufacturers offer cabinet doors that emulate the look of historic mullion windows found in Colonial times, when glass was so difficult to produce it could only be made in small panes. These are typically called "mullion" or "muntin" doors. This accent door may have an arch at the top or be a square design. The mullions may only be on the face of the door backed by a solid piece of glass, or may be True or Tru divided-light mullions with individual panes of plain glass, specialty glass or beveled glass painstakingly placed within each opening.

CABINET MILLWORK DESIGN DETAILS

To accentuate fine cabinetry, Traditional rooms today oftentimes feature architectural details from the past. These include:

- **Columns** to surround a specially designed sink or cooktop cabinet, or to frame tall armoire cabinetry.

- **Turnings**—either half turnings flat against a cabinet, or full turnings at the edge of islands, on the face of wall cabinets or, again, around a special purpose cabinet.

- **Brackets** (sometimes called "corbels") in carved detail to support mantel hoods, countertop overhangs and decorative shelves.

- **Curved molding** that may have classical shapes, such as a crown molding, with carved details in the form of flowers, leaves or stylized patterns.

Each manufacturer's offering of such architectural accoutrements are specific to that manufacturer; therefore, the designer will find a wide array of products to accentuate a kitchen or bathroom from the manufacturer.

Figure 1.38 *The Storage Systems: A Close-up of Architectural Millwork Elements*
Turnings on the side of the vanity, an appliqué and decorative bracket, and dentil molding below the crown molding are architectural elements that help make special design statements. (Courtesy of Wood-Mode Inc.)

Figure 1.39 *The Storage Systems: An Example of Cabinet Architectural Millwork Details*
Architectural details can be easily combined with open storage cabinets or glass door cabinets. (Courtesy of Wellborn Cabinet Inc.)

KCMA CERTIFICATION PROGRAM

While many good quality cabinets are not certified, in some markets and situations it is important to the end-user to have certified cabinets. Therefore, it is important for you as a designer to be aware of the certification requirements for cabinet construction and durability. Cabinets and bath vanities bearing the Kitchen Cabinet Manufacturers Association (KCMA) Certification have met or exceeded the necessary requirements and are recommended by KCMA.

You should also be aware of the KCMA Certification requirements so you may recommend cabinets that meet or exceed these standards of manufacturing to your clients.

About the KCMA Certification Program

(Reprinted Courtesy of Kitchen Cabinet Manufacturers Association)

Encouraged by HUD and a need to better define a growing market in 1965, member companies of the Kitchen Cabinet Manufacturers Association (KCMA) came together to develop the national performance standard, ANSI/KCMA A161.1, and a nationally recognized testing and certification program utilizing independent laboratories. Every five years, the standard is revised through a demanding review process as required by the American National Standards Institute (ANSI), to incorporate material and technological changes in the industry.

The KCMA Certification Program assures the specifier or user of kitchen cabinets and bath vanities that the cabinet bearing the blue and white seal complies with the rigorous standards developed by the industry, and approved by ANSI through a canvas review process which includes government and private sector users, general interest groups and producers. Cabinets bearing the certification seal are exact duplicates of samples that have been independently tested for conformance to ANSI/KCMA A161.1.

The KCMA Certification Program is open to all cabinet manufacturers including non-KCMA members. Manufacturers may certify one, several, or all of their cabinet lines. Only those lines certified are listed in the annual KCMA Directory of Certified Cabinet Manufacturers.

Compliance with ANSI/KCMA standards is assured by initial cabinet testing, periodic unannounced plant pick-up and testing, and additional testing resulting from complaints. All testing is performed by an experienced independent laboratory.

These cabinets also comply with the provision of Paragraph 611-1.1, "HUD Minimum Property Standards—Housing 4910.1" 9/8/86.

Companies not licensed with the KCMA Certification Program may not claim or imply conformance with these standards for their products. KCMA, as the proprietary sponsor, reserves the right to question any claims of conformance and to test the products of any manufacturer making such claims. Should KCMA discover that a manufacturer is falsely representing that its products meet these standards, KCMA will take appropriate legal action.

Requirements For Earning The KCMA Certification Seal

- All cabinets shall be fully enclosed with backs, bottoms, sides, and tops on wall cabinets; and backs, bottoms, and sides on base cabinets, with certain specified exceptions on kitchen sink fronts, sink bases, oven cabinets, and refrigerator cabinets.

- All cabinets designed to rest on the floor must be provided with a toe space at least 2" deep and 3" high.

- All utility cabinets shall meet the same construction requirements as wall cabinets.

- Doors shall be properly aligned, have means of closure, and close without excessive binding or looseness.

- All materials must ensure rigidity in compliance with performance standard.

- Face frames, when used, shall be of thickness to provide rigid construction.

- For frameless cabinets, the ends, tops/bottoms, and back shall be of thickness necessary to provide rigid construction.

- Corner or lineal bracing shall be provided at points where necessary to ensure rigidity and proper joining of various components.

- All wood parts must be dried to a moisture content of 10 percent or less at time of fabrication.

- All exterior exposed surfaces and edges, except the edges of end panels and the edges of back panels, shall be free of saw marks and other imperfections and shall be filled and sanded, edge-banded, or otherwise finished to ensure compliance with the performance standards.

- All exterior exposed parts of cabinets shall have nails and staples set and holes filled.

- All exposed construction joints must be fitted in a workman-like manner consistent with specifications.

- All interior exposed surfaces shall be free of saw marks and poor workmanship, and shall be covered with a laminate material or have a minimum of one coat of clear or pigmented finish.

- Exposed cabinet hardware must comply with Builders Hardware Manufacturing Association finishing standards.

Test Cabinets Must Pass To Earn The KCMA Certification Seal

Five Structural Tests Measure Cabinet's Structural Integrity, Installation

- All shelves and bottoms are loaded at 15 pounds per square foot, and loading is maintained for seven days to ensure that there is no excessive deflection and no visible sign of joint separation or failure of any part of the cabinets or the mounting system.

- Mounted wall cabinets are gradually loaded to 500 pounds without any visible sign of failure in the cabinet or the mounting system.

- To test the strength of base-front joints, a load of 250 pounds is applied against the inside of cabinet-front stiles for cabinets with drawer rail, or 200 pounds is applied for cabinets without drawer rail, to ensure reliable front joints that will not open during stress in service or during installation.

- To test the ability of shelves, bottoms, and drawer bottoms to withstand the dropping of cans and other items, a three-pound steel ball is dropped from six inches above the surface. After the test, the drawer shall not be damaged and must operate as before the test with no visible sign of joint separation or failure of any part of the cabinet or mounting system.

- To test the ability of cabinet doors and connections to withstand impacts, a 10-pound sandbag is used to strike the center of a closed cabinet door and repeated with the door opened to a 45-degree angle. The door shall operate as before the test and show no damage or sign of separation or failure in the system.

Two Drawer Tests Required

- To test the ability of drawers and drawer mechanisms to operate with loading during normal use, drawers are loaded at 15 pounds per square foot and operated through 25,000 cycles. The drawers shall then remain operable with no failure in any part of the drawer assembly or operation system, and drawer bottoms must not be deflected to interfere with drawer operation.

- To test the ability of the drawer-front assembly to withstand the impact of closing the drawer under normal use, a three-pound ball is dropped 8 inches against the drawer assembly. After 10 drops, there shall be no evidence of looseness or structural damage to the drawer-front assembly that impairs operation.

Four Finish Tests Conducted

These tests create, in accelerated form, the cumulative effects of years of normal kitchen conditions of pre-finished cabinets. Cabinet finishes are inspected to ensure that stringent standards of appearance are also met.

- To test the ability of the finish to withstand high heat, a cabinet door is placed in a hotbox at 120 degrees Fahrenheit and 70 percent relative humidity for 24 hours. After this test the finish shall show no appreciable discoloration and no evidence of blistering, checks, or other film failures.

- To test the ability of the finish to withstand hot and cold cycles for prolonged periods, a cabinet door is placed in a hotbox at 120 degrees Fahrenheit for one hour, removed and allowed to return to room temperature and humidity conditions, and then placed in a cold box for one hour at -5 degrees Fahrenheit. The cycle is repeated five times. The finish shall then show no appreciable discoloration and no evidence of blistering, cold checking, or other film failure.

- To test the ability of the finish to withstand substances typically found in the kitchen and bath, exterior exposed surfaces of doors, front frames, and drawer fronts are subjected to vinegar, lemon, orange and grape juices, tomato catsup, coffee, olive oil, and 100-proof alcohol for 24 hours and to mustard for one hour. After this test, the finish shall show no appreciable discoloration, stain, or whitening that will not disperse with ordinary polishing and no indication of blistering, checks, or other film failure.

- To test the ability of the finish to withstand long periods of exposure to a detergent and water solution, a cabinet door edge is subjected to exposure to a standardized detergent formula for 24 hours. The door edge shall then show no delamination or swelling and no appreciable discoloration or evidence of blistering, checking, whitening, or other film failure.

GENERIC KITCHEN NOMENCLATURE

Cabinet manufacturers use a code to designate each cabinet's size, use and placement within the kitchen. The following pages will help you understand a generic nomenclature along with illustrations of various cabinets. This sample "manufacturer's specification list" will be similar to brochures provided to you by the various manufacturers you sell. This list would represent a stock manufacturer, and will include only a fraction of the many products available to you through a custom manufacturer. Also, this list will include only sizes and illustrations of framed cabinets. Most of the information for framed cabinets is typical for frameless cabinets.

After your review of this material, compare your manufacturer's specification brochures with this list. You will notice many similarities in both nomenclature and cabinetry.

General industry nomenclature is that the first two digits represent the width of the cabinet (12, 15, 18, 21, 24, etc.). The other sets of figures indicate height and/or depth choices when available.

The letters generally indicate types of cabinets: B (base cabinets), W (wall cabinets) and specialty cabinets. For example, (BCW) is a blind corner wall. The letters L or R generally indicated left or right hinging.

Thus, a U151284L is a utility cabinet 15" wide, 12" deep and 84" high, with the hinge on the left.

Base Cabinet Nomenclature

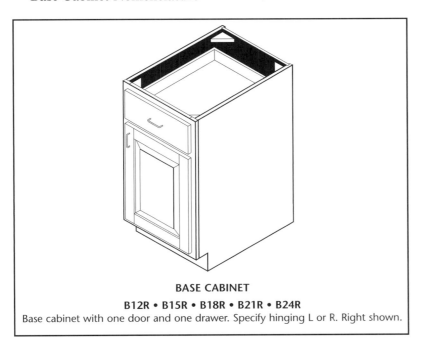

BASE CABINET

B12R • B15R • B18R • B21R • B24R

Base cabinet with one door and one drawer. Specify hinging L or R. Right shown.

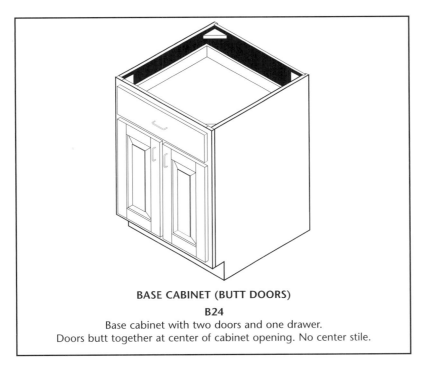

BASE CABINET (BUTT DOORS)

B24

Base cabinet with two doors and one drawer.
Doors butt together at center of cabinet opening. No center stile.

(Courtesy of David Newton Associates)

Base Cabinet Nomenclature

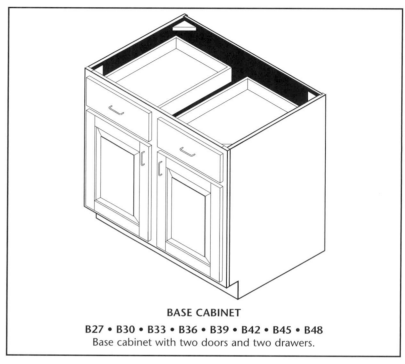

BASE CABINET

B27 • B30 • B33 • B36 • B39 • B42 • B45 • B48

Base cabinet with two doors and two drawers.

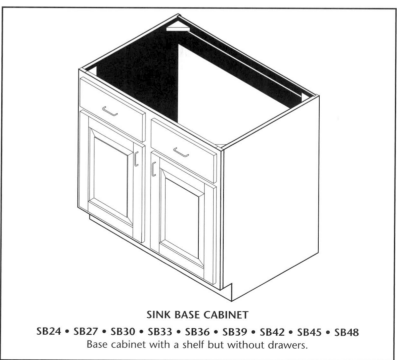

SINK BASE CABINET

SB24 • SB27 • SB30 • SB33 • SB36 • SB39 • SB42 • SB45 • SB48

Base cabinet with a shelf but without drawers.

(Courtesy of David Newton Associates)

Base Cabinet Nomenclature

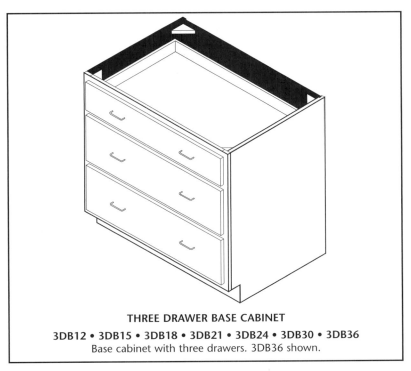

THREE DRAWER BASE CABINET
3DB12 • 3DB15 • 3DB18 • 3DB21 • 3DB24 • 3DB30 • 3DB36
Base cabinet with three drawers. 3DB36 shown.

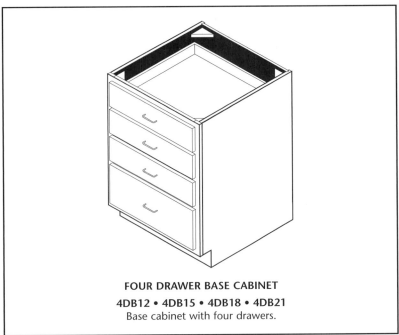

FOUR DRAWER BASE CABINET
4DB12 • 4DB15 • 4DB18 • 4DB21
Base cabinet with four drawers.

(Courtesy of David Newton Associates)

Base Cabinet Nomenclature

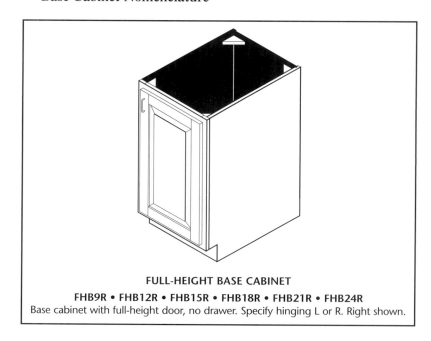

FULL-HEIGHT BASE CABINET

FHB9R • FHB12R • FHB15R • FHB18R • FHB21R • FHB24R

Base cabinet with full-height door, no drawer. Specify hinging L or R. Right shown.

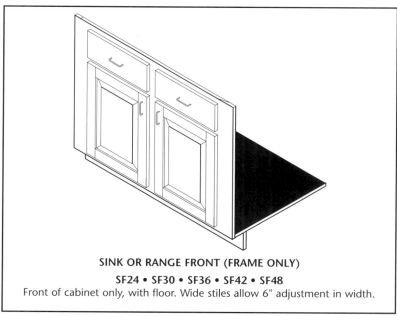

SINK OR RANGE FRONT (FRAME ONLY)

SF24 • SF30 • SF36 • SF42 • SF48

Front of cabinet only, with floor. Wide stiles allow 6" adjustment in width.

(Courtesy of David Newton Associates)

Base Cabinet Nomenclature

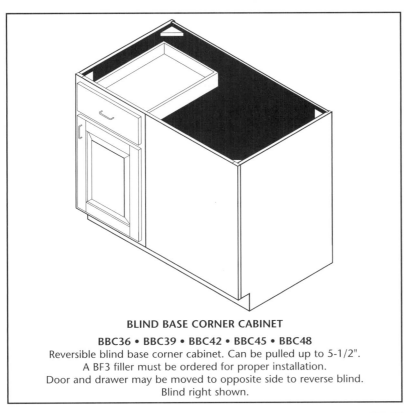

BLIND BASE CORNER CABINET

BBC36 • BBC39 • BBC42 • BBC45 • BBC48
Reversible blind base corner cabinet. Can be pulled up to 5-1/2".
A BF3 filler must be ordered for proper installation.
Door and drawer may be moved to opposite side to reverse blind.
Blind right shown.

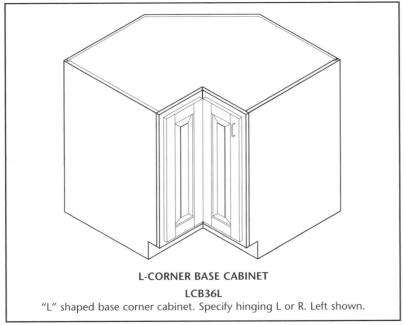

L-CORNER BASE CABINET

LCB36L
"L" shaped base corner cabinet. Specify hinging L or R. Left shown.

(Courtesy of David Newton Associates)

Base Cabinet Nomenclature

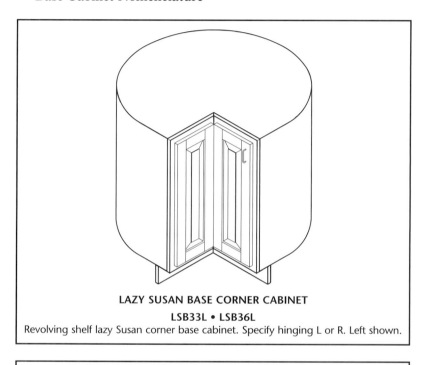

LAZY SUSAN BASE CORNER CABINET

LSB33L • LSB36L

Revolving shelf lazy Susan corner base cabinet. Specify hinging L or R. Left shown.

DIAGONAL CORNER BASE CABINET

DCB36L

Diagonal base cabinet for corner application. Specify hinging L or R. Left shown.

(Courtesy of David Newton Associates)

Base Cabinet Nomenclature

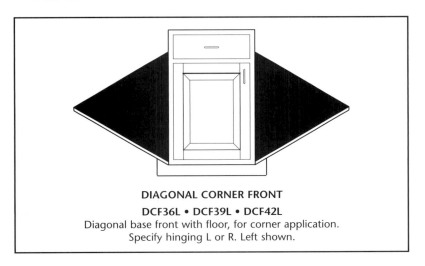

DIAGONAL CORNER FRONT

DCF36L • DCF39L • DCF42L

Diagonal base front with floor, for corner application.
Specify hinging L or R. Left shown.

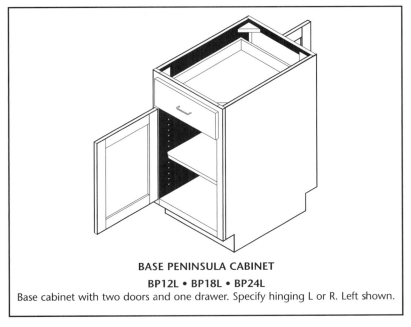

BASE PENINSULA CABINET

BP12L • BP18L • BP24L

Base cabinet with two doors and one drawer. Specify hinging L or R. Left shown.

(Courtesy of David Newton Associates)

Base Cabinet Nomenclature

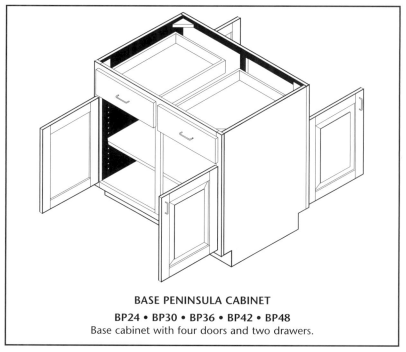

BASE PENINSULA CABINET

BP24 • BP30 • BP36 • BP42 • BP48

Base cabinet with four doors and two drawers.

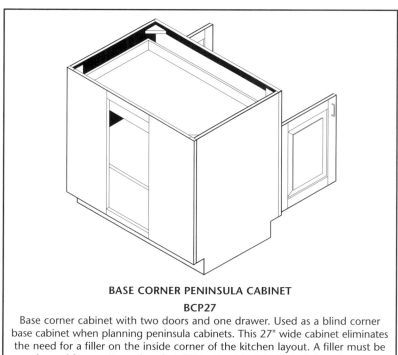

BASE CORNER PENINSULA CABINET

BCP27

Base corner cabinet with two doors and one drawer. Used as a blind corner base cabinet when planning peninsula cabinets. This 27" wide cabinet eliminates the need for a filler on the inside corner of the kitchen layout. A filler must be planned for any item placed at 90° to the BCP27. Blinded view shown.

(Courtesy of David Newton Associates)

Wall Cabinet Nomenclature

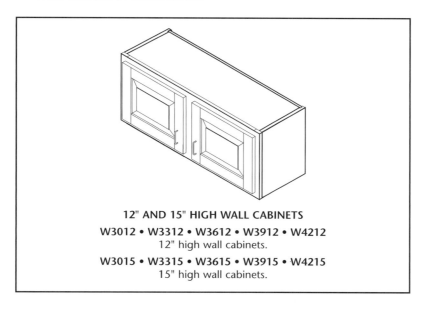

12" AND 15" HIGH WALL CABINETS
W3012 • W3312 • W3612 • W3912 • W4212
12" high wall cabinets.
W3015 • W3315 • W3615 • W3915 • W4215
15" high wall cabinets.

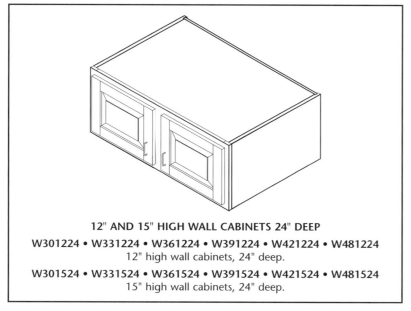

12" AND 15" HIGH WALL CABINETS 24" DEEP
W301224 • W331224 • W361224 • W391224 • W421224 • W481224
12" high wall cabinets, 24" deep.
W301524 • W331524 • W361524 • W391524 • W421524 • W481524
15" high wall cabinets, 24" deep.

(Courtesy of David Newton Associates)

Wall Cabinet Nomenclature

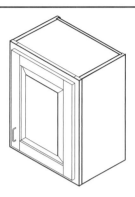

18" AND 24" HIGH WALL CABINETS

W1818R • W2118R • W2418R

18" high wall cabinet, single door. Specify hinging L or R. Right shown.

W1824R • W2124R • W2424R

24" high wall cabinet, single door. Specify hinging L or R. Right shown.

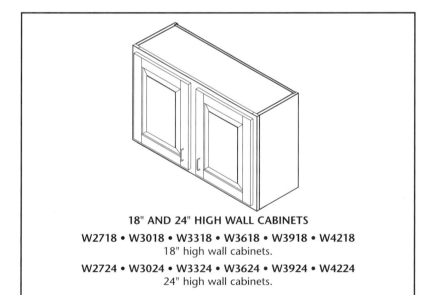

18" AND 24" HIGH WALL CABINETS

W2718 • W3018 • W3318 • W3618 • W3918 • W4218

18" high wall cabinets.

W2724 • W3024 • W3324 • W3624 • W3924 • W4224

24" high wall cabinets.

(Courtesy of David Newton Associates)

Wall Cabinet Nomenclature

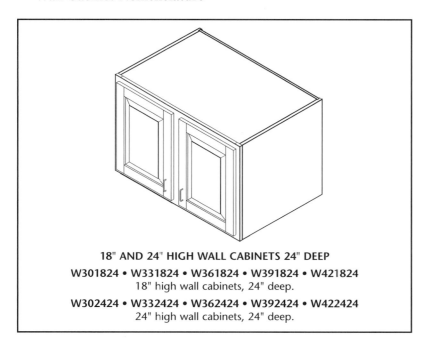

18" AND 24" HIGH WALL CABINETS 24" DEEP

W301824 • W331824 • W361824 • W391824 • W421824
18" high wall cabinets, 24" deep.

W302424 • W332424 • W362424 • W392424 • W422424
24" high wall cabinets, 24" deep.

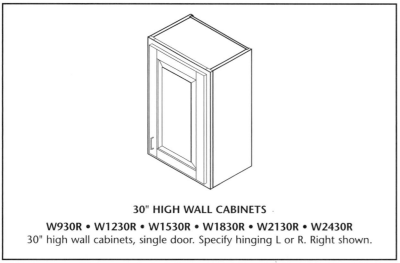

30" HIGH WALL CABINETS

W930R • W1230R • W1530R • W1830R • W2130R • W2430R
30" high wall cabinets, single door. Specify hinging L or R. Right shown.

(Courtesy of David Newton Associates)

Wall Cabinet Nomenclature

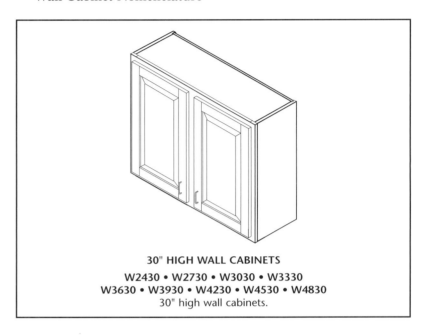

30" HIGH WALL CABINETS

W2430 • W2730 • W3030 • W3330
W3630 • W3930 • W4230 • W4530 • W4830
30" high wall cabinets.

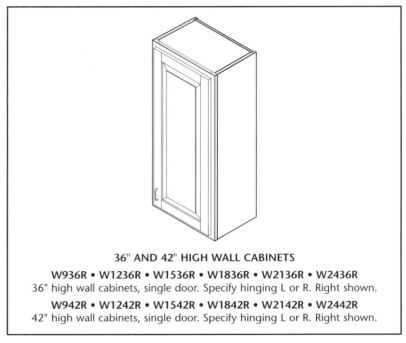

36" AND 42" HIGH WALL CABINETS

W936R • W1236R • W1536R • W1836R • W2136R • W2436R
36" high wall cabinets, single door. Specify hinging L or R. Right shown.

W942R • W1242R • W1542R • W1842R • W2142R • W2442R
42" high wall cabinets, single door. Specify hinging L or R. Right shown.

(Courtesy of David Newton Associates)

Wall Cabinet Nomenclature

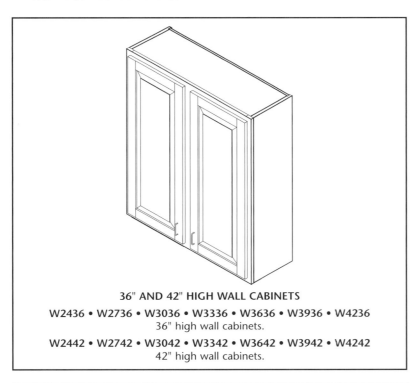

36" AND 42" HIGH WALL CABINETS

W2436 • W2736 • W3036 • W3336 • W3636 • W3936 • W4236
36" high wall cabinets.

W2442 • W2742 • W3042 • W3342 • W3642 • W3942 • W4242
42" high wall cabinets.

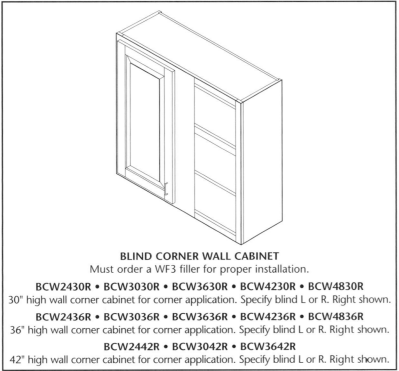

BLIND CORNER WALL CABINET
Must order a WF3 filler for proper installation.

BCW2430R • BCW3030R • BCW3630R • BCW4230R • BCW4830R
30" high wall corner cabinet for corner application. Specify blind L or R. Right shown.

BCW2436R • BCW3036R • BCW3636R • BCW4236R • BCW4836R
36" high wall corner cabinet for corner application. Specify blind L or R. Right shown.

BCW2442R • BCW3042R • BCW3642R
42" high wall corner cabinet for corner application. Specify blind L or R. Right shown.

(Courtesy of David Newton Associates)

Wall Cabinet Nomenclature

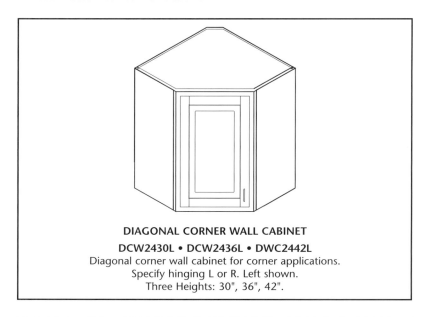

DIAGONAL CORNER WALL CABINET

DCW2430L • DCW2436L • DWC2442L

Diagonal corner wall cabinet for corner applications.
Specify hinging L or R. Left shown.
Three Heights: 30", 36", 42".

"L" CORNER WALL CABINET

LCW2430L • LCW2436L • LCW2442L

"L" corner wall cabinet for corner applications.
Specify hinging L or R. Left shown.
Three Heights: 30", 36", 42".

(Courtesy of David Newton Associates)

Wall Cabinet Nomenclature

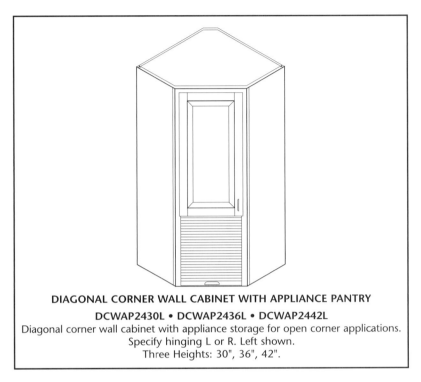

DIAGONAL CORNER WALL CABINET WITH APPLIANCE PANTRY
DCWAP2430L • DCWAP2436L • DCWAP2442L
Diagonal corner wall cabinet with appliance storage for open corner applications.
Specify hinging L or R. Left shown.
Three Heights: 30", 36", 42".

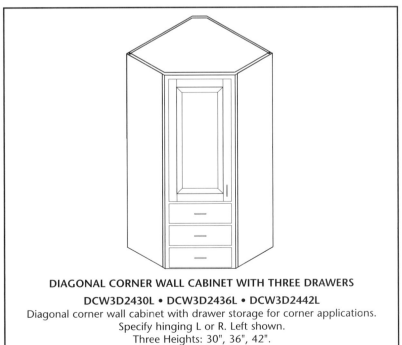

DIAGONAL CORNER WALL CABINET WITH THREE DRAWERS
DCW3D2430L • DCW3D2436L • DCW3D2442L
Diagonal corner wall cabinet with drawer storage for corner applications.
Specify hinging L or R. Left shown.
Three Heights: 30", 36", 42".

(Courtesy of David Newton Associates)

Wall Cabinet Nomenclature

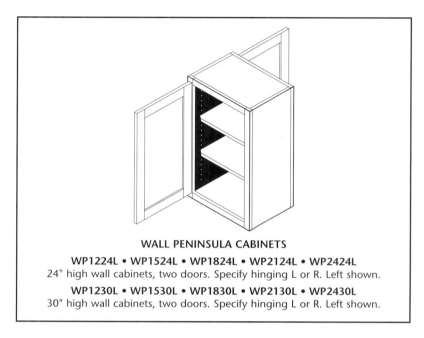

WALL PENINSULA CABINETS

WP1224L • WP1524L • WP1824L • WP2124L • WP2424L
24" high wall cabinets, two doors. Specify hinging L or R. Left shown.

WP1230L • WP1530L • WP1830L • WP2130L • WP2430L
30" high wall cabinets, two doors. Specify hinging L or R. Left shown.

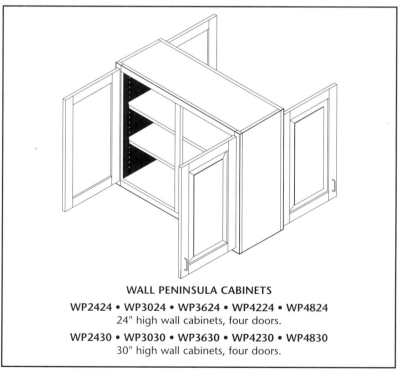

WALL PENINSULA CABINETS

WP2424 • WP3024 • WP3624 • WP4224 • WP4824
24" high wall cabinets, four doors.

WP2430 • WP3030 • WP3630 • WP4230 • WP4830
30" high wall cabinets, four doors.

(Courtesy of David Newton Associates)

Tall Cabinet Nomenclature

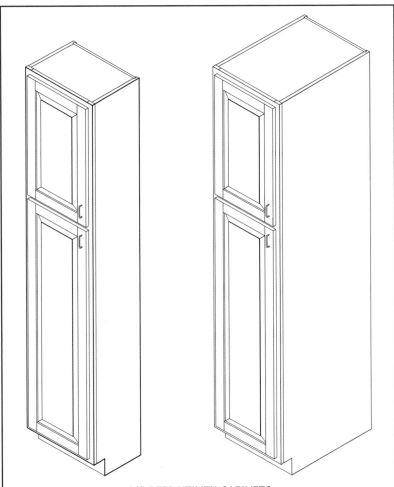

12" DEEP UTILITY CABINETS

U151284L • U181284L • U241284L
Single door, 12" deep, 84" high utility cabinets. Specify hinging L or R. Left shown.

U151290L • U181290L • U241290L
Single door, 12" deep, 90" high utility cabinets. Specify hinging L or R. Left shown.

U151296L • U181296L • U241296L
Single door, 12" deep, 96" high utility cabinets. Specify hinging L or R. Left shown.

24" DEEP UTILITY CABINETS

U152484L • U182484L • U242484L
Single door, 24" deep, 84" high utility cabinets. Specify hinging L or R. Left shown.

U152490L • U182490L • U242490L
Single door, 24" deep, 90" high utility cabinets. Specify hinging L or R. Left shown.

U152496L • U182496L • U242496L
Single door, 24" deep, 96" high utility cabinets. Specify hinging L or R. Left shown.

(Courtesy of David Newton Associates)

Tall Cabinet Nomenclature

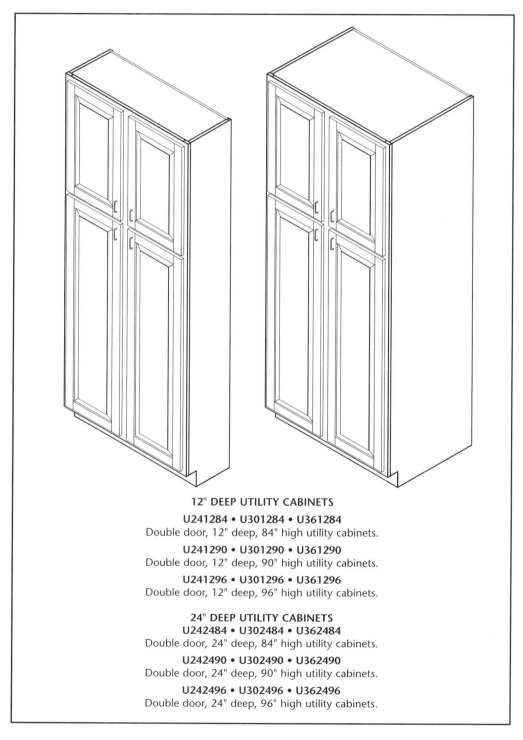

12" DEEP UTILITY CABINETS

U241284 • U301284 • U361284
Double door, 12" deep, 84" high utility cabinets.

U241290 • U301290 • U361290
Double door, 12" deep, 90" high utility cabinets.

U241296 • U301296 • U361296
Double door, 12" deep, 96" high utility cabinets.

24" DEEP UTILITY CABINETS
U242484 • U302484 • U362484
Double door, 24" deep, 84" high utility cabinets.

U242490 • U302490 • U362490
Double door, 24" deep, 90" high utility cabinets.

U242496 • U302496 • U362496
Double door, 24" deep, 96" high utility cabinets.

(Courtesy of David Newton Associates)

Tall Cabinet Nomenclature

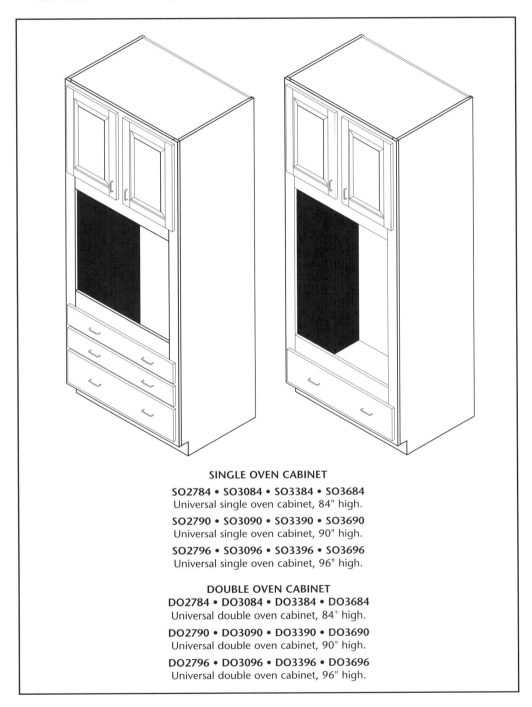

SINGLE OVEN CABINET

SO2784 • SO3084 • SO3384 • SO3684
Universal single oven cabinet, 84" high.

SO2790 • SO3090 • SO3390 • SO3690
Universal single oven cabinet, 90" high.

SO2796 • SO3096 • SO3396 • SO3696
Universal single oven cabinet, 96" high.

DOUBLE OVEN CABINET
DO2784 • DO3084 • DO3384 • DO3684
Universal double oven cabinet, 84' high.

DO2790 • DO3090 • DO3390 • DO3690
Universal double oven cabinet, 90" high.

DO2796 • DO3096 • DO3396 • DO3696
Universal double oven cabinet, 96" high.

(Courtesy of David Newton Associates)

Filler Nomenclature

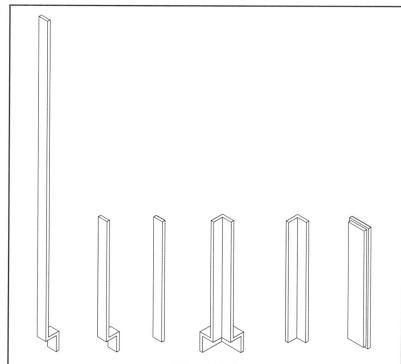

TALL FILLERS

TF3 • TF6

96" high in two widths (3" and 6").
Fillers can be cut in height and width for correct fit.

BASE FILLERS

BF3 • BF6

34-1/2" high in two widths (3" and 6").
Fillers can be cut in height and width for correct fit.

WALL FILLERS

WF3 • WF6

30" high in two widths (3" and 6"). Fillers can be cut in height and
width for correct fit. For taller wall fillers, order TF3 or TF6.

CORNER FILLERS

CBF3 • CWF3

Corner wall fillers can be cut in height.
Both base and wall fillers can be cut in width.

FULL OVERLAYS

TF03 • TF06 • BF03 • BF06 • WF03 • WF06

Overlays are available for all standard fillers. Designed for use with full-overlay
door styles. Specify door style to match door material, finish and edging profile.

(Courtesy of David Newton Associates)

Specialty Base Cabinet Nomenclature

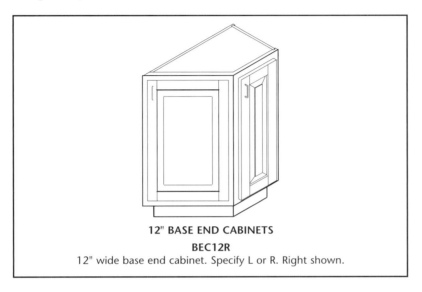

12" BASE END CABINETS

BEC12R

12" wide base end cabinet. Specify L or R. Right shown.

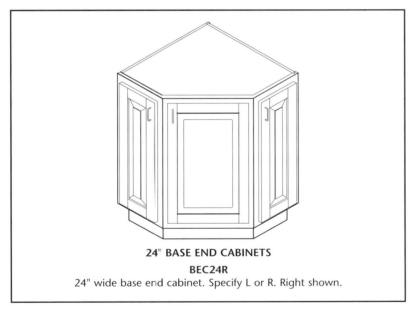

24" BASE END CABINETS

BEC24R

24" wide base end cabinet. Specify L or R. Right shown.

(Courtesy of David Newton Associates)

Specialty Base Cabinet Nomenclature

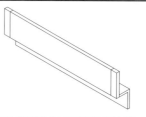

30" DROP-IN RANGE PANEL

RP30
A 30" wide panel placed below a drop-in range.
Height is adjusted to fit a drop-in range. Toekick is attached.

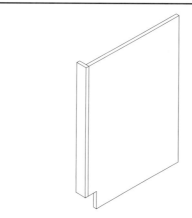

END PANEL (BEP-3R SHOWN)

WEP • WEP1 1/2 • WEP 3
Wall end panels 12" deep and 30" high without toekick notch shown above.
Reverse for R or L

BEP • BEP1 1/2 • BEP 3
A base panel usually placed beside a dishwasher at the end of a base cabinet run.
Stile widths of 3/4", 1-1/2" and 3". Larger sizes can be reduced in width.
Specify L or R. Right shown

TEP • TEP1 1/2 • TEP 3
A tall panel usually placed beside a refrigerator. Widths of 3/4", 1-1/2" and 3". The
two larger sizes can be trimmed to a smaller dimension. No toekick. Reverse R or L.

COUNTERTOP BRACKET (CORBEL)

CB
12" x 12" bracket to support countertop.

(Courtesy of David Newton Associates)

Specialty Wall Cabinet Nomenclature

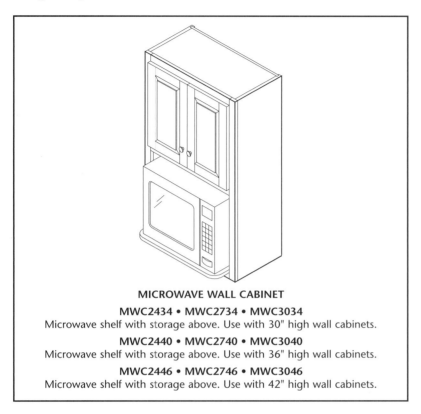

MICROWAVE WALL CABINET

MWC2434 • MWC2734 • MWC3034
Microwave shelf with storage above. Use with 30" high wall cabinets.

MWC2440 • MWC2740 • MWC3040
Microwave shelf with storage above. Use with 36" high wall cabinets.

MWC2446 • MWC2746 • MWC3046
Microwave shelf with storage above. Use with 42" high wall cabinets.

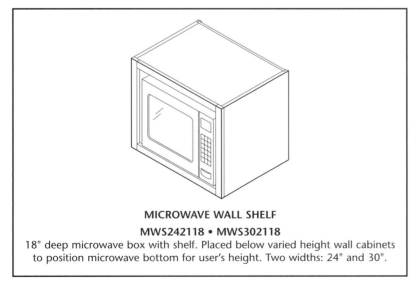

MICROWAVE WALL SHELF

MWS242118 • MWS302118
18" deep microwave box with shelf. Placed below varied height wall cabinets to position microwave bottom for user's height. Two widths: 24" and 30".

(Courtesy of David Newton Associates)

Specialty Wall Cabinet Nomenclature

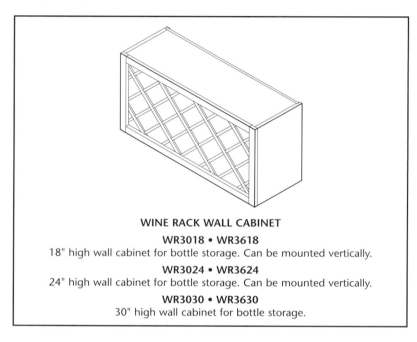

WINE RACK WALL CABINET

WR3018 • WR3618

18" high wall cabinet for bottle storage. Can be mounted vertically.

WR3024 • WR3624

24" high wall cabinet for bottle storage. Can be mounted vertically.

WR3030 • WR3630

30" high wall cabinet for bottle storage.

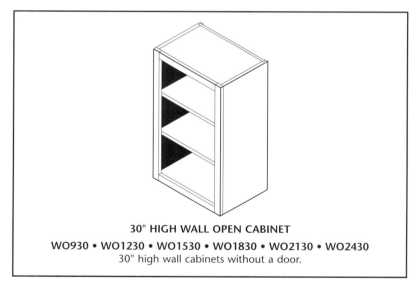

30" HIGH WALL OPEN CABINET

WO930 • WO1230 • WO1530 • WO1830 • WO2130 • WO2430

30" high wall cabinets without a door.

(Courtesy of David Newton Associates)

Specialty Wall Cabinet Nomenclature

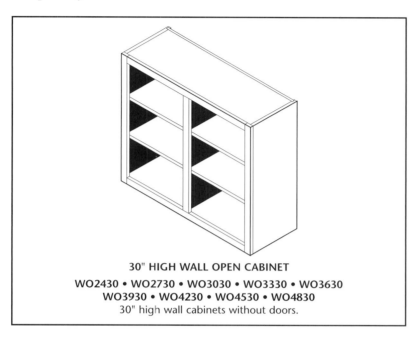

30" HIGH WALL OPEN CABINET
WO2430 • WO2730 • WO3030 • WO3330 • WO3630
WO3930 • WO4230 • WO4530 • WO4830
30" high wall cabinets without doors.

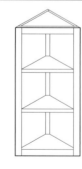

WALL END CABINETS

WEC1230R
30" high wall end cabinets. Order with or without door. Specify L or R.

WEC1236R
36" high wall end cabinets. Order with or without door. Specify L or R.

WEC1242R
42" high wall end cabinets. Order with or without door. Specify L or R.

(Courtesy of David Newton Associates)

Specialty Wall Cabinet Nomenclature

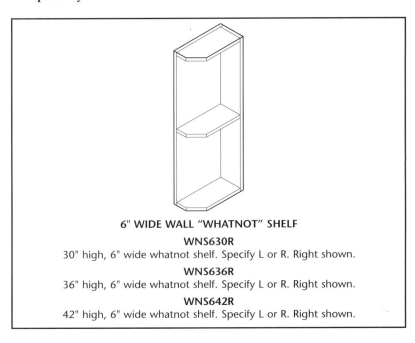

6" WIDE WALL "WHATNOT" SHELF

WNS630R
30" high, 6" wide whatnot shelf. Specify L or R. Right shown.

WNS636R
36" high, 6" wide whatnot shelf. Specify L or R. Right shown.

WNS642R
42" high, 6" wide whatnot shelf. Specify L or R. Right shown.

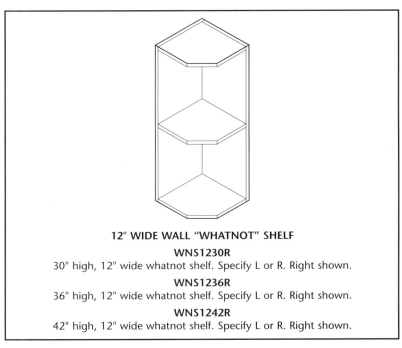

12" WIDE WALL "WHATNOT" SHELF

WNS1230R
30" high, 12" wide whatnot shelf. Specify L or R. Right shown.

WNS1236R
36" high, 12" wide whatnot shelf. Specify L or R. Right shown.

WNS1242R
42" high, 12" wide whatnot shelf. Specify L or R. Right shown.

(Courtesy of David Newton Associates)

Specialty Wall Cabinet Nomenclature

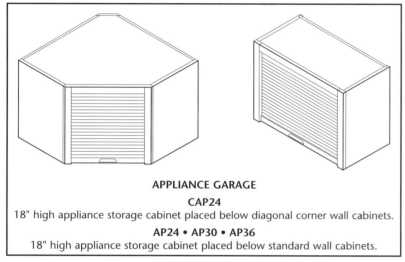

APPLIANCE GARAGE

CAP24
18" high appliance storage cabinet placed below diagonal corner wall cabinets.

AP24 • AP30 • AP36
18" high appliance storage cabinet placed below standard wall cabinets.

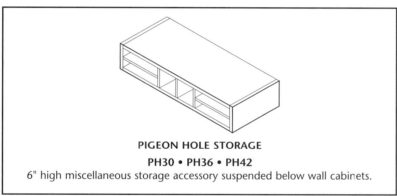

PIGEON HOLE STORAGE

PH30 • PH36 • PH42
6" high miscellaneous storage accessory suspended below wall cabinets.

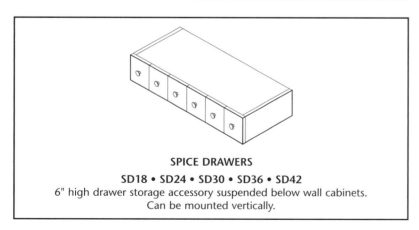

SPICE DRAWERS

SD18 • SD24 • SD30 • SD36 • SD42
6" high drawer storage accessory suspended below wall cabinets.
Can be mounted vertically.

(Courtesy of David Newton Associates)

Specialty Wall Cabinet Nomenclature

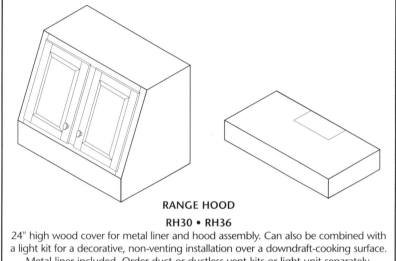

RANGE HOOD

RH30 • RH36

24" high wood cover for metal liner and hood assembly. Can also be combined with a light kit for a decorative, non-venting installation over a downdraft-cooking surface. Metal liner included. Order duct or ductless vent kits or light unit separately.

VALANCE BOARDS

Valance boards are placed between or under cabinets to hide light fixtures. These 4-1/2" high boards are available in 6" increments from 24" to 96" and can be reduced in width for exact fit as needed.

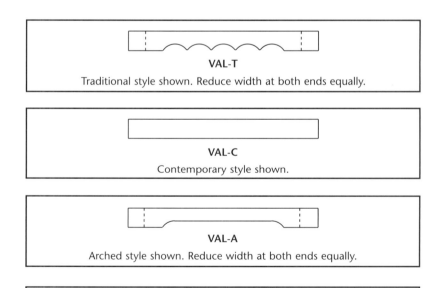

VAL-T

Traditional style shown. Reduce width at both ends equally.

VAL-C

Contemporary style shown.

VAL-A

Arched style shown. Reduce width at both ends equally.

VAL-EC

English Country style shown. Reduce width at both ends equally.

(Courtesy of David Newton Associates)

GENERIC BATHROOM NOMENCLATURE

Cabinet manufacturers use a code to designate each cabinet's size, use and placement within the bathroom. The following pages will help you understand a generic nomenclature along with illustrations of various cabinets and accessories. This sample "manufacturer's specification list" will be similar to brochures provided to you by the various manufacturers you represent. This list would represent a stock manufacture and will include only a fraction of the many products available to you through a custom manufacturer. Also, this list will include only sizes and illustrations of framed cabinets. Most of the information for framed cabinets is typical for frameless cabinets.

Vanity base cabinets are available in several heights depending on the manufacturer. These sizes range in height from 28-1/2" to 34-1/2" high for a finished countertop height of 30" to 36". This sample nomenclature will use a vanity base cabinet height of 32-1/2". The finished counter height would be 34".

After your review of this material, compare your manufacturer's specification brochures with this list. You will notice many similarities in both nomenclature and cabinetry.

Vanity Base Cabinet Nomenclature

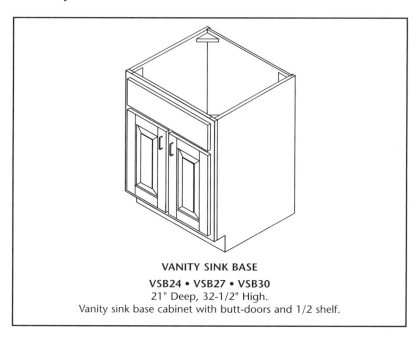

VANITY SINK BASE

VSB24 • VSB27 • VSB30

21" Deep, 32-1/2" High.
Vanity sink base cabinet with butt-doors and 1/2 shelf.

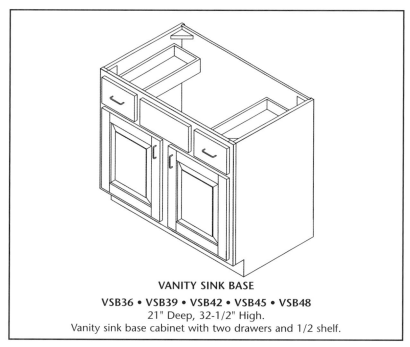

VANITY SINK BASE

VSB36 • VSB39 • VSB42 • VSB45 • VSB48

21" Deep, 32-1/2" High.
Vanity sink base cabinet with two drawers and 1/2 shelf.

(Courtesy of David Newton Associates)

Vanity Base Cabinet Nomenclature

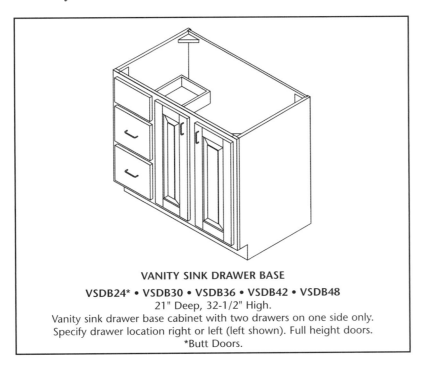

VANITY SINK DRAWER BASE
VSDB24* • VSDB30 • VSDB36 • VSDB42 • VSDB48
21" Deep, 32-1/2" High.
Vanity sink drawer base cabinet with two drawers on one side only.
Specify drawer location right or left (left shown). Full height doors.
*Butt Doors.

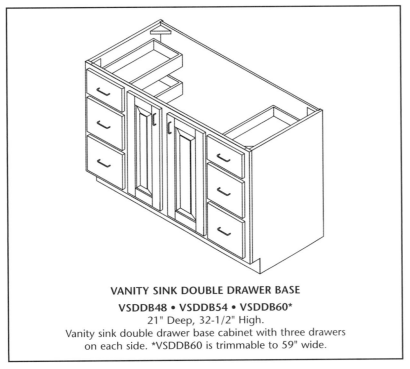

VANITY SINK DOUBLE DRAWER BASE
VSDDB48 • VSDDB54 • VSDDB60*
21" Deep, 32-1/2" High.
Vanity sink double drawer base cabinet with three drawers
on each side. *VSDDB60 is trimmable to 59" wide.

(Courtesy of David Newton Associates)

Vanity Base Cabinet Nomenclature

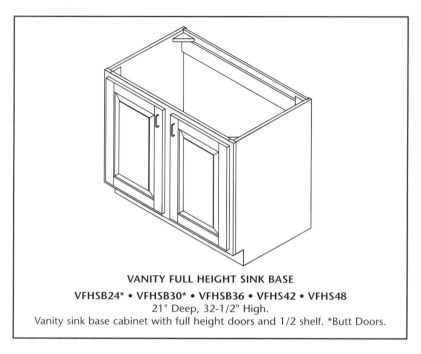

VANITY FULL HEIGHT SINK BASE
VFHSB24* • VFHSB30* • VFHSB36 • VFHS42 • VFHS48
21" Deep, 32-1/2" High.
Vanity sink base cabinet with full height doors and 1/2 shelf. *Butt Doors.

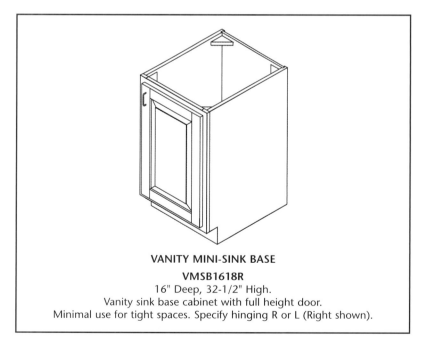

VANITY MINI-SINK BASE
VMSB1618R
16" Deep, 32-1/2" High.
Vanity sink base cabinet with full height door.
Minimal use for tight spaces. Specify hinging R or L (Right shown).

(Courtesy of David Newton Associates)

Vanity Base Cabinet Nomenclature

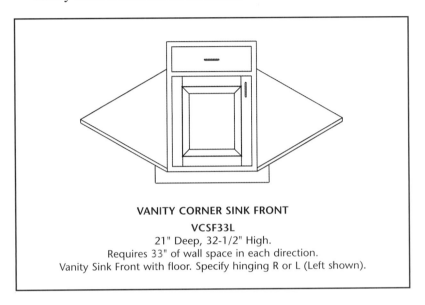

VANITY CORNER SINK FRONT
VCSF33L
21" Deep, 32-1/2" High.
Requires 33" of wall space in each direction.
Vanity Sink Front with floor. Specify hinging R or L (Left shown).

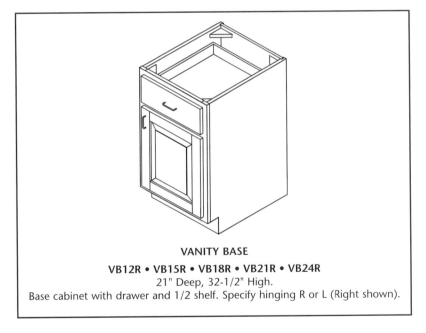

VANITY BASE
VB12R • VB15R • VB18R • VB21R • VB24R
21" Deep, 32-1/2" High.
Base cabinet with drawer and 1/2 shelf. Specify hinging R or L (Right shown).

(Courtesy of David Newton Associates)

Vanity Base Cabinet Nomenclature

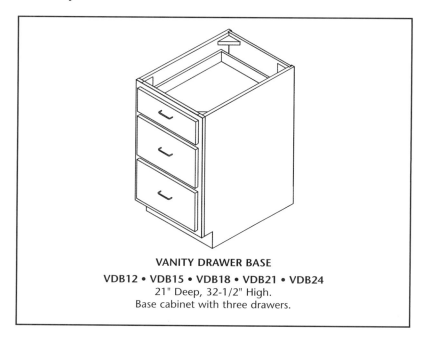

VANITY DRAWER BASE
VDB12 • VDB15 • VDB18 • VDB21 • VDB24
21" Deep, 32-1/2" High.
Base cabinet with three drawers.

(Courtesy of David Newton Associates)

Vanity Tall Cabinet Nomenclature

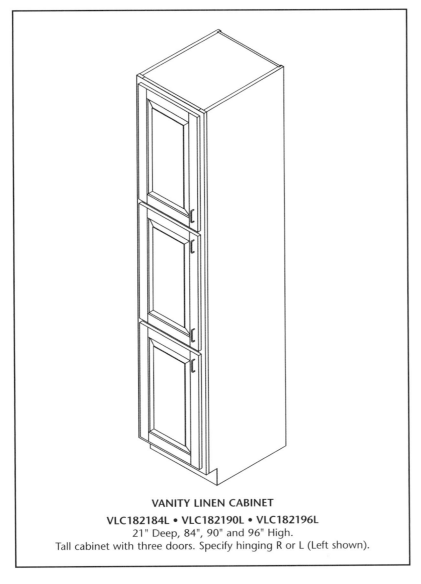

VANITY LINEN CABINET
VLC182184L • VLC182190L • VLC182196L
21" Deep, 84", 90" and 96" High.
Tall cabinet with three doors. Specify hinging R or L (Left shown).

(Courtesy of David Newton Associates)

Vanity Wall Cabinet Nomenclature

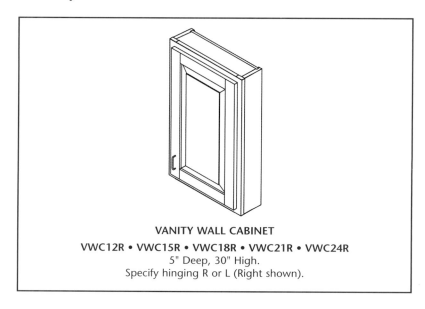

VANITY WALL CABINET
VWC12R • VWC15R • VWC18R • VWC21R • VWC24R
5" Deep, 30" High.
Specify hinging R or L (Right shown).

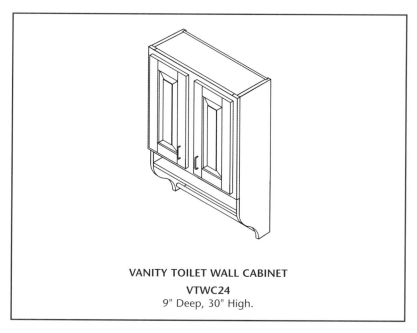

VANITY TOILET WALL CABINET
VTWC24
9" Deep, 30" High.

(Courtesy of David Newton Associates)

Miscellaneous Vanity Cabinet Nomenclature

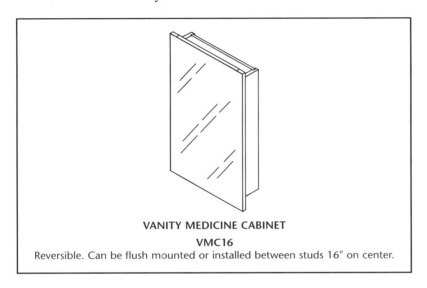

VANITY MEDICINE CABINET

VMC16
Reversible. Can be flush mounted or installed between studs 16" on center.

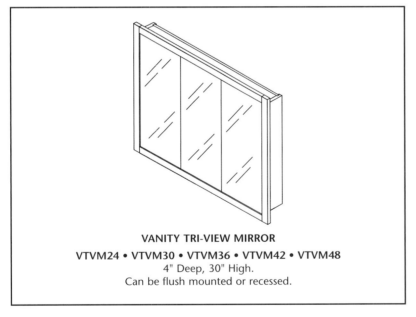

VANITY TRI-VIEW MIRROR
VTVM24 • VTVM30 • VTVM36 • VTVM42 • VTVM48
4" Deep, 30" High.
Can be flush mounted or recessed.

(Courtesy of David Newton Associates)

Miscellaneous Vanity Cabinet Nomenclature

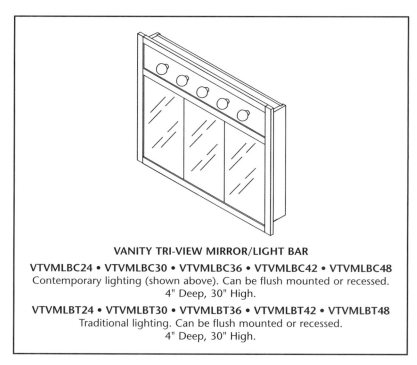

VANITY TRI-VIEW MIRROR/LIGHT BAR

VTVMLBC24 • VTVMLBC30 • VTVMLBC36 • VTVMLBC42 • VTVMLBC48
Contemporary lighting (shown above). Can be flush mounted or recessed.
4" Deep, 30" High.

VTVMLBT24 • VTVMLBT30 • VTVMLBT36 • VTVMLBT42 • VTVMLBT48
Traditional lighting. Can be flush mounted or recessed.
4" Deep, 30" High.

(Courtesy of David Newton Associates)

Miscellaneous Vanity Cabinet Nomenclature

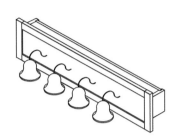

VANITY TRADITIONAL LIGHT BAR

VLBT24 • VLBT30 • VLBT36 • VLBT42 • VLBT48

Traditional lighting (shown above). Can be flush mounted or recessed.
4" Deep, 7-3/4" High.

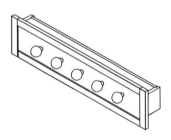

VANITY CONTEMPORARY LIGHT BAR

VLBC24 • VLBC30 • VLBC36 • VLBC42 • VLBC48

Contemporary lighting (shown above). Can be flush mounted or recessed.
4" Deep, 7-3/4" High.

(Courtesy of David Newton Associates)

Miscellaneous Vanity Cabinet Nomenclature

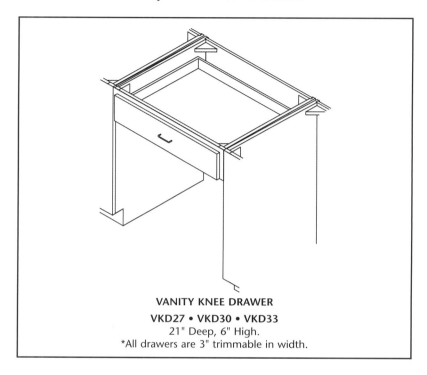

VANITY KNEE DRAWER
VKD27 • VKD30 • VKD33
21" Deep, 6" High.
*All drawers are 3" trimmable in width.

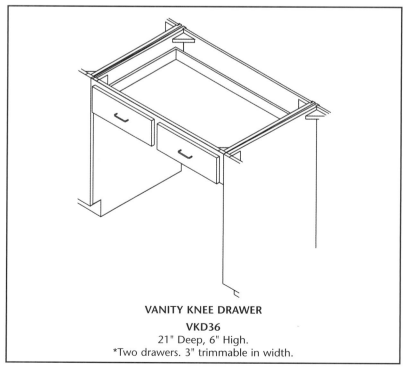

VANITY KNEE DRAWER
VKD36
21" Deep, 6" High.
*Two drawers. 3" trimmable in width.

(Courtesy of David Newton Associates)

Miscellaneous Vanity Cabinet Nomenclature

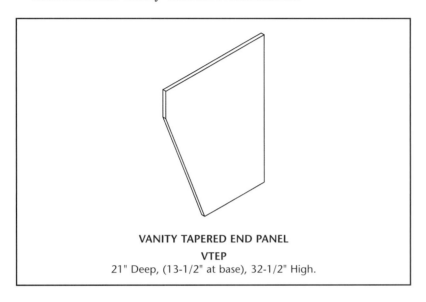

VANITY TAPERED END PANEL
VTEP
21" Deep, (13-1/2" at base), 32-1/2" High.

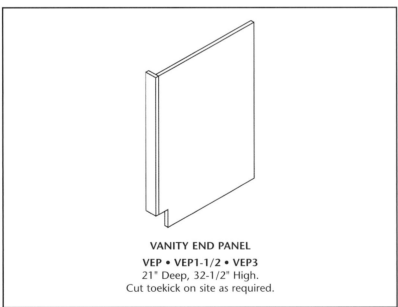

VANITY END PANEL
VEP • VEP1-1/2 • VEP3
21" Deep, 32-1/2" High.
Cut toekick on site as required.

(Courtesy of David Newton Associates)

Filler Nomenclature

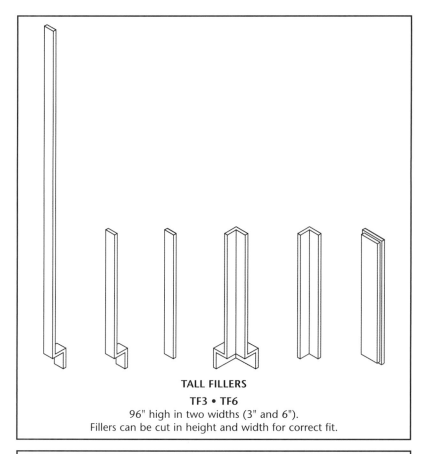

TALL FILLERS

TF3 • TF6

96" high in two widths (3" and 6").
Fillers can be cut in height and width for correct fit.

VANITY BASE FILLERS

VBF3 • VBF6

32-1/2" high in two widths (3" and 6").
Fillers can be cut in height and width for correct fit.

WALL FILLERS

WF3 • WF6

30" high in two widths (3" and 6"). Fillers can be cut in height and
width for correct fit. For taller wall fillers order TF3 or TF6.

CORNER FILLERS

CBF3 • CWF3

Corner wall fillers can be cut in height.
Both base and wall fillers can be cut in width.

FILLER OVERLAYS

TFO3 • TFO6 • F03 • BF06 • WFO3 • WFO3

Overlays are available for all standard fillers. Designed for use with full-overlay
door styles. Specify door style to match door material, finish and edging profile.

(Courtesy of David Newton Associates)

GENERIC DESK
NOMENCLATURE

Cabinet manufacturers use a code to designate each cabinet's size, use and placement within the desk or menu-planning center. The following pages will help you understand a generic nomenclature along with illustrations of various cabinets. This sample "manufacturer's specification list" will be similar to brochures provided to you by the various manufacturers you represent. This list would represent a stock manufacture and will include only a fraction of the many products available to you through a custom manufacturer. Also, this list will include only sizes and illustrations of framed cabinets. Most of the information for framed cabinets is typical for frameless cabinets.

Desk cabinets are typically available with a height of 28-1/2" for a finished countertop height of 30".

After your review of this material, compare your manufacturer's specification brochures with this list. You will notice many similarities in both nomenclature and cabinetry.

Desk Base Cabinet Nomenclature

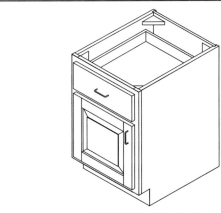

FURNITURE DESK BASE

FDB1224L • FDB1524L • FDB1824L • FDB2124L • FDB2424L
24" Deep, 28-1/2" High.
Furniture Desk Base cabinet with 1 door, 1 drawer and 1/2 shelf.
Specify hinging right or left (Left shown).

FDB1221L • FDB1521L • FDB1821L • FDB2121L • FDB2421L
21" Deep, 28-1/2" High.
Furniture Desk Base cabinet with 1 door, 1 drawer and 1/2 shelf.
Specify hinging right or left (Left shown).

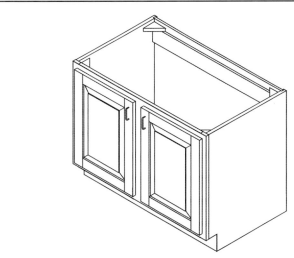

FURNITURE DESK BASE NO DRAWER

FDBND2424
24" Deep, 28-1/2" High.
Furniture desk base with full height doors and full shelf.

FDBND2421
21" Deep, 28-1/2" High.
Furniture desk base with full height doors and full shelf.

(Courtesy of David Newton Associates)

Desk Base Cabinet Nomenclature

FURNITURE DESK DRAWER BASE
FDDB1224 • FDDB1524 • FDDB1824 • FDDB2124 • FDDB2424
24" Deep, 28-1/2" High.
Furniture desk drawer base cabinet with 3 drawers.

FDDB1221 • FDDB1521 • FDDB1821 • FDDB2121 • FDDB2421
21" Deep, 28-1/2" High.
Furniture desk drawer base cabinet with 3 drawers.

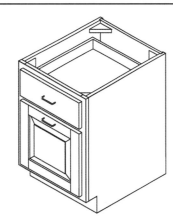

FURNITURE DESK FILE BASE
FDFB1824
24" Deep, 28-1/2" High.
Furniture desk file base cabinet with 1 standard drawer and 1 hanging file drawer.
FDFB1821
21" Deep, 28-1/2" High.
Furniture desk file base cabinet with 1 standard drawer and 1 hanging file drawer.

(Courtesy of David Newton Associates)

Desk Base Cabinet Nomenclature

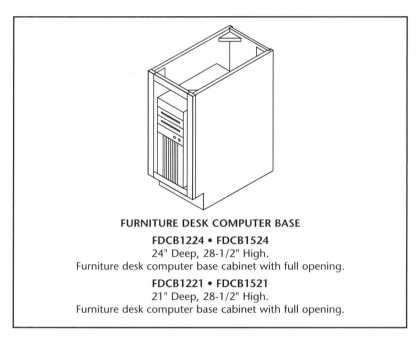

FURNITURE DESK COMPUTER BASE

FDCB1224 • FDCB1524
24" Deep, 28-1/2" High.
Furniture desk computer base cabinet with full opening.

FDCB1221 • FDCB1521
21" Deep, 28-1/2" High.
Furniture desk computer base cabinet with full opening.

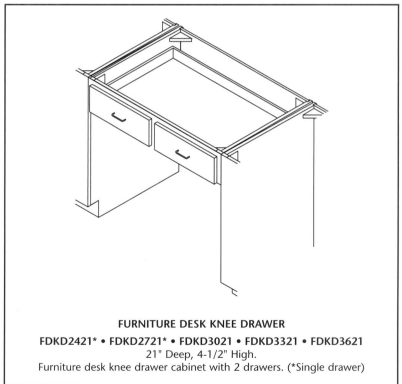

FURNITURE DESK KNEE DRAWER
FDKD2421* • FDKD2721* • FDKD3021 • FDKD3321 • FDKD3621
21" Deep, 4-1/2" High.
Furniture desk knee drawer cabinet with 2 drawers. (*Single drawer)

(Courtesy of David Newton Associates)

Desk Base Cabinet Nomenclature

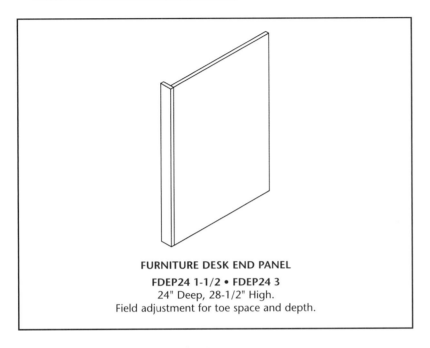

FURNITURE DESK END PANEL
FDEP24 1-1/2 • FDEP24 3
24" Deep, 28-1/2" High.
Field adjustment for toe space and depth.

(Courtesy of David Newton Associates)

Furniture Bookcase Nomenclature

FURNITURE BOOK CASE

FBC241248 • FBC301248 • FBC361248
12" Deep, 48" High. Three adjustable shelves. (FBC301248 shown above).

FBC241260 • FBC301260 • FBC361260
12" Deep, 60" High. Three adjustable shelves.

FBC241272 • FBC301272 • FBC361272
12" Deep, 72" High. Four adjustable shelves.
To match style of cabinets, kitchen cabinet valances can be field installed.

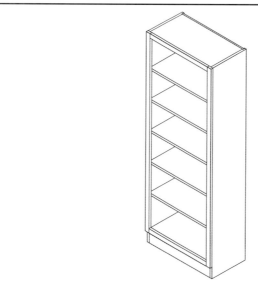

FURNITURE BOOK CASE

FBC241284 • FBC301284 • FBC361284
12" Deep, 84" High. Five adjustable shelves. (FBC301284 shown above).

FBC241290 • FBC301290 • FBC361290
12" Deep, 90" High. Five adjustable shelves.

FBC241296 • FBC301296 • FBC361296
12" Deep, 96" High. Five adjustable shelves.
To match style of cabinets, kitchen cabinet valances can be field installed.

(Courtesy of David Newton Associates)

CHAPTER 2: Appliance Types And Planning Considerations

For many years North Americans have recognized the importance of "thinking green"—living environmentally conscious lives. Only recently have kitchen and bathroom professionals been given the tools and training to incorporate environmentally safe products and practices into their design practice.

Responsible designers and homeowners know that the phrase "think globally, act locally" applies as much to the design of the room, the family's purchasing habits and the use of the space and its equipment, as it does to other planning and usage of the kitchen and bathroom.

Because the international need to understand and employ conservation tactics and waste-management techniques is so important, we begin this section on appliances by tackling these two key topics first.

SELECTING MORE EFFICIENT APPLIANCES

When it comes to residential conservation, just how can the designer and the homeowners help limit world energy consumption? Most energy specialists agree on three key actions that provide an excellent foundation for residential energy conservation.

- Install more efficient appliances and equipment.

- Adapt better everyday energy usage habits.

- Improve the thermal integrity of the building.

Over the past 35 years, federal regulations have continuously challenged appliance manufacturers to develop new energy efficient and environmentally safe equipment. The first milestone was the introduction of the Energy Guide label in 1972. These bright yellow labels continue to provide important data during the equipment selection phase of the kitchen planning process.

Some appliances also may feature the Energy Star logo, which means the appliance is significantly more energy efficient than the average comparable model. Energy Star products exceed minimum U.S. Government energy standards by 10% or more. A list of appliances that qualify for the Energy Star label can be found on its website at www.energystar.gov.

Energy Guide And Energy Star Labels

The Energy Guide and Energy Star labels rate energy and water use —not performance. Because some appliances use less amounts of heated water, saving water equates to saving money. These energy guides tell you the following:

- The capacity of the particular model.

- For refrigerators, freezers, dishwashers, clothes washers and water heaters, the estimated annual kilowatt hour energy consumption of the model. (For air conditioners, heat pumps, furnaces, boilers and pool heaters, the energy efficiency rating.)

- The range of estimated annual energy consumption, or energy efficiency ratings of comparable models.

Energy experts and appliance specialists recommend an appliance shopping strategy that focuses as much on the cost to operate the appliance as the purchase price. The more energy and water an appliance uses, the more it will cost to run. Consulting the Energy Guide and Energy Star label will allow you and your clients to compare the energy use of different models. The difference on their monthly utility bill can be significant, especially when considered over the 10 to 20 year life of the appliance. The client will save money over the long-run by choosing a model that is more energy efficient, even if the purchase price is higher than another model being considered.

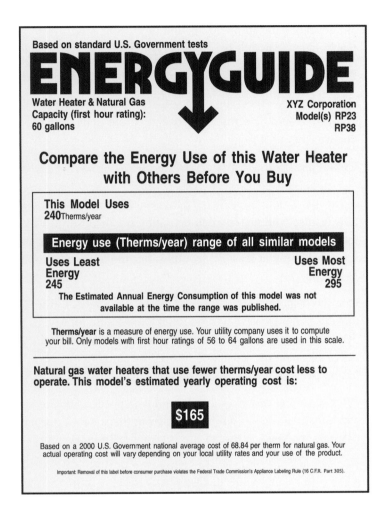

Based on standard U.S. Government tests

ENERGYGUIDE

Water Heater & Natural Gas
Capacity (first hour rating):
60 gallons

XYZ Corporation
Model(s) RP23
RP38

Compare the Energy Use of this Water Heater with Others Before You Buy

This Model Uses
240 Therms/year

Energy use (Therms/year) range of all similar models

Uses Least
Energy
245

Uses Most
Energy
295

The Estimated Annual Energy Consumption of this model was not available at the time the range was published.

Therms/year is a measure of energy use. Your utility company uses it to compute your bill. Only models with first hour ratings of 56 to 64 gallons are used in this scale.

Natural gas water heaters that use fewer therms/year cost less to operate. This model's estimated yearly operating cost is:

$165

Based on a 2000 U.S. Government national average cost of 68.84 per therm for natural gas. Your actual operating cost will vary depending on your local utility rates and your use of the product.

Important: Removal of this label before consumer purchase violates the Federal Trade Commission's Appliance Labeling Rule (16 C.F.R. Part 305).

Figure 2.1 *Appliance Types: The Energy Guide Label* (Courtesy of the Federal Trade Commission)

Adopting Better Everyday Usage Habits

However, your assistance in helping the client select the most energy-efficient appliance is not enough. All family members must adopt new ways to minimize the energy and water consumption of each appliance. The following guidelines may help your clients become more conscious of the residential appliance energy usage in their own home.

DISHWASHER

- Scrape but do not pre-rinse dishes, especially under a steady stream of water. A study, conducted at Ohio State University, concluded a dishwasher required 9.9 gallons (37.47 liters) of water (without pre-rinsing), while washing by hand used 15.7 gallons (59.43 liters) with rinsing under a running stream of water.

Figure 2.2 *Appliance Types: The Energy Star Logo* (Courtesy of U.S. Dept. of Energy)

143

- Do not block the spray arm action or prevent water from reaching some dishes by improperly loading the dishwasher.

- Wash full loads, use the energy-saving drying cycle.

- Pots and pans with charred-on soils from delayed meals or fast cooking should be scraped or soaked before placing in the dishwasher.

- Do not use the dishwasher to warm plates.

FOOD WASTE DISPOSER

- Always use cold water when operating the disposer to solidify fatty and greasy wastes. Use a strong flow of cold water and keep it running at least 30 seconds after the noise of grinding has stopped.

- Run the disposer each time food waste is put in it. Before leaving home for several days, check to be sure all wastes have been flushed out of the disposer to avoid odors developing. If odors do occur, they can be removed by running orange or lemon peels or ice cubes through the disposer.

- When washing dishes in a sink with a disposer, check to be sure all small objects are removed from the sudsy water before draining the sink.

- Periodically (and always after disposing of fibrous food wastes) purge the drain line by filling the sink with 2" to 3" of cold water. Turn on the disposer and allow this water to run through with no wastes added.

- If the home uses a septic tank, plan on cleaning the tank about twice as often as normally scheduled.

KITCHEN WASTE MANAGEMENT

Kitchen waste management is another important part of residential energy conservation.

The solution to our management problem seems to be centered in three areas: reduction, recycling and control. We can produce less waste, we can reuse more of what we would otherwise throw away, or we can allow the consumer product itself to be controlled by virtue of its disposability.

- Recycling: Well-planned kitchens include multiple recycling bins in or near the primary cleanup area, allowing easy sorting of materials to be recycled and those to be disposed.

REFRIGERATOR/FREEZER

- Open the door only when necessary and for a minimum amount of time. Organize the storage items in the refrigerator. Label all frozen food packages.

- Do not overload the food storage compartment, especially with items that do not require refrigeration.

- Cover all liquids and most foods before placing in the refrigerator. The food will retain its quality better and not allow extra moisture to escape, which places an extra load on the defrost system.

- Keep the freezer compartment as full as possible. This will reduce cold air lost when the door is opened.

- Locate the refrigerator-freezer away from other heat-producing equipment, such as the range or heat vents, and out of direct sunlight.

- Check to make sure there is the proper amount of clearance for a refrigerator/freezer with back mount condenser coils.

- Make sure the doors seal tightly. To check the gasket, close the door on a dollar bill and pull the dollar bill straight out. There should be some resistance. On models with magnetic door seals, an even more effective test is to place a light inside, close the door and inspect the perimeter of the seal in a dark room to see if light is coming through the cracks.

- Vacuum/clean the condenser coils on the back or the bottom of the refrigerator at least twice a year.

GAS AND ELECTRIC RANGES

- Select small appliances for some cooking jobs. Small electrical appliances often require less energy for the cooking job than the oven or the surface cooktop of a range because they have an enclosed heating element and often a thermostatic control.

- Defrost frozen foods before cooking to cut down on the cooking time. A defrosted roast requires 33% less cooking time than one still frozen.

- Preheat the oven only as long as necessary, usually for no longer than 10 minutes. Many recipes do not need a preheated oven.

- For more efficient range top cooking on glass ceramic and electric coil surfaces, use pots and pans with flat bottoms. Use tight fitting covers on pots. Turn off the surface units as soon as you have finished, or shortly before and allow foods to finish cooking on retained heat.

- If the range has two ovens, use the smaller one whenever possible. Bake several food items at once and then freeze for future dinners.

- When using the broiler, put the food under the broiler before turning it on. Turn it off before removing food.

- Don't peek! The temperature may drop as much as 25° or more every time the door is opened.

- Never use the oven to heat the kitchen.

- Keep the oven clean. Make sure the gaskets on the oven door provide a good, tight seal. Maintain the drip bowls under coil cooking elements so they can efficiently reflect the heat upward.

- When cooking with gas, use a low or medium flame. Cooking seldom requires a high flame and then only for a short while. Tailor the size of the flame to the size of the pan. A high flame licking up the sides of a pan wastes gas.

Selecting Appliances

After considering the positive ramifications of specifying energy-efficient appliances, as well as learning "use and care" recommendations useful to the client, designers should familiarize themselves with the basics of appliance operation and planning guidelines.

The Metric Conversion

Once again, we must address the sizing differences between American appliances sized in inches and European appliances sized in metric—or, sometimes, in inches.

- American manufacturers build all appliances to dimensions in inches, and then parenthetically qualify these dimensions in metric in the technical section of their websites.

- International manufacturers build in metric sizing and expect the designer to convert the metric size to American inches. Rarely do their websites' specifications list both dimensions.

- If an international manufacturer is launching a product exclusively for the United States market, they may choose to engineer, manufacture and specify on the technical side of their website all dimensions in inches.

The first home delivery of ice in America occurred in 1802. This necessitated the inclusion of an ice chest (a heavy wooden box, large enough to hold both ice and food together in a single compartment) in the kitchen. Today, refrigeration and freezing may be provided by a combined single vertical appliance or by several separate models. Regardless of configuration, the cooling system remains the same.

Selection Criteria

- Size of family, type of cooking and entertaining plans determine recommended cubic footage of fresh and frozen storage space.

- Decor of room, size of room and project budget will be used as a guide to select between built-in/freestanding and the use of panels with cabinetry material/appliance color.

- Family kitchen usage and room size are primary considerations when planning point-of-use refrigeration beyond the primary appliance.

KITCHEN REFRIGERATION CENTER

Method of Cooling

The most important concept to grasp is that refrigeration is the removal of the heat which causes food to deteriorate. Tests have shown that bacteria multiply rapidly at warm temperatures; therefore, all modern refrigerators are constructed to maintain temperatures at no more than 40° (4.45° C). Lower temperatures are usually recommended for specific foods: between 32° F (0° C) and 35° F (1.67° C) for milk and 25° F to 31° F (-3.89 C to -.56° C) for fresh meat, for example. It is because of these different temperature requirements that many refrigerator models include different compartments for meats and vegetables so currents of extra cold air can be circulated around the specific compartment. The appliance design elements are as follows:

Figure 2.3 *Appliance Types: How a Refrigerator Works*

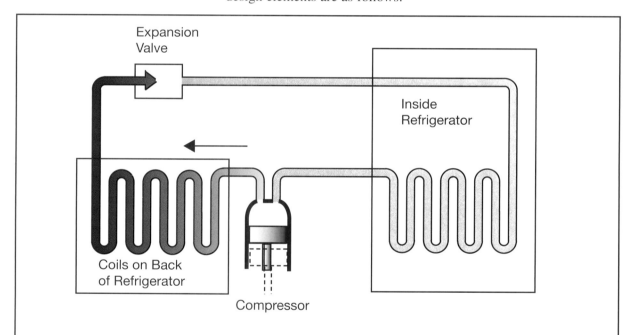

1. The compressor compresses a gas that has a low boiling point, such as ammonia. As it compresses, the gas heats up.

2. The coils on the back of the refrigerator allow the gas to cool to room temperature, but it is still under high pressure.

3. The gas flows through the expansion valve, which releases the pressure, thus cooling gas below room temperature. The now cold gas flows through coils inside the refrigerator, cooling the interior.

4. The gas flows back to the compressor to repeat the cycle.

THE ENCLOSURE

Refrigerator cabinets are made of various materials designed to create an inner and outer shell with insulation between. Experiments have proven that 80% to 90% of the heat that gets into the refrigerator comes through the walls of the appliance. Consequently, a great deal of engineering and design time is spent perfecting the insulation and making sure the door gaskets provide a tight seal.

THE COMPRESSOR

The compressor consists of a motor and pump sealed inside a steel case concealed within the refrigerator structure. The pump compresses refrigerant vapor that concentrates the heat and sends it to the condenser.

The majority of manufacturers have engineered an appliance with one compressor used to support both the fresh food and frozen food refrigeration temperature and air-quality requirements.

Luxury appliance manufacturers have engineered a dual refrigeration system. Pioneered by Sub-Zero Freezer Co., the dual refrigeration system keeps fresh food fresh longer and preserves frozen food longer because of the two separate self-containing cooling systems—one for the refrigerator and one for the freezer. As Sub-Zero explains, "The system insures there is no transfer of air from the fresh food compartment to the frozen food compartment. A refrigerator/freezer is like a duplex, where the residents of one apartment like moist, 38 degree air and the residents of the other like dry, 0 degree air. If the two must share a cooling system, both will be uncomfortable. With dual refrigeration...both the fresh food compartment and the frozen food compartment get exactly what they need."

Specific benefits of dual refrigeration engineered systems include:

- Higher humidity (moist air) in the fresh food compartment.

- No transfer of air from refrigerator to freezer, no transfer of food odors.

- Dry air in the freezer compartment, which prevents excessive freeze/defrost. Uniform temperature in the fresh food compartment, resulting in more accurate temperature control.

- Greater energy efficiency in the overall appliance.

THE CONDENSER

The condenser is a long folded tube that receives hot, high-pressure refrigerant vapor pumped by the compressor. As the heat leaves, the vapor inside it cools and condenses back to liquid. Condensers in many built-in refrigerators are located at the top of the appliance. Free-standing refrigerators are engineered with the condenser on the back or underneath the appliance. The capillary tube connects the condenser to the evaporator, metering the flow of liquid refrigerant to the evaporator.

THE EVAPORATOR

The evaporator, also a long tube, receives liquid refrigerant from the condenser. The liquid boils and vaporizes as it picks up heat from inside the cabinet. In a side-by-side refrigerator, it may be found behind the rear wall of the freezer, whereas in a top- or bottom-mount, it is usually found between the refrigerator and freezer.

Basic Types of Refrigerators

Before selecting a specific piece of equipment for a project, you should consider all of your options from the sizing, configuration and installation standpoints.

There are two basic types of refrigerators to choose from.

- **Combination Refrigerator and Freezer**: The most common unit is the combination refrigerator/freezer where one-quarter to one-half of the unit is a separate freezer section that maintains 8° F (-13.33° C), or below and that can be adjusted to 0° F (-17.78° C). This appliance has the freezer above the refrigerator or in a drawer below. The two sections may also be next to one another, called a "side-by-side."

- **Stand-alone Refrigerator and Freezer**: Another choice is the "all refrigerator" with no freezer compartment or only a very small one (0.50 cubic feet or less). This single-purpose appliance can be an upright vertical appliance with a large capacity, a drawer unit that fits under the counter, or a single door unit for a refreshment center.

All types of refrigerators should maintain 33° F to 38° F (.56° C to 3.33° C) in a fresh-food section. A few refrigerators/freezers have special compartments with temperatures a few degrees cooler or warmer than the rest of the fresh food section. An example of a cooler area is a meat keeper compartment that is connected to the air circulating around the freezer section. A refrigerator has a single temperature control, while the refrigerator/freezer model has either single or multiple controls for the fresh food and freezer sections. In most models with multiple controls the primary sensor is in the fresh food section. In these models the refrigerator may not run enough to keep the freezer temperature low enough if the room temperature around the refrigerator is lower than 60° F (15.56° C), or if the fresh food section has large amounts of very cold food in it (such as frozen food defrosting). A few multiple-control models have dual compressors and the sections are cooled independently.

Point-of-Use Refrigeration

Appliance manufacturers offer a wide variety of point-of-use refrigeration systems designed to provide smaller versions of a typical refrigerator, or custom designed units for specific food/drink products. The majority of these appliances are designed to slip underneath a normal countertop; several wine storage units are available in full refrigerator height. Popular models are:

- Under-counter refrigerator drawer appliances that can be two refrigerator drawers, two freezer drawers or a combination.

- Under-counter "mini-refrigerators." These range from the very affordable college dorm room-type of appliance, to elegantly styled and engineered under-counter refrigerators that may include a separate ice making compartment—an appliance perfect for a refreshment center in a specialty area in an upscale residential kitchen.

- Wine storage units designed to be under a counter or in a tall stand-alone appliance.

- Matching refrigerator/freezer separate under-counter with left- and right-hinged doors. These small appliances are occasionally substituted for full-sized equipment in urban living environments. They are also quite suitable for specialty kitchens planned in outdoor living areas, mini-kitchens, an adult master suite, or fully equipped second kitchens in a game room environment.

Planning Tips From Kitchen Pros

Experienced designers suggest the following considerations when selecting a new refrigerator.

Accessibility. In side-by-side and three-door models, the vertical door split minimizes the door projection into walkway spaces. The interior is also easier to access for people with limited reach. Unfortunately, though, the left and right hinging configuration blocks adjacent countertops on either side of the appliances. Additionally, in smaller models, the freezer may be so narrow that a frozen pie package will not fit into the space, let alone the 25-pound Thanksgiving turkey.

Appliance Placement. If a client is going to reuse an existing refrigerator that only has a few more years of service, do not plan the entire kitchen around this outdated appliance. While many refrigerators are permanently hinged in one direction, some models today have reversible doors, so there is no longer a left hinge or right hinge limitation. If the refrigerator will be replaced in a short time, design the best kitchen first. Then suggest to your clients they work with the old appliance until it is replaced with a new one with the proper hinging to support the overall design concept.

Boxed-in vs. Built-in vs. Integrated. If the appliance is framed with panels that extend to the floor, it is called a "boxed-in" look. Experienced pros caution, "Do not call this a built-in look." The necessary air space on each side and above the refrigerator, as well as the oversized depth of this type of free-standing unit prohibits it from being a true "built-in" look. A built-in refrigerator is only 24" deep and is designed to be flush with the adjacent cabinets. An integrated refrigeration or freezer appliance is completely concealed—or integrated into the cabinetry.

Figure 2.4 *Appliance Types: Free-standing Refrigerator*
In this application, cabinetry surrounds or boxes in the refrigerator which is deeper than the cabinets. (Courtesy of Sandy Hayes, CKD, CBD – Portland, Oregon)

Decorative Panel. If you are selecting a decorative wood panel for the refrigerator, be cautious about specifying a 1/4" sheet of paneling in a kitchen that features solid-wood raised panel doors. The graining difference between the veneer panel and the solid-wood panel might be unacceptable. If you have a heavily styled raised panel door on the cabinetry, suggest to the client that an equally intricate styled panel be ordered for the refrigerator.

Door Swing. If you are planning to reuse an existing refrigerator, verify if there are any door swing engineering problems which limit access to the crisper bins within. Some models require doors open far beyond 90° to allow bins to be pulled out from the interior. This will severely limit where that appliance can be placed.

Freezer Location. Because the most accessible shelf space is located between 22" and 56" off the floor, appliances that are designed with a lower freezer are more desirable than top freezer models. Ideally, the lower freezer should be a bin that pulls out to the user.

Glass Doors. Many point-of-use specialty appliances have glass door options.

Separate Units. The all-refrigerator and all-freezer residential units that are available are ideal for large kitchens where the appliances are heavily used. Two general sizes are available: a pair of 27" units equaling 54" of total space, or a pair of 36" units requiring a total of 72" of space.

Storage Above. Ideally, a 24" deep cabinet should be placed above the refrigerator so that this cabinet is accessible. A good use for this type of cabinet is vertical tray storage.

Figure 2.5 *Appliance Types: An Integrated Refrigerator*
A refrigerator easily integrates with the cabinetry. (Courtesy of Pietro Giorgi, Sr., CMKBD – Wilmington, Delaware)

KITCHEN WASTE MANAGEMENT

Food Waste Disposer

The disposer is a popular means of disposing of food waste products. Clients value this appliance because it removes food waste products efficiently. This eliminates concerns with odors and rodent/insect problems associated with garbage placed in the normal trash receptacle.

There is a great deal of difference of opinion about whether a disposer can be installed in a home with a septic tank system. Plumbers generally recommend that if you have a home that is on a septic system and you are adding a dishwasher and a food waste disposer, the septic system should be 40% to 50% larger than one for a house without these appliances. In a renovation situation, the tank should be cleaned out twice as often if these appliances are added. Therefore, instead of every six years, it should be cleaned out every three years.

In addition to the concerns about a food waste disposer installed in a home using a septic system, verify if local codes will allow the use of this appliance. In some high-rise condominium developments, you cannot install a food waste disposer. In some municipalities, they are simply not allowed; in others, they are required.

Selection Criteria

- The location for a wall-mounted electric switch, a deck-mounted air switch or a batch feed appliance cap switching system will be of concern when the sink is placed on an island or if there is a decorative backsplash planned.

- Better disposals featuring near silent operation are good investments in open-plan kitchens.

- The space required by the disposal inside the sink cabinet will determine the available remaining space for under-sink storage plans.

Operation Choices

- **Continuous Feed.** This appliance operates from a toggle switch on the wall or an air switch on the sink. It operates continuously as it is fed refuse; consequently, the name. It allows the most flexibility in use, but it is also the most dangerous because a person's hand or a utensil can unexpectedly be caught in the disposer when it is turned on.

- **Batch Feed**. This appliance is activated when the lid is turned. This is a safer appliance because it cannot be in operation unless the lid is in-place. However, it can be more complicated to use: to activate the disposal, the lid must be in a half-way position; to use it as a stopper for the sink, it must be pushed to a full close position. This action can be confusing and require dexterity difficult for a child or an elderly family member.

Regardless of the method of activation, the disposer actually disposes food waste in the same manner.

Basically, six types of action are employed in the waste disposal process: hammering, shredding, cutting, grinding, rubbing and pulverizing. As waste reaches the bottom of the shredding compartment, the whirling impeller comes in contact with the food. The centrifugal force presses the waste against the impeller arms, the fibrous waste cutting blades and the grind positioner. As the action continues, waste is finally divided into particles small enough to pass through into a lower evacuation chamber. From this point, the particles enter the drain and flow through the drain system to exit the house. Because of the movement of food waste particles to the drain system, it is imperative the drain line enter the wall low enough so the food waste is not forced to "flow up hill." Generally, the centerline to the drain pipe at the wall should be between 17" and 19" high.

Many people do not realize the effectiveness of the operation of the disposer is directly related to the rate of flow of cold water. Cold water should be flowing during the entire process of disposing of food and several minutes afterwards to clear the waste line. Cold water is used, not hot, so fat or grease can be hardened so it can be cut and flushed away with other types of waste. If warm water is used, grease will be melted and as it comes in contact with lower waste pipes in the system, it may harden and cause a stoppage. Many specialists recommend periodically flushing the drain lines through the disposer by filling the sink with 3" to 4" of cold water and then activating the disposer.

Disposers come with different amounts of insulation and different grind chamber sizes. Motor sizes also vary; larger motors provide extra thrust for tough-to-grind loads. The increased sound insulation makes it much more pleasant for the cook to use the disposer because noise levels are kept low. When reviewing the noise of a disposer in operation, designers must also alert the client about the impact the sink material can have on noise transmission.

157

All disposals have some type of an anti-jam feature: it may simply be a reset button at the bottom of the disposer, or it may be an automatic reversing action. In this latter case, if the disposer jams, the unit will pause for a brief time and then automatically reverse the direction of the impeller blades.

In addition to a larger motor and more insulation, better disposers also use better interior materials to improve the durability of the appliance.

If you are working on a renovation project and the client wants to reuse their food waste disposer, be cautious. Typically, when you remove an existing disposer and dishwasher and leave them inoperable for several weeks during the renovation, these appliances will not function properly when reinstalled.

If the disposer is older than three or four years, recommend the client purchase a new one or add a clause in your contract stipulating you will not be responsible for the operation of this appliance once reinstalled. The same concern exists for a dishwasher if it is ten years or older.

Trash Compactor

Environmentalists do not recommend trash compactors because the compacted mixed refuse slows down the decomposition process. However, you may have a client who has had a compactor in the past and wishes to have a new version of the appliance.

On the other side of the argument, trash compactor manufacturers feel the concern for the environment is one of the rallying cries for purchasing a trash compactor. Their argument is that when you have compacted refuse that is one-quarter the volume of that found in a loose trash can, you minimize the burden on garbage company landfills. A discussion worth continuing.

Under-countertop trash compactors are 12" or 15" wide. Some models are 18" wide. They may have a charcoal filtering system built-in or use a deodorizer to minimize the odors associated with refuse that is left at room temperature for an extended period of time in the compactor. Even with this deodorizing mechanism, the appliance's use and care manual will instruct the user to carefully rinse all containers before placing them in the compactor.

Some units have pull-out bin doors, others have doors that swing to the left or right and then include a pull-out bin within the opening. Several models have a small tilt-out door at the top to facilitate disposing of one small container or such.

The compactor plugs into a standard household circuit, much like the dishwasher and disposer. They are operated by motors that vary in size. The motor drives a single ram down that compacts the trash. Some of the appliances on the market can be operated by a foot pedal, and most have a key lock to prevent children from playing with the appliance.

Dishwasher

A dishwasher is typically installed as a built-in appliance adjacent to the sink. It may have a fold-down door or be a series of drawers. Drawers come individually or as a stacked pair. Some appliances are designed to be totally concealed in the cabinetry. Interiors are available in plastic, stainless steel and porcelain. The most popular size is 24" wide (23-5/8" for European manufactured appliances). Both 18" and 30" wide models are also on the market.

Selection Criteria

- Large households or families who entertain extensively may require two dishwashers.

- The dishwasher location should be carefully plotted in relationship to landing counter space for stacked soiled dishes and in relationship to storage cabinetry/pantry areas.

- Raised dishwasher installations can provide an attractive special height pedestal cabinet and make the appliance much easier to access.

The type of dishwashing action varies to some degree with each manufacturer. Rotating arms, fan jets and other enhancements are used to maximize the effectiveness of the washing actions. In most machines, the water is filtered and recirculated during the washing process, thereby reducing the amount of water required. In fact, a recent research study demonstrated that dishwasher wash cycles used less energy, less time and less water than hand washing.

Better dishwashers are insulated and engineered to reduce or eliminate any noise when the appliance is in operation.

When evaluating a dishwasher, first look at the racks. Better units offer some flexibility in racking arrangements and provide various rack height options. Most manufacturers have two racks that accommodate glasses in the top, plates and larger pieces on the bottom rack. One manufacturer reverses this rack design. Another has three racks, rather than two. One design features a third small rack placed close to the top of the appliance cavity for knives and other serving pieces.

One of the most important things to understand about well-designed dishwashers is that, because of the improved washing action and better filters, pre-rinsing is not necessary. Filters built into the dishwasher trap food particles and prevent them from being redeposited on the dishes. To overcome the necessity of cleaning filters, some models feature a small disposer that chops food particles and discharges them into the drain. An important feature is a rinse agent dispenser to prevent spotting and lubricate the pumps and seals.

The best water temperature for dishwashing is between 140° F and 160° F (60° C and 71.11° C). This is important both from the standpoint of sanitation and from the requirement for hot water of at least 140° F (60° C) to dissolve typical dishwasher detergents. While many families do set their hot water tanks at 140° F (60° C), many people today are turning down their domestic water heaters to conserve energy. Therefore, newer dishwashers have thermostatically controlled delay features to allow the built-in heating element to raise the water temperature to 140° F (60° C) before beginning the washing cycle. All dishwashers have one or more washing cycles and one or more rinsing cycles, as well as a drying cycle. Drying is generally done by warm air blowing across the dishes, heated by an internal heating element. Many models today have an "energy saver" switch that turns off the heating element during the drying cycle, and simply relies on heat within the dishwasher and room air for drying.

Many municipal codes call for an "air-gap" to be installed as an overflow protection device for the dishwasher. This mechanical planning consideration is covered in *Kitchen & Bath Systems*, part of the NKBA's Professional Resource Library.

Figure 2.6 *Appliance Types: Dishwasher Panels*
The dishwasher panel may contrast with the adjacent cabinetry. (Courtesy of KraftMaid Cabinetry)

Figure 2.7 *Appliance Types: An Integrated Dishwasher*
A dishwasher may be designed to receive a wood panel to match the cabinetry. (Courtesy of Plain & Fancy Custom Cabinetry)

Figure 2.8 *Appliance Types: A Raised Dishwasher*
A dishwasher may have the controls at the top of the door so it completely disappears within the elevation. In this example, an integrated dishwasher is installed in a mid-way unit adjacent to a concealed microwave. (Courtesy of Tom Trzcinski, CMKBD – Pittsburgh, Pennsylvania.)

THE COOKING CENTER

Cooking: that's what most people think about when they hear the word "kitchen." A kitchen specialist needs to carefully select the equipment that will help the cook roast, bake, broil and sauté delectable meals for family and friends. The quandary of determining which appliance (or a combination of appliances) will best suit the work space available and the homeowner's cooking style can only be resolved by adapting a systematic approach to the selection process. Surprisingly, the old "gas vs. electric" issue should not be your first decision.

- **Step one** is based on the method of heat transference selected: conduction, convection, induction and radiation.

- **Step two** involves the heat source.

- **Step three** is choosing the appliance style: built-in, drop-in, slide-in.

- **Step four** is the ventilation system.

Methods of Heat Transference

When it comes to oven cooking, we need to turn our attention away from heat sources and consider methods of heat transference. Whatever form of energy is used to create heat, the transference of it is what cooks the food.

There are four general ways by which heat is transferred.

CONDUCTION

Conduction is a process by which heat is transferred through a substance, or from one substance to another that is in direct contact with it by molecular activity. In conventional cooking, the source of heat starts the molecules at the bottom of a pan into rapid vibration. They strike other molecules in the metal, putting them in motion. The molecules on the inside of the pan put the layer of water molecules next to them in motion and they, in turn, start other water molecules moving. The motion of molecules, called heat, has been given to the water in the pan. Heat has been transferred by conduction from the heat source to the pan and from the pan to the water touching it.

In microwave and magnetic cooking, the energy is placed in direct contact with the food substance, bypassing the cooking vessel. Normal conduction activity then takes place.

CONVECTION

Convection is a more rapid process of heat transfer involving the motion of heated matter itself from one place to another. This transference of heat appears in both liquid currents and in air currents. On the range surface, water is kept in motion by convection while it heats. The layer of water at the bottom of the pan is heated first by conduction. Because of the rise in temperature, the water expands and becomes lighter. The lighter water is then displaced by the heavier cold water. In the oven, air is heated by the electric element or gas burner at the bottom of the oven. It expands and rises to the top of the oven, allowing the cooler, heavier air to come to the bottom to be heated.

INDUCTION

Induction cooktops are more energy efficient, have greater control, and are considered safer than either electric or gas cooktops. These advantages are easily explained by discussing how the induction cooktop works. Each hob contains one or more coils made of ferromagnetic material. When an alternating current is passed through these coils, a magnetic field of the same frequency is produced. If a magnetic-based pan is placed on the hob, the magnetic field induces a current in the pan. The internal resistance of the pan causes heat to be dissipated, following the "Joule" effect. Therefore, it is the pan itself, and not the cooktop, that heats up and cooks the food. Once the pan is removed from the cooktop, the energy transfer stops. The result is a flame-less method of cooking in which it is nearly impossible to start a fire by forgetting to turn off the stove.

RADIATION

Radiation of heat takes place at the speed of light (186,300 miles per second) in electromagnetic waves. No material medium is required for its transmission. Heat transfers by conduction and convection are involved in cookery on top of the range. Radiation and convection are of primary concern in oven cookery. All bodies warmer than their surroundings radiate heat. If a cold object is brought into a warm room, the walls of the room radiate heat to the cold object and the cold object, when heated, radiates heat to the walls of the room. Since the walls are at a higher temperature, they give more heat per second to the cold object than the cold object gives up. The temperature of the cold object, therefore, rises until it comes to the same temperature as the room. When an oven is heated, the bottom and sides of the oven become hot and radiate heat directly to utensils and foods in the oven. In a conventional oven, 60% to 70% of the heat is radiant heat.

Heat Sources

The designer now has finally arrived at the factor foremost in most consumers' minds as they talk about a cooking appliance: the decision between a gas or electric heat source.

NATURAL GAS

Gourmet cooks usually prefer gas because it permits precise control of heat and offers an instant "on/off" feature. Gas appliances feature pilotless ignition systems that eliminate continuously burning pilot lights and save about 30% of the gas used by the range when compared with older equipment.

Designers should understand how gas cooking works. Gas is composed of molecules continually in motion. Since a gas tends to expand and diffuse, the molecules completely fill the containing vessel and their motion is limited only by the size of the enclosed space. They exert equal pressure in all directions. The tendency of gas to diffuse is the fundamental essential for gas flow.

Just as water flows from a higher to a lower level and heat flows from a hotter to a cooler body, gas flows from a place of higher pressure to one of lower pressure.

The heating value of a gas is the amount of heat produced when a unit quantity is burned. It is measured in Btus (British Thermal Units) per cubic foot. A Btu is a unit of heat energy; the amount of heat required to raise the temperature of one pound of water by 1° F. This amount of heat is equal to that produced by burning an ordinary wooden match.

The standard cubic foot of gas, as defined by the American Gas Association, is the quantity contained in one cubic foot of volume at a barometric pressure of 30° of mercury, and at a temperature of 60° F.

Gas is regulated by a meter on the house exterior. Gas travels through a pipe from the meter to the appliance. The Btu rating of the appliance determines the diameter of the pipe. The flow of gas is directed by the turning of a valve handle. A horizontal pipe through which gas flows from the fuel line to the different orifices is called the manifold. Attached to the manifold are burner valve handles that direct the gas through the orifice and mixer head into the burner.

Forced through the orifice at velocities of 100 to 160 feet per section, the gas develops sufficient suction to draw air through the partly open shutter. This air, called the primary air, mixes with the gas before it is ignited in a porcelain-lined mixing tube, the smooth finish of which increases the injection of primary air and gives a clean, sharp blue flame.

The gas/air mixture now flows through the ignition port on the side of the burner head. This port is connected to the solid-state ignition. The spark that ignites the gas when the burner is turned on is caused by the electric ignition. It is also the electric system that turns the gas off.

Gas cooking appliances incorporate a grate over the flame to allow for the necessary oxygen for correct combustion of the gas.

Gas burners are designed to give a circular flame pattern, the size of which can be controlled, to some degree, by the amount of gas delivered to the burner. The burners are usually controlled by a throttling valve that resembles a rotary switch in appearance. The intensity of the flame can be controlled on a graduated basis from low to high. Some burners are equipped with special simmer units which are, in effect, a very small burner located in the center of the main burner. Although gas burners differ somewhat in form, the principle parts are the same, and the way the gas is ignited is the same.

ELECTRICITY

Alternatively, an electric heat source can be specified. There are four types of electric cooktops generally available for home kitchens today.

Conventional Coil Elements

The cooktops we all grew up with have maintained their popularity for a good reason. This is the most inexpensive of all available electric cooktops and has a good heating speed.

Coil elements are versatile, as well. If equipped with a special raised canning element or a contoured wok element, they will accept large canners or woks. With conventional coils, electrical resistance is used to create heat. Wire is encased in a metallic tube filled with an insulation material. The tube is shaped into a coil and flattened for maximum contact with cooking utensils. Heat travels from the hot coils to the cookware both by conduction (where there is contact) and radiation.

Solid Disk Elements (Electric Hobs)

Originally from Europe, the solid disk elements are popular today because of their sleek lines and cleanability. The cast iron surface, which contains electric resistance wires below, has a non-corrosive coating and is grooved for traction. It is surrounded by a stainless steel spill ring and sealed to the cooktop. With the solid elements, the entire disk becomes hot and conducts heat to the cookware. Since the solid element disk is cast iron, it shares many of the positive qualities of cast iron: gradual heat up and heat retention so the cook can finish cooking after the power has been turned off.

There are two types of solid disk elements available: the thermostatically controlled version has a central thermostat that senses the temperature of the pan bottom. Controls can be set for a range of temperatures. The second version has a thermal protector or limiter that assures the long life of the element by preventing overheating in situations in which heat is not properly conducted away from the element surface. Regardless of the type of control, solid elements do not glow red, an indication the temperature of the element does not become high enough to be a fire hazard. Because the element is a thick plate of metal, the problem of warping is eliminated. Sealing the element into the cooktop eliminates the need for cleaning drip pans or the area underneath. Periodic treatment may be needed to prevent rusting, but generally is not necessary if the manufacturer's directions for care are followed. Heavy gauge, flat bottom metal cookware of the same diameter as the element is recommended.

Glass Ceramic Cooktops

These cooktops have been available for nearly 20 years. Electric resistance coils under the attractive smooth glass ceramic top are the source of heat. The heat radiates to the glass surface where it is transferred to the pot by conduction and some radiation. In order to efficiently conduct heat, contact between the pan bottom and the cooktop must be good. Designs on the cooktop indicate heating areas. Early glass tops were not as quick or as cleanable as promised, but glass ceramics are again hot news—especially in white and black. Withstanding temperatures to 1300° F (704.44° C) without expanding or contracting, the new glass ceramics will not warp and are very hard to break. Yellowing of white ceramic surfaces has been eliminated, and elements have been redesigned to achieve faster heating.

In addition to conventional radiant heat, two other technologies are used with glass ceramic cooking surfaces. The first is induction, the second halogen.

Induction

As outlined earlier, in induction cooking solid-state power causes induction coils, located beneath the glass ceramic surface, to generate a magnetic field that induces current within ferromagnetic cookware. Ferromagnetic cookware is a material, such as iron, which reacts to a magnetic field. Magnetic utensils are made of materials such as cast iron, porcelain enamel on steel, porcelain enamel on cast iron, triple stainless steel and magnetic stainless steel.

Because the vessel is heated, induction cooking is cooler, faster and cleaner than conventional cooktop methods. Little heat is generated in the room, and total control is possible over the cooking source. Much like gas, it is instant on and off and easily controlled down to very low temperatures. It is also a safe method of cooking because the cooking surface is only heated by bounced-back heat from the cooking vessel, so it is safe to the touch.

Halogen

Halogen range burners combine the elegance of smooth glass ceramic cooktops without giving up cooking performance. Whereas a conventional electric burner gets hot because of electrical resistance as electricity flows through a nichrome wire, a halogen burner works like an incandescent light bulb. Electricity passes through a tungsten filament inside a quartz-glass tube. Resistance causes the filament to heat up and, in the process, tungsten particles boil off. Therefore, conventional electric energy is converted into light and heat beneath the glass ceramic surface.

In conventional light bulbs, the tungsten particles settle inside the glass which darkens it. In a halogen bulb, halogen gas combines with the evaporated tungsten to form tungsten halide. When this compound nears the filament, the heat breaks down and redeposits the tungsten on the filament, so the lamp does not darken and the filament lasts longer. The energy emitted is mostly infrared and wavelength. Therefore, the waves pass readily through the glass ceramic cooktop. About 10% of the output is visible light. Consequently, the burner's red glow instantly shines through the translucent cooktop. This allows the cook to know immediately if the burner is on, overcoming a problem with traditional glass top cooktops.

Thermostatically Controlled Surface Units

Some cooking surfaces on the market have one or more surface units that are thermostatically controlled. This type of element has a central sensitive disk backed by a spring that holds the disk in contact with the bottom of the utensil. The control is connected to the switch or valve handle, and operates to maintain the temperature for which the dial is set. Such a controlled burner is equivalent to using a small electric appliance and helps to eliminate scorching of food. Since the action of the thermostat is regulated by the temperature of the center of the pan in contact with the disk, it is good practice to have the food cover the center of the pan. Additionally, utensils used with these thermostatically controlled burners should be made of heavy gauge material that is a good conductor of heat. The pan must also have a flat bottom.

METHODS OF HEATING

Gas Ovens

The gas oven is heated by a burner which is beneath the oven floor. The floor plate has openings at the corners or along the sides through which the convection currents rise to circulate throughout the oven. The food in the oven is heated partly by these convection currents and partly by the radiation that occurs once the lining of the oven becomes heated. Because oxygen must be available for the combustion of gas, gas ovens are generally not as tightly constructed as electric ovens.

Gas ovens offer pilotless ignition systems, which have eliminated the need for a constantly burning pilot flame. It is estimated this innovation has saved up to 30% of the gas used in residential cooking.

Most gas ovens have broiler drawers below the oven, some appliances have a waist-high broiling element that allows oven broiling.

Electric Ovens

Because electric heat is flameless, the electric heating units are placed within the oven itself, which is of a tight construction. Generally, there is a heating element at the top and another at the bottom of the oven. There may be tubular enclosed or open wiring. The lower unit is usually a single coil, and the top unit will be either a single coil, several loops or it may be two coils. The oven vents through the center of the reflector pan beneath one of the back surface units.

Temperature in both gas and electric ovens is controlled by a thermostat. However, the thermostatic action is different in gas and electric ovens. For example, if the thermostat in an electric oven has been set for 325° F (162.77° C) and the switch is turned on, the unit will operate until a temperature of about 400° F (204.44° C) is reached. This temperature is known as the preheat overshoot—it allows the door to be opened and cool food to be placed within the oven without losing too much heat. At the end of this preheat period, the electricity cycles off automatically and the temperature drops somewhat lower than the 325° F (162.77° C) setting. The current then turns on again and continues to cycle on and off usually 10° above and below the 325° F (162.77° C) setting.

In a gas oven, there is also a preheat overshoot. However, the gas does not shut off completely, rather the valve partially closes, reducing the flame size to maintain a fairly constant preset temperature. Ranges that feature the low 140° F to 250° F (60° C to 121.11° C) temperature may use the cycling method, but the curves have smaller aptitudes than the electric range. Temperature in the food does not cycle, but continues to rise until the food is cooked.

TYPES OF OVENS

Convection Ovens

Convected hot air for baking was introduced to the baking industry as a commercial advantage in the 1950s. It was an immediate success, creating considerable savings in energy and time, offering greater flexibility in baking with a more even bake. Virtually all bakeries and restaurants now use convection ovens and the convection cooking principle is now widely available for home use in several brands of ovens.

A convection oven simply means an element heats the air and a fan then circulates this air evenly throughout the oven cavity. The circulating hot air penetrates food faster than the motionless air in a conventional oven. Therefore, several cooking advantages are offered to the consumer.

The circulating hot air cooks foods evenly and in a shorter period of time. Eggs and cheese dishes bake higher and lighter. Meats and poultry remain juicy, tender and brown beautifully. Any dish normally baked in a standard oven can be cooked in a convection oven with no special bakeware required. Additionally, several items can be baked at the same time or the oven can be filled with several trays of the same item because air circulation space need not be so generous around all the foods as in a conventional oven.

On the down side, baking pans and casseroles must have low sides and be uncovered to take advantage of the circulating air. For cooking covered foods, convection ovens offer no time or energy savings.

171

Additionally, converting recipes to convection ovens can be tricky. The cook needs to take the time to experiment to find the best combination of time and temperature for favorite recipes.

Microwave Ovens

Microwave energy is a form of non-ionizing radiation. Ionizing radiation (X-ray, gamma, cosmic rays) can cause chemical changes to take place with little or no temperature rise. Non-ionizing radiation (infrared, microwaves, broadcasting waves) in sufficient intensity will cause a rise in temperature, but will not cause cell changes. Radiant waves are characterized by their wavelength and their frequency of vibration.

Microwaves vibrate millions of times per second, and are therefore very short waves, hence the term "microwave." There is one microwave frequency in general use for microwave ovens, 2450 MHz (wave length 5" long). The term MHz stands for megahertz and means a million cycles. The 2450 MHz stands for 2450 million cycles per second. The 2450 MHz is considered the most successful wavelength because it cooks faster. This wave has a vibration amplitude about the thickness of a pencil. This thickness prevents the waves from passing through the small metal mesh installed in the oven doors.

The microwave oven cooks food within the oven by activating the dipolar (water) molecules so they rotate in a rapidly alternating electrical field. Thus, the amount of moisture in food has a direct bearing on its heating rate in the oven. The molecular rotation occurs as the molecules behave like microscopic magnets and attempt to line up within the field. However, when the electrical field is changing millions of times each second, these tiny magnets are unable to keep up because of other forces acting to slow them down. Such forces which restrict their movement may be mechanical, such as ice, or viscous, such as syrup. The energy of the microwave in trying to overcome these forces is converted into heat. Thus, the heat is restricted to within the food product and the cool oven interior is explained.

Microwave energy penetrates deeply into the food materials and produces heat instantaneously as it penetrates. This is a sharp contrast to conventional heating, which depends on the conduction of heat from the food surface to the inside.

Because of this energy penetration, the highest temperature occurs 1" in from the surface. The remaining interior is cooking by conduction. The cooking by conduction takes place during the recommended standing time. Because the heat is generated within the food substance, the heat conduction process should occur without the continuing input of microwave energies. Disregard for this principle will result in overcooking of the outer surface. Because of the penetration limitation, the ideal food configuration is that of a doughnut. This allows a maximum of surface area for maximum penetration.

The exterior surface of an item cooked in a microwave oven will be lower in temperature than the interior. This is caused by radiation of heat from the food surface to the cooler surroundings of cooking vessel or oven interior. Thus, the homemaker cannot judge the doneness of a food product by the outer temperature. Nor should he or she be told that the cooking vessel will always be cool. Some utensils will require the use of a potholder for removal.

The magnetron is the device that creates the waves. It is a little broadcasting station with an antenna. It has a central cathode from which electrons escape, pressured by high voltage, and as they move outward circularly, they pass by many little charged cavities in the surrounding anode. This sets up a vibration that creates the electro-magnetic microwaves. These are discharged by the antennae into the wave guide. The waves enter the cavity through the wave guide, and are circulated by the stirrer. It diffuses the waves in order for them to enter the food material from all directions. A transformer within the oven converts the ordinary 120 or 240 volts to a voltage between 3,000 to 6,000 volts. This high voltage is needed for the magnetron to operate.

To develop a sense of timing in microwave cooking, it is first necessary to know how much power is available in the oven. Research has shown that it is not uncommon for the actual available power to be 10% to 15% less than that specified by the manufacturers. The cooking wattage is a major factor in cooking times. Other factors include the food density, arrangement, quantity, temperature, moisture content and bone conformation. A local manufacturer's demonstrator or utility home can elaborate on these items for your staff or client.

OVEN CLEANING SYSTEMS

Pyrolytic System (Self-cleaning)

Pyrolysis is a chemical change brought about by the action of heat. "Heat" is the key word in describing this self-cleaning or pyrolytic oven. In this system, the oven is heated at temperatures ranging from 850° F (454.44° C) to 1000° F (537.78° C). At the end of the completed cycle, after the cool down period, all that remains of the food soil is a powdery ash that is easily removed with a damp cloth.

To activate the cleaning system, a lever is moved to lock the oven door and two controls are set. An inner lock is provided so the oven door cannot be unlocked when the oven temperature is too high for safety. An electrostatic precipitator is usually included to remove the smoke that would otherwise come from the oven vent. However, do warn the clients that they will probably smell an odd odor during the cleaning process. Supporters of the pyrolysis system claim that with this method all six sides of the oven interior are cleaned completely and no special care is required to prevent scratching or damage to the oven surface. Additionally, the extra insulation provided in these ovens to protect against heat transference from the oven to the adjacent living spaces means cooler cooking throughout the year, and less cycling on and off of the heating element.

Catalytic System (Continuous Cleaning)

The catalytic system is designed to eliminate the need for cleaning an oven. A catalytic material is mixed into the porcelain enamel coating on the oven liner panels. This material causes a chemical reaction at normal cooking temperatures that oxidizes food soils continuously as they occur during the cooking operation. This method, then, does not require a separate cleaning cycle at high temperatures because the cleaning takes place simultaneously as the food is cooked. Manufacturers using this system emphasize three points:

- Heavy spill-overs will not be cleaned without first wiping up the excess with a damp cloth.

- Harsh abrasives, chemical oven cleaners and scouring pads should not be used on excessive soil or stubborn stains.

- Certain types of food stains may not disappear in one operation, but will fade during continuous subsequent use of the oven.

You will find this type of catalytic system is the most commonly specified cooking appliance in Europe. When combined with a true convection oven, the continuous cleaning cycle works in an acceptable fashion. However, when it is not a part of a convection oven, many people find the oven is unacceptable for a clean appearance. Advocates of the catalytic approach point out that the oven is always available for cleaning, since the cleaning is continuous during normal usage. All that continuous cleaning prevents any build-up of soil and very little basic redesign of existing ovens is required since high temperatures are not used. This is another reason why this system is employed in European appliances, which are generally smaller than domestically produced ones. If the interior oven size of a European manufacturer model were further reduced because of the extra insulation required for the pyrolysis system, it would probably not be a usable appliance.

Major appliance manufacturers are constantly devoting resources to product improvement; therefore, appliance specifications change regularly. Additionally, new innovative appliances are introduced to the kitchen and bathroom industry on a frequent basis. Therefore, on a regular basis, designers should study manufacturers updated literature, visit manufacturer web sites, and attend national and local trade shows where new products are introduced to the market.

Primary Cooking Center

The next decision lies in determining which style unit or units will suit the space and cooking needs of the client.

BUILT-IN EQUIPMENT

Ovens

The family's cooking patterns will direct the recommendation for a single, double or a combination of single and micro convection equipment.

Ovens built into a tall tower offer the convenience of one oven at waist height, and one below in the case of double ovens. Some ovens are designed to be placed in the base cabinet so counter space is not lost. An oven should be placed at a comfortable, accessible level. Under-counter installations should only be suggested with ovens engineered for such a location. Single oven(s) can also be placed in "mid-height" base units, which make the appliance more accessible and maintains a landing space above the appliance.

One of the biggest advantages of built-in oven/cooktop units is the designer and client have complete freedom and flexibility in placement. The two appliances can be placed side-by-side or separated to create distinct work cells.

Built-in appliances have a higher cost than a free-standing range, which combines both oven and cooking surface. Additionally, installation fees and electrical wiring requirements will be greater than needed for a single appliance.

A planning concern is the wall space required for ovens placed apart from the cooktop. Oven cabinets are 27", 30" or 33" wide for single- or double-stack ovens. Placed side-by-side, ovens can require as much as 66" of wall space. The two built-in units also use a minimum of 55" to 60" of wall space, which might cramp countertops in a compact kitchen. Lastly, the interior dimension of most built-in ovens is smaller than a 30" wide free-standing range oven.

Appliance manufacturer specifications guide designers in proper placement off the floor, as well as heat concerns related to cabinetry above the oven.

Figure 2.9 *Appliance Types: Built-in Oven Configurations*
Built-in ovens are available in single or double configurations and with bottom or side hinged doors. Typically, they are installed in a tall cabinet above one another or in conjunction with a microwave or warming drawer. (Courtesy of GE)

Figure 2.10 *Appliance Types: Built-in Oven Configurations*
Alternatively, ovens may be placed below the countertop. (Courtesy of Sandra L. Steiner-Houck, CKD – Mechanicsburg, Pennsylvania)

COOKTOPS/RANGE TOPS

Built-in cooktops come in two configurations. The first is a self-contained surface unit, which drops into a cut-out in the countertop and is called a "cooktop." The second popular style is a front controlled unit, which requires a lowered cabinet height to accommodate the front panel controls and is called a "range top."

Cooktops come in a wide variety of sizes and configurations. Simple four-burner cooktops are often used in more modest projects. For the serious cook, five- or six-burner range tops are often specified.

The method of ventilating the cooktop must be determined in the early design phase. If a downdraft separate ventilation system is going to be used, the overall depth of the cabinet may need to be increased.

Figure 2.11 *Appliance Types: Cooktop Choices Focus on the Placement of the Controls*
A cooktop has the controls on the surface, a range top has the controls on the front of the appliance. (Courtesy of Wolf Appliance Co.)

SLIDE-IN AND FREE-STANDING RANGES

Slide-in and free-standing ranges feature an oven below the cooking surface. The least expensive of this type of appliance may suit the client's cooking needs, space limitations and budget. However, it will not add the sleek look of built-in models, nor the gourmet cooking style of commercial-type free-standing equipment. Regardless of expense, models with the controls along the range's backsplash should be avoided. They are awkward to use and potentially dangerous to the cook.

If the slide-in or free-standing range being considered has the controls along the top and can accommodate a down-draft ventilation system, designers may need to increase the depth of the adjacent cabinetry to accommodate the down-draft appliance.

Figure 2.12 *Appliance Types: A Slide-in Range*
This type of range suits a variety of cooking needs and is very cost-effective for many clients. (Courtesy of GE)

Commercial-type Cooking Equipment

When it comes to free-standing equipment, many cooks are attracted by the high-tech styling and extra power of commercial ranges. Commercial-type cooking equipment is available in a free-standing configuration designed for residential applications. Several manufacturers offer a range (called a "dual fuel") which has a gas cooktop above an electric oven. This advantage provides a high heat self-cleaning feature for the oven. The big difference between residential and commercial equipment is the burner Btu (British Thermal Units) rating. The higher Btu rating is an important criterion for successful gourmet cooking. The Btu rating per hour of the burner must be high enough to generate intense heat for some types of cooking. Typical residential equipment provides a burner at 9,000 to 12,000 Btus per burner. Commercial sized burners approved for residential use offer 15,000 (+) Btus. Appliances engineered for home use include the more powerful burner, yet are sized to fit a residential environment. They also offer features important to the consumer, such as easy to clean parts. Free-standing ranges are most frequently 30 inches wide. Professional-type equipment is available in 36 inches, 49 inches or 60 inches wide appliances.

Figure 2.13 *Appliance Types: Commercial-type Ranges*
Commercial-type ranges are now engineered to be suitable and safe for residential use. (Courtesy of Viking Range Corporation)

DROP-IN RANGE

Your third option is a drop-in range. Although similar in looks and price to the slide-in, this appliance is installed between base cabinets and supported by the range deck or by adjacent cabinetry. There is a rim to provide the transition from range to countertop that helps avoid cleaning problems. Generally, the controls are placed along the front of these 27" to 30" so they are simple to reach and safe to use.

If the drop-in range will be combined with a down-draft ventilation system, extra cabinets around the range and on each side may need to be planned.

MICROWAVE COOKING

The last cooking appliance that will be considered is the microwave oven. After debuting in American kitchens almost 50 years ago, the microwave oven is now a household staple. Estimates claim that 90% of all U.S. homes own at least one microwave oven. To insure user satisfaction, designers must be able to provide information about how microwave energy provides a heat source of energy to generate heat in the food, and then carefully question the family to find the right place in the plan for the oven.

Microwave ovens are designed to sit on a counter or shelf in an "open air" environment, built-in with a steel "trim kit," integrated into a hood, or serve as part of a combination oven. Some models have bottom-mounted doors and most have left-side hinged doors with the controls to the right.

Special features useful to the client are inverters, recessed turntables and preprogrammed buttons. Some space-saver models have controls on the top. Specify a model with easy-to-understand controls!

Figure 2.14 *Appliance Types: Microwave Oven Placement*

Microwave ovens can be placed above the cooking surface (with proper clearance from the range top) or below countertop height. They can also be in a special purpose wall cabinet or in a cabinet that sits on the countertop. In this example the microwave is built in to a wall cabinet. (Courtesy of Plain & Fancy Custom Cabinetry)

Figure 2.15 *Appliance Types: Microwave Oven Placement*
A microwave placed in a counter-level special purpose cabinet. (Courtesy of Erica Westeroth, CKD and Co-designer Tim Scott – Toronto, Ontario)

Planning Tips from Kitchen Pros

- Although available, avoid over-the-range combination microwave/hood appliances when possible. This type of appliance requires a cook to reach (dangerously) high to retrieve foodstuffs in the microwave. The installation reduces the available clear space for quantity cooking at the cooktop. The ventilation system is marginally successful.

- Select the appliance and its door hinging configuration before finalizing the design. The door should swing away from the user, avoiding the need for a family member to walk around an open door.

- When installing a microwave oven in a wall cabinet, select the appliance before completing the design to determine:

  1. Is the microwave shallow enough that it can fit in a standard 12" wide cabinet, or is an oversized cabinet needed?

  2. Does the appliance require a trim kit, or can it simply sit in an "open air" opening?

  3. Is there room to completely conceal the microwave within a cabinet and cover the exterior with a door mounted on special purpose cabinet hardware?

- If the microwave is installed in a cabinet extending to the counter, hold the microwave off the countertop 3/4" to 1-1/2" to make sure the door does not hit the counter, nor hit a shaped "no-drip" edge of the countertop.

- When space is limited, a full-size microwave oven that is combined with a convection oven can serve as the second oven for the cook. The appliance is still smaller in size than a normal oven and may give the designer more flexibility to plan workable counter space for the cook.

SPECIALTY APPLIANCES

- *Coffeemakers*: Built-in coffeemakers are available in both plumbed and non-plumbed configurations. Engineered to recess into a normal wall thickness, they can provide a coffee station for the consumer, yet remove the bulky coffeemaker appliance from sitting on the countertop.

- *Electric Fryer Cooktop*: An electric fryer cooking module is another specialty cooking appliance. A deeply drawn pan is an integral part of this unit, into which a series of baskets are used to deep-fry food. Accurate temperature control is essential; therefore, the better units have a digital temperature readout to provide complete control.

- *Electric Grills*: Individual electric grills can be incorporated under an overhead ventilation system, or as part of a combination cooktop vented with a down-draft system. Extra attention must be paid to the ventilation system when planning an integrated grill cooktop. Typically, high wattage or Btu-rated elements provide heat under a low-profile, one-piece grilling grate. For ease of cleaning, there will be some type of plate or removable tray to accumulate unwanted grease and make removal and disposal easy.

- *Griddle*: Oftentimes, cooktops and range tops with six burners have an interchangeable griddle available that can take the place of two burners for specialty cooking.

- *Steam Ovens:* New to the residential market, they come as a steam oven alone, or as a combination of steam and convection. The steam oven provides a moist, humid heat; therefore, food is cooked in a gentle environment to retain its flavor and moisture. This type of cooking reduces the shrinkage in meats and fish, infuses texture in pastries and bread, and reduces overall cooking time. The combination convection and steam oven allows the cook to sear and brown meats in the same oven - without having to use another oven or pan. Steam ovens are also easier to clean than conventional ovens.

- *Steamer Cooktop*: Steamer modules are used to provide temperatures of 140° F, allowing food to be kept hot for long periods of time or defrost easily without drying out or losing the flavor. A typical steamer will have a 2-gallon capacity, which can hold up to 14 cups of cooked food, and will feature a dome lid to maximize the interior space.

- *Warming Drawers*: Warming drawers are available in single and double configurations. They may have a decorative door or be concealed to match the cabinetry. Featuring both moist and dry settings, they are used to maintain food at a serving temperature after the product has been cooked. Some homeowners also use them to heat plates.

185

- *Wok Cooking*: Several custom manufacturers offer a built-in wok to augment normal cooktop/range top cooking. Other manufacturers design their high rated Btu burners to accommodate a surface wok, insuring sufficient heat for the quick stir fry nature of wok cooking.

Ventilation

Please review the material in *Kitchen & Bath Systems* to refamiliarize yourself with the basic engineering and mechanical concerns of a well-designed ventilation system.

Once you have considered the categories of equipment available, you should evaluate whether the model you are considering has the type of ventilation system available that will enhance your design as well.

There are several ventilation systems the designer must be familiar with:

- *Proximity or down-draft ventilation systems*, allowing design freedom and creativity above and around the cooking surface.

- *Decorative metal or wood* with an integral or a remote located blower.

- *Overhead ventilation systems* which can be concealed within the cabinets or be a low-profile, pull-out hood.

- *An appliance that is a combination microwave and hood.* This combination, oftentimes, does not provide an ideal location for the microwave oven, and does not always allow for a proper holding canopy for an effective hood.

- *Mantel or chimney hood* where a ventilator is housed in a custom enclosure, which acts as a focal point in the space. Again, the motor may be part of the interior structure or remote mounted. Designers typically purchase an interior liner, including the ventilator and lighting portion of the system surrounding it with a job-built frame, or incorporate it in a prefabricated plaster-like enclosure. This decorative hood may be mounted on brackets returning to the wall, or be completely enclosed with a mantel-type extension to the countertop. Providing proper landing space is critical with this type of hood.

Figure 2.16 *Appliance Types: Down-draft Ventilation*
When a down-draft ventilation is used, an open, airy feeling can be maintained in the kitchen. (Courtesy of KraftMaid Cabinetry)

Figure 2.17 *Appliance Types: Overhead Ventilation System*
If an overhead ventilation system is included, it may become part of the cabinets. (Courtesy of Fantech)

Figure 2.18 *Appliance Types: Decorative Hood*
A stainless steel hood becomes a sculpture against the back wall. (Courtesy of GE)

Figure 2.19 *Appliance Types: Cooking Niche Hood*
The hood is part of a tiled cooking niche in this kitchen. (Courtesy of Cameron Snyder, CKD – Norwell, Massachusetts)

APPLIANCE CHECKLIST

Use the Appliance Checklist as you complete the final specifications for each kitchen project you work on. It will help you estimate and specify all the planning details of appliance placement.

REFRIGERATOR INSTALLATION CONSIDERATIONS

1. Required door swing/drawer opening dimension verified. _____

2. Overall appliance depth (including air space and handles) listed on plans. _____

3. Overall width, including air space and countertop overhang dimension determined before overhead cabinet width size and height specified. _____

4. Appliance doors drawn in an open position on the plan to verify walkway clearances. _____

5. Ice maker copper water lines/water filter specified. _____

6. Trim kits and/or panels have been ordered. Labor to install has been included in estimate. _____

7. Special handles ordered for integrated units. _____

DISHWASHER INSTALLATION CONSIDERATIONS

1. Trim kits and/or panels have been ordered. Labor to install has been included in estimate. _____

2. Existing water lines and drain location to be reused. _____
    New water line to be installed. _____

3. Existing dishwasher circuit to be reused. _____
    New dishwasher circuit to be added. _____

4. Appliance door drawn in an open position on the plan to verify walkway clearances. _____

TRASH COMPACTOR INSTALLATION CONSIDERATIONS

1. Trim kits and/or panels have been ordered. Labor to install has been included in estimate. _____

2. Existing compactor wiring to be reused. _____

3. New compactor wiring to be added. _____

4. Appliance door drawn in an open position on the plan to verify walkway clearances. _____

FOOD WASTE DISPOSER INSTALLATION CONSIDERATIONS

1. Unit to be batch fed _____ or switch operated _____. _____

2. Switch location located after considering primary user's handedness. _____

    Wall location _____ or countertop location _____.

3. Waste line no higher than 17" on center off the floor. _____

BACKSPLASH CONVENIENCE APPLIANCE INSTALLATION CONSIDERATIONS

1. Backsplash appliance does not interfere with wall stud placement. _____

2. Recess required for appliance is not obstructed by vents, ducts or pocket doors. _____

3. Recessed convenience appliances do not interfere with backsplash design or use. _____

4. Convenience outlets along backsplash do not interfere with built-in backsplash appliance location. _____

5. Heat generating backsplash appliances are not specified below task lighting that features a plastic diffuser. _____

DROP-IN OR FREE-STANDING RANGE INSTALLATION CONSIDERATIONS

1. Gas or electrical requirements:

   Gas Size of existing gas line. _____
   Existing gas line to be reused in its existing location. _____
   Existing gas line to be relocated. _____
   Diameter of new gas line required. _____

   Electric Electrical amperage of existing line:
   30 amp _____ 40 amp _____ 50 amp _____

   Electrical amperage requirement of new appliance:
   30 amp _____ 40 amp _____ 50 amp _____

   Existing electrical line to be reused in its existing location. _____
   Existing electrical line to be relocated. _____
   New electrical line to be added. _____

2. Ventilation system specified on plans. _____

3. Drop-in range method of support and distance from floor to bottom of range specified on plans. _____

4. Countertop cut-out for drop-in units specified on plans. _____

5. Side clearance for drop-in units which have a flange overlapping adjacent cabinetry has been considered in the planning process. _____

6. Appliance overall depth, including handles, listed on the plans. _____

7. Appliance door drawn in an open position to verify walkway clearances. _____

BUILT-IN OVEN INSTALLATION CONSIDERATIONS

1. Gas or electrical requirements:

   Gas   Size of existing gas line.   _____
   Existing gas line to be reused in its existing location.   _____
   Existing gas line to be relocated.   _____
   Diameter of new gas line required.   _____

   Electric   Electrical amperage of existing line:
   30 amp _____ 40 amp _____ 50 amp _____

   Electrical amperage requirement of new appliance:
   30 amp _____ 40 amp _____ 50 amp _____

   Existing electrical line to be reused in its existing location.   _____
   Existing electrical line to be relocated.   _____
   New electrical line to be added.   _____

2. Ventilation requirement for new oven: Ducted _____ Non-ducted _____

3. Countertop overhang treatment against oven cabinet side to be:

   Countertop extends past oven case.   _____
   Countertop ties into side of special depth oven cabinet.   _____

   Case depth to be _____.
   Toe kick to be _____.

4. All dimensions are included in specifications and plans:

   Overall appliance depth (including handles).   _____
   Appliance height placement in relationship to primary cook's height.   _____
   Cut-out and overall dimensions.   _____

5. For under-counter installation, manufacturer's specifications have been verified   _____
   for minimum cut-out height from the floor.

COOKTOP INSTALLATION CONSIDERATIONS

1. Gas or electrical requirements:

   Gas   Size of existing gas line. _____

             Existing gas line to be recessed in its present location. _____

             Existing gas line to be relocated. _____

             Diameter of new gas line required. _____

   Electric   Electrical amperage of existing line:

             30 amp _____ 40 amp _____ 50 amp _____

             Electrical amperage requirement of new appliance:

             30 amp _____ 40 amp _____ 50 amp _____

             Existing electrical line to be reused in its existing location. _____

             Existing electrical line to be relocated. _____

             New electrical line to be added. _____

2. Ventilation system specified on plans. _____

3. Can cabinet drawers be installed below the cooktop? _____

4. Can roll-outs be installed below the cooktop? _____

5. All dimensions (cut-out and overall) are listed on the plan _____

MICROWAVE OVEN INSTALLATION CONSIDERATIONS

1. Dedicated electrical circuit specified. _____

2. Trim kit ordered with appliance. _____
   Labor to install trim kit included in estimate. _____

3. Microwave oven placement is away from other heat generating appliances. _____

4. Microwave oven placement is away from television set in the kitchen. _____

5. Appliance height has been determined in relation to the height of the primary cook _____
   for both safety and convenience.

6. Cut-out and overall dimensions are listed on the plan. _____

VENTILATION HOOD INSTALLATION CONSIDERATIONS

1. Length of duct path from ventilation system to exterior termination point. _____

2. Number of elbow turns along duct path. _____

3. Ventilating unit's (free air pressure) CFM rating. _____
   Exit (static air pressure) CFM rating estimate. _____

4. Hood depth in relation to adjacent cabinetry. _____

5. Hood distance from cooking surface. _____

6. Hood width in relationship to cooktop width below. _____

CHAPTER 3: Fixture Materials

Before we discuss the materials used for fixtures, let's define some key words.

- **Accessory**. Although some accessories are specified for kitchens, they are a far more integral part of bathroom planning. Towel bars, handrails, toilet paper holders and various other items that complement the fixtures and fittings are an important part of each bathroom center of activity. Their design and placement are detailed in the *Bath Planning* book.

- **Fixture**. A kitchen sink, bathtub, shower, lavatory (bathroom sink), toilet (water closet), bidet or urinal that receives water.

- **Fitting**. A faucet, bathtub filler spout, showerhead, body spray, body mist or other finished piece through which water passes and then enters a fixture. For simplicity, we will use the word "fitting" to refer to all of these types of water-delivering devices.

Your company may have specific terminology policies. So ask how you should refer to the various fixtures in your specifications. When speaking with a client, use terms that are familiar to the average homeowner, or explain a new name to the client the first time you use it.

To introduce you to the most popular materials and construction methods used to manufacture fixtures, we have listed the widely used materials in alphabetical order. There is an ever-changing collection of special materials available for unique, one-of-a-kind fixtures today – notably for lavatories. Unique bathing pools/bathtubs are also available. To learn more about these special fixture materials, collaborate with your manufacturing representative and/or manufacturing companies.

FIXTURE CONSTRUCTION

Cast Iron

You may have heard the term "cast iron," but have never known what the term really means. "Cast iron" actually describes a manufacturing process used for more than a century to produce bathtubs and kitchen sinks. The molten iron is "cast" in a sand mold.

Sand is used to shape the cavity of the mold. The reclaimed molten iron, at 2700° F (1482° C), is poured into a channel, filling the cavity. After the molten iron has cooled and solidified, the sand cast is removed (the sand is recycled) and the exposed product is ready for finishing. The exterior surface must be smoothed to a uniform finish. Once this is done, the final enamel finish coat is added. This finish is a combination of clay, frit, color oxides and opacifiers. It is applied to the exposed surfaces of the fixture in powder form, and then fired at 1250° F (676.67° C), which melts the powder uniformly into a smooth coating which fuses to the cast iron base material.

The enamel coating on iron is much thicker, and the cast iron more resistant to movement than is the case with an enameled steel fixture. Therefore, a cast iron product is more chip-resistant.

HEAT TRANSFERENCE

Cast iron fixtures are cool to the touch and, therefore, may be momentarily uncomfortable for the bather as he/she reclines against the backrest above the water line. Because the cast iron is a conductor of heat, the bath water will cool more rapidly in a cast iron bathtub than it will in one made out of a plastic material, which has better insulating properties.

WEIGHT FACTOR

Kitchen sinks and bathroom lavatories are heavy, but can be carried by one person. Cast iron bathtubs are heavy, and therefore generally limited to sizes up to 72" x 36" and 60" x 42". Attention to this weight factor is important if you are designing a bathroom that is accessible only up a long flight of stairs. It can easily require four strong men to wrestle a cast iron bathtub up to a second floor location. Check the manufacturer's specifications to verify the exact weight of the fixture, and verify clearances to assure the bathtub can be moved into the bathroom.

Figure 3.1 *Fixture Materials: Composite*
Natural granite is mixed with acrylic resin to form a composite sink that is highly resistant to scratching and chipping. (Courtesy of Blanco)

Composite

The use of composite kitchen sinks is growing rapidly. However, because there are many types of composite sinks, there is much confusion in differentiating one from another. In general the main types are acrylic/polyster, granite-based and quartz composite.

Acrylic/Polyester. Of all the types of composite sinks available, acrylic/polyester are the lowest performing in terms of scratch and stain resistance, because they are made from soft materials that can cut and nick easily. On the positive side, acrylic/polyester-based composites tend to have a "shiny" look that appeals to many homeowners because they brighten up the kitchen. They are also popular because they come in a variety of colors.

Granite Based. The most scratch-resistant sink material on the market today is a "granite" composite. These sinks offer stain, chemical and scratch resistance. They also offer the highest level of durability because of the extremely high density of rock particles at the sink's surface. Granite based sinks are available only in matte finishes; therefore, the consumer is not offered the "glossy" look of other options.

Quartz Composite. With a combination of 70% quartz and 30% resin filler, quartz composite sinks provide a durable surface. These sinks can resist everyday cuts, scuffs and dents, and can easily stand up to harsh cleaning materials or liquids that might stain other sinks. Quartz composite sinks are available in a variety of colors. Because the color is uniform throughout, the material never loses its original color. Once again, quartz sinks are available in a matte finish only, rather than the glossy look of a cast iron sink.

Enameled Steel

Bathtubs and lavatories can be constructed out of enameled steel. This material is fabricated by forming steel in a cold state, then applying a coating of enamel, and finally firing the finished piece in an oven.

To fabricate an enameled steel fixture, a sheet of metal is pressed into a die so it forms the desired shape. This process is called "drawing" because the process results in creating a shape that has depth. The fixture is also subject to mechanical operations, called "stamping," to cut or form the individual parts of the fixture. Some enameled steel fixtures also require sections to be welded together.

After the form and shape have been finalized, an enamel coating is sprayed onto the fixture. It is then fired in a furnace.

In the showroom, an enameled steel fixture looks quite similar to a cast iron one. However, there are dramatic differences between these two types of fixtures. Enameled steel fixtures are more susceptible to damage than some other fixture materials because when an object is dropped on the fixture, the smooth formed steel will flex on impact. Because of the smooth nature of the enameled finish, it does not follow the movement of the steel and may, therefore, chip. Such fixtures also require a stainless rim for mounting purposes.

Enameled steel bathtubs are also noisy and good heat conductors causing the bath water to cool quickly. On the plus side, they are the least expensive fixture you can specify, and they are easy to handle because of their light weight.

PROPRIETARY MATERIALS

In an effort to maintain the weight benefits and the cost savings of enameled steel fixtures, yet overcome the material's susceptibility to damage, major manufacturers have introduced proprietary fixture materials over the last several years. These special materials combine various layers of structural composite backing products (an enamel grade metal and high quality porcelain enamel) to provide a lightweight—but durable—fixture. Pioneered by American Standard 20 years ago as "Americast," the manufacturing process forms the layered material in a closed mold manufacturing process similar to an enameled steel manufacturing system, but results in a more durable product for the bath because of increased shock resistance. This system is also used for kitchen sinks as well.

To learn more about the benefits of these special products, read the manufacturer's literature or consult with a company representative.

Fire Clay

Fire clay is a compound ceramic material that includes pre-fired clay particles mixed with ball and china clays. The pre-fired clay particles (called "grog") are ground into small grains and added to the liquid casting slip, giving it a unique and distinct appearance. Up to 40% of the slip can be pre-fired particles that allow the fired product to be more porous. This extra porosity requires that a material called "angobe" be applied to the surface before glazing. Such an extra step in the glazing process gives the finish a deeper color throughout the piece. Fire clay colors—notably white—are typically more brilliant than the colors of cast iron products. The porosity also makes the fire clay more resistant to shock than vitreous ware; therefore, its durability characteristics are similar to cast iron.

Lastly, fire clay products are distinctly different from cast iron in that they are lighter in weight. One of the advantages of the lighter weight material and less shrinkage in fire clay is that considerably larger pieces can be manufactured with less warpage and crisper design details. However, the porosity makes fire clay products non-code compliant for toilets and urinals—all surfaces containing water must be glazed.

Plastics

Novice bathroom designers are often confused by all the terms that relate to bathroom fixtures made from man-made materials. Some fixtures are identified by the reinforcing material used: fiberglass. Other fixtures are identified by the exterior finish material used: acrylic. And, still others are identified by the manufacturing process employed to fabricate the fixture: injection molded.

To understand the differences among these fixtures you need to understand the differences between a reinforcing material and a finishing one. Plus, you should be familiar with the different attributes of each one of the popular finishing materials.

ACRYLIC

The first manufacturing approach is to create the fixture by forming it out of 1/8" – 1/10" sheet of acrylic or acrylonitrile-butadiene styrene (ABS). In this thermo-forming method, the temperature of a thermo-plastic material, such as acrylic or ABS, is elevated to a level that makes it pliable and workable; it is then vacuum formed into a mold, creating the desired shape. All fixtures requiring structural support are sprayed with resin and chopped strands of glass in much the same manner as the fiberglass spray-up method of construction detailed on the following page. The application of reinforcement boards or braces is also the same for both materials.

Acrylic and ABS thermal plastics are harder materials than polyester gel coat and the color goes all the way through the material. They also offer deeper color tones and are more resistant to abrasion, high heat scarring and sun fading than fiberglass. Although acrylic can be scratched, it is repairable. As you might expect, acrylic fixtures are also more expensive than gel coat finished fixtures.

Figure 3.2 *Fixture Materials: Acrylic*
An array of shapes, configurations and sizes is available in acrylic tubs, including jetted versions. Color goes all the way through the material. (Courtesy of Americh)

FIBERGLASS

Fixtures that are generally referred to as "fiberglass" refer to the backing material used to reinforce a polyester gel coat finishing surface. A mold receives a layer of gel coat and then fiberglass strands immersed in a polyester resin is sprayed on or placed on top of the mold in mat form. Additional reinforcing, in the form of wood or metal strips or braces, is attached at this stage of the manufacturing process.

The polyester gel coat is not as durable as other finish surface layering materials in use today. However, it is generally the least expensive finish and the easiest of the plastic fixtures to repair. Much like cultured marble (cast polymer) products, such fixtures are widely produced by small factories. Therefore, quality levels can vary widely.

INJECTION MOLDING

Injection molding is the third method of manufacturing plastic fixtures. The plastic material is heated until it reaches a liquid state, at which time it is injected into the cavity of a mold. With this process, the color you see on the surface goes all the way through the material.

All plastic fixtures are warm to the touch and, therefore, are comfortable for the bather to lean against. These fixture materials act as insulators so the water in the bathtub does not cool too rapidly. Noise can be reduced by including a sound-deadening undercoating.

Figure 3.3 *Fixture Materials: Solid Surface Vanity Top*
A solid surface vanity top includes an easy-to-clean integral bowl. (Courtesy of Charles A. Ward, CKD, and Co-designer Lisa Anderson, CKD, ASID – Omaha, Nebraska)

Solid Surfacing

Solid surfacing materials are excellent products for bathroom wall panels and countertops, molded one-piece lavatories and custom shaped shower pans, as well as kitchen sinks and countertops. Manufactured from acrylic, polyester or a combination of acrylic and polyester base materials, these homogeneous (color all the way through) materials can be machined by a skilled fabricator and are repairable if damaged. The hard, non-porous surfaces are stain and burn resistant.

There are differences between acrylic-based and polyester-based materials. A more detailed discussion of solid surfacing follows later in Chapter 7.

Vitreous China

Vitreous china is used in the manufacture of lavatories, toilets, bidets and urinals. Vitreous china is a form of ceramic/porcelain that is vitrified or "glass-like." It is used for lavatories and toilets because of its formability and sanitary characteristics. Vitreous china has less than $1/_2$ of 1% moisture absorption compared to other types of ceramics, such as wall tile, that may have as much as 10% moisture absorption.

A MOLDED PRODUCT

Vitreous china fixtures are a pottery product. To begin the manufacturing process, flint, feldspar and water are mixed with different types of clays. Once combined, the mixture is poured into a Plaster of Paris mold, where it remains during the curing process. The mold is cast from a "master mold," which is reused. These molds consist of two sections that form the inside and outside profile of the piece. In solid casting, the mixture is poured into the area between these mold sections. This mixture, called a "slip," then conforms to the interior profile of the mold. For thicker elements of vitreous china fixtures, such as the rim of a pedestal lavatory, an alternative method called "drain casting" is used. This permits the forming of a hollow section without the use of an interior mold.

QUALITY STANDARDS

When the fixture is removed from the mold, it is inspected for imperfections. Different manufacturers have different definitions of acceptable quality. Generally, it pays to stay with reputable brands and deal only with firms who have a good reputation for quality.

The number of times a Plaster of Paris mold is used affects the incidence of imperfections in the fixture. To maintain a high-quality product, first class manufacturers use the molds fewer times. Some fixture imperfections are repairable. Others are not, which then require that the fixture be destroyed. Therefore, an unacceptable flaw in the tank of a one-piece unit will require destruction of the entire fixture. This is one reason why these fixtures cost more than two-piece toilets.

Figure 3.4 *Fixture Materials: Vitreous China*
Vitreous china is used for pedestal lavatories. (Courtesy of American Standard Inc. and Porcher)

THE GLAZE

After a fixture passes inspection, a glaze is applied. The fixture is fired in a kiln for an average of 24 hours at temperatures reaching up to 2250° F (1232° C). Once the fixture is removed from the kiln, it is again inspected for imperfections in the glaze surface. Fixtures that meet all standards are boxed and shipped.

Figure 3.5 *Fixture Materials: Decorated Vitreous China*
Decorated vitreous china fixtures add a touch of elegance to guest bathroom spaces. (Courtesy of Kohler Company)

DECORATED VITREOUS CHINA

Some vitreous china fixtures are enhanced with the application of a decorative decal, the addition of striping in a precious metal, or the application of an accent color and/or pattern. A decal or decorative striping is applied after the china fixture has been glazed and fired. The fixture is then refired a second time. If this additional firing is at 800° F (426° C), the decoration is "on-glaze." If the firing is at a higher temperature, the decoration is "in-glaze." If the decorative detail is "on-glaze," it will require more care than a typical fixture. To determine just how careful your client must be when using or cleaning the fixture, find out at what temperature the final firing took place.

Specialty Materials

Specialized fixtures are also available in spun glass, plastic products, copper and brass. Your product research for these unique designs, typically proprietary, should focus on the manufacturer's information on sizing, material composition, plumbing/hook-up requirements, and use and care instructions when specifying these "one-of-a-kind" items.

LAVATORIES

Cast Glass. Glass lavatories in various sizes are cast by space-age glass products to create unique vessel or over-the-vanity type of lavatories.

Hand-painted. Many vitreous china lavatories (below counter, above counter and pedestal) are part of an artist's collection that has a beautifully rendered hand-painted pattern.

Glass. High-tech glass materials—a spin-off from the space industry—is used to create glass lavatory bowls. They spin layers of metallic oxides, such as titanium, silicone and magnesium, between two sheets of glass, which is then fused into a flat sheet. These unique lavatories are then placed over a mold and heated to the final shape. Because each of these bowls is hand-crafted by artists, there will be slight variations in color, layout, texture and finish.

Metal Finishes. An innovative range of sculptural bathroom shapes is available from several manufacturers. Typically, these lavatories have a smooth, polished interior finish, and they have a textured design on the exterior of vessel bowls. These lavatories have a "living" finish; therefore, they require constant cleaning.

Figure 3.6 *Fixture Materials: An Overview of Kitchen Sinks Available in Stainless Steel* (Courtesy of Elkay)

Stainless Steel

Stainless steel fixtures are generally formed following the same process described for enameled steel fixtures. However, no surface coating is applied to a stainless steel fixture.

Stainless steel quality is generally judged by the steel gauge, the nickel content of the fixture and the finishing technique.

The higher the gauge number, the thinner the steel.

- A 22 gauge, mirror-like stainless steel sink is the least expensive and the least desirable stainless steel product. Because of its thinness, it will dent easily and its mirror finish will show scratches.

- A 20 gauge brush finished stainless steel sink that has a high nickel content will resist water spotting, conceal fine scratches within the brush finish, and is thick enough to resist dents.

- The most durable stainless steel sink is an 18 gauge, brushed finish, high nickel content sink that has an undercoating on the back side to control noise transmission.

Stone – Natural

Granite or marble slabs may be used to create custom one-of-a-kind lavatories. Typically, these natural stone products are reserved for wall, counter or floor surfacing in a slab or tile format.

A detailed discussion of surfacing materials and their application appears later in this book.

Wood – Natural

Several manufacturers offer wood bathtubs and lavatories. Wood fixtures are generally constructed from solid strips of oak or teak. Teak wood is considered more desirable than any other species because of its oily composition, which minimizes its expansion and contraction properties. This is why teak is used extensively in marine applications.

Once constructed, the fixtures are finished with a polyethylene coating to protect and enhance the beauty of the wood. To add to the structural integrity of the fixture, as well as to aid in heat retention, the outside of wood bathtubs is generally sheathed in fiberglass.

Wood fixtures should not be exposed to constant, direct sunlight. They need to be wiped down after each use to avoid the development of a permanent, unattractive water line. If damaged, the polyethylene finish can be repaired.

CHAPTER 4: Fixture Design And Planning Considerations

KITCHEN SINK AND BATHROOM LAVATORY FIXTURES

The bathroom sink is called a lavatory, basin or bowl. In this book, they are identified as "lavatories." The main kitchen sink is called just that: the kitchen sink. Smaller secondary sinks may be specified as a refreshment center sink, a vegetable sink, or decorative apron front fixture with an exposed front panel.

Kitchen Sink Configuration Choices

Kitchen sinks are made out of many materials. Integrated solid surface, cast iron, composite and stainless steel are the most popular today. Brass, copper, soapstone and other specialty materials are also used. We will be addressing sink construction and configuration as it relates to sizes and mounting methods.

Sinks come in a variety of sizes.

Single Sinks. 24" to 30" wide. In small kitchens (less than 150 square feet in size), it is not uncommon to have one single-bowl sink specified. This sink is generally 24" x 22" in size. This sink can fit in a 27" wide cabinet.

Double Sinks. Double, varying depth double, or triple-bowl sinks are more often specified in kitchens larger than 150 square feet.

Special Purpose Sinks. Second sinks in kitchens are often single sinks. Round or other shaped configurations are popular today. Several manufacturers offer elongated "ribbon" shaped specialty sinks.

Apron Panel Sinks. Specially designed sinks featuring an exposed or decorative front apron are available in double and single configurations.

Sink/Counter-Section Combinations. A sink "center" rather than a plain sink is also available in corner configurations and in 36" to 60" sink/counter combinations. Built-in front towel bars, adjacent drain boards or customized-raised compartmentalized storage areas behind the faucet are available.

Accessories. A variety of sink accessories are also available.

- Plastic covered wire or stainless steel baskets are useful for washing and peeling fresh vegetables. They take the place of a colander.

- Plate racks that fit inside the sink.

- Wire racks.

- Specialized chopping surfaces that completely or partially cover the sink are also available.

These accessories may match the sink color, contrast with the sink color, or be a combination of the sink's color and stainless steel. They enhance the sink's function, as well as its appearance. Do not overlook them.

Figure 4.1 *Fixture Design: Typical Kitchen Apron/Farmhouse Sink Configuration* (Courtesy of Rohl)

Planning Tips From Kitchen Pros

Bowl Arrangement. Unless your client is going to wash and rinse dishes in a double sink configuration, demonstrate how a sink with one large compartment and one small compartment functions. This configuration gives you the largest sink for everyday use, and then a smaller—yet usable—compartment for other uses.

Corner Sinks. When placing a sink in a corner, do not push it back more than 2" or 3" away from the front edge of the countertop. That is the normal installation location and it should be maintained (even in a custom design) so the client has comfortable access to the water source.

Damage. Make sure your client realizes that cast iron, self-rimming sinks are susceptible to damaged edges or to warpage. This is particularly a problem with larger sinks. Make sure you inspect the sink before it goes to the jobsite. Look for chips along the lead edge. The client must accept the possibility of a wide caulking joint connecting the sink to the countertop for large sink configurations. If this will not be acceptable, specify another type of sink. With these self-rimming sinks, also make sure you specify caulking that will either match the countertop or the sink so the joint compound does not become a focal point in the sink area.

Depth. The deeper the sink, the straighter the sides of the sink. The tighter the angle where the sink side and bottom meet, and the flatter the sink bottom, the bigger the interior space is.

Drain Boards. A sink with an attached drain board is an excellent accessory to specify for a client who does a lot of fresh food preparation.

Food Waste Disposer Compartment. Some sink configurations are a single size (24" x 21"), but have a small, round compartment for the food waste disposer in one back corner. Because the compartment for the food waste disposer is almost too small to use, this is not the most desirable sink configuration.

Holes. Make sure you know how many holes are on the back ledge of the sink and how many holes you need for the faucet and water attachments. If a hot water dispenser, a faucet, a dishwasher air gap, other dispensers and/or water treatment spouts are planned, you may run out of pre-drilled holes. Typically, cast iron sinks have four holes. A fifth hole can be drilled, but it is expensive and the sink may be damaged. Adding extra holes is much easier in a stainless steel sink. In solid surface sinks, the holes are drilled in the countertop deck so the number and placement is flexible.

Overall Size. When specifying a solid surface integral sink, verify what the actual overall dimensions of the sink are. The sink literature may list the interior dimension of the sink, not the overall dimension. This overall dimension will determine your spacing in a standard side-by-side double configuration. You may find it necessary to increase the cabinet size if you are planning to create a "butterfly" corner arrangement with such sinks.

Recycle Center. Some sinks on the market have an opening within the sink that allows access to a chute for a compost container or a waste receptacle below.

Round Shapes. If you are going to specify two round sinks as the primary sink arrangement, make sure your client understands the interior space of these sinks is less than a comparable square model. Also, realize these sinks require deck-mounted faucet locations; therefore, you must specify the faucet location on your plan.

Small Sinks. Avoid small, 12" x 12" sinks. They have a drain that does not accept a food waste disposer, and are so small there will be a water-splash problem when the cook uses the sink for food preparation.

Strainer. If you are not ordering a food waste disposer to be mounted on the sink, make sure you order a good quality strainer.

Under-mounted Sinks. If you use separate under-mounted sinks in place of a sink manufactured in a double configuration, warn your client that if water is running and the faucet is swung from one sink to the other, water will splash on the countertop. Consider routing down the countertop section that separates the two sinks, or recessing the entire configuration into the counter surfaces 1/4" or so in order to eliminate the potential for water to run across the countertop and down to the floor as the spout is moved from sink to sink while water is running.

Bathroom Lavatory Configuration Choices

Know the different types of lavatories available to you.

Console Table. A separate or integral fixture that is installed above or below a countertop material that is supported by decorative legs, creating a console piece of furniture. Plumbing lines are partially concealed by the front edge of the console furniture piece.

Countertop. A separate fixture installed above or below the level of the countertop material. Plumbing lines are concealed in the cabinetry.

Integral. A fixture that is fabricated from the same piece of material as the countertop material. Plumbing is concealed in the cabinetry.

Pedestal. A free-standing fixture. The water supply lines are visible. The trap is partially concealed by the base.

Vessel/Above Counter. A decorative lavatory which sits on top, or is partially recessed into a vanity countertop.

Wall-hung. A fixture that hangs from the wall. The plumbing lines and trap are visible, unless a shroud is used to cover them.

Planning Tips From Bathroom Pros

INTEGRAL LAVATORY

Integral bowls are the easiest to clean because of their seamless configuration. Be forewarned—they are also typically the shallowest types of bowls available. Therefore, in a shallow integral bowl, a high arched spout might cause a splash-back problem that the client finds unacceptable. If you are dealing with an integral bowl that is shallow, stick with standard type faucets to minimize the splash-back problem. Additionally, it is a good idea for clients to understand that splashing may occur until they grow accustomed to using the faucet at the lavatory.

PEDESTAL LAVATORY

A variety of sizes are available. The smallest pedestal lavatory is little more than a bowl on a base. Larger pedestal lavatories offer a generous bowl and counter space on each side of the lavatory. Plumbing specialists suggest the following checklist for you to think through when you specify a pedestal lavatory.

Open Pedestal Base. The pedestal base may be open all the way down the back, may be solid up to 16" off a finished floor, or may have a horizontal support bar connecting both sides of the pedestal base somewhere along the back. These last two fixture designs may interfere with the drain location. Therefore, read the manufacturer's specifications to verify what the back of the pedestal base looks like and where the drain line should be roughed in.

Finishing the Pipes. Because the pedestal base is at least partially open, do not install a mirror behind the unit. To maintain continuity, remember to consider the decorative finish on the shut-off valves, P-trap, box flange and supply lines as you select the other fittings in the bathroom.

Blocking in the Wall. If the pedestal lavatory does not completely support its own weight, the installation may require reinforcement behind the finished wall surface.

Vertically Align the Pedestal. Because the plumbing lines are exposed behind the vertical pedestal base, it is critical that the drain and supply lines are dimensionally balanced behind the pedestal. This is far less critical inside a vanity cabinet, where the supply lines can be anywhere within the open cabinet space. For a pedestal lavatory, the rough-in dimensions must be perfectly centered on the pedestal—make sure your plans are accurate.

Selecting the Right Faucet. Your choices of faucet handle style and escutcheon plate diameter may be limited if the pedestal lavatory has a small back deck, or if there is an integral splash along the back of the fixture. If you are specifying a fitting that has not been designed to fit on the pedestal lavatory by the fixture manufacturer, verify that these two items are compatible by reviewing the dimensional information from both companies.

Specifying the Height. The design of some pedestal lavatory bases limit the shut-off valves to about 16 inches off the finished floor. This height dimension is as important as the vertical arrangement mentioned above.

SELF-RIMMING LAVATORY

If the lavatory is designed to sit on top of the countertop, it is called "self-rimming." If not, it will require a rim as discussed earlier in this chapter. The lavatory features a rim around the edge of the bowl which overlaps a cut-out in the countertop. A bead of sealant is placed between the bowl rim and the countertop to prevent water seepage. The weight of the fixture, the sealant, the supply lines, and the trap hold the lavatory in place.

Warpage. Self-rimming lavatories are also susceptible to warpage. Large lavatories, and particularly oval designs, may not fit flush on the countertop. Because they do not rest perfectly on the countertop surface, they will require a larger caulking line. The client must understand this and must be willing to accept the fixture with this installation.

Templates. For some hand-made china self-rimming bowls, no template will be available. In a bathroom with more than one lavatory, do not allow the installer to use one bowl to template all the lavatories—there may be a slight difference. Therefore, each lavatory should be used for its own template in this unusual decorative situation. As a general rule, make sure the self-rimming lavatory is on the job when the countertop is cut. That way there will be no mistakes!

Ledge Drilling. The drilling location for a self-rimming lavatory must be verified before the cabinetry is ordered. Most standard self-rimming lavatories have one hole: a 4" center set drilling or 8" to 12" widespread drilling as part of their back ledge. Therefore, no special dimensioning is required because the overall depth of the lavatory will accommodate the bowl, the overflow and the plumbing lines to the faucet.

However, pay particular attention to the number and diameter of the holes drilled in the lavatory. As you will learn when we talk about lavatory faucets, a mini-widespread faucet does not use an escutcheon plate and has rigid piping, so there is no flexibility in the distance separating the valves from the spout. Therefore, if there is any discrepancy between the drilling holes on the lavatory and the faucet drilling it will not work.

Another compatibility problem may occur when you attempt to specify a single-hole faucet with an escutcheon plate on a lavatory faucet that has been drilled with three holes. Sounds simple enough—you are going to use the escutcheon plate to cover the two unused holes. The problem is the diameter of the hole. On many lavatories drilled for a standard 4" center set, the center hole will only be 1-1/8" in diameter. For a single hole faucet, you need 1-1/4". It is difficult, and expensive, to drill a cast iron lavatory. The potential for damage is great, as well.

VESSEL/ABOVE COUNTER BOWLS

Installing a sink that sits on the bathroom counter or is partially recessed in the counter has special planning concerns. These concerns revolve around the height of the user, the faucet location, and the relationship of the vessel bowl to the countertop.

User's Height. Placing a vessel bowl atop a typical 32" to 36" high vanity cabinet may be too high for a more petite user, and definitely inappropriate in a children's bathroom. Consider the actual physical height of the individual who will be using the vessel sink: if need be, partially recessing the vessel fixture may give you the "look" without the added height.

Faucet Location. Plumbers are not accustomed to vessel bowls—the craftspeople on the project need to be aware that the faucet positioning will be very different for this type of special lavatory. A wall-mounted faucet needs to be exactly positioned by the designer for the craftsperson on the job. If a wall-mounted faucet is not being used, special decorative deck mounted faucets that are installed adjacent to the vessel sink (not behind because you cannot reach the overflow or the controls) need to be specified.

Relationship of the Vessel Bowl to the Actual Countertop. The designer needs to think through the material of the countertop, the material of the vessel bowl, and the waterproof caulking compound that will be used to join the two together. In many installations today we see beautiful glass vessel bowls in glass countertops—once again, the finish and fit of all plumbing (which is now dramatically exposed) must be thought through before the project is finalized—from a planning and budgeting standpoint.

MOUNTING METHODS FOR KITCHEN SINKS AND BATHROOM LAVATORIES

There are several ways to mount a sink or lavatory.

Flush Mounted. The sink is recessed into the countertop substrate material so it is even with the counter material. This is particularly effective in a ceramic tile top. Special sinks are designed which have square ledges so the sink sits on the countertop and can flush-out with the ceramic tile on the deck.

Integral. As the name implies, the sink and countertop are all made out of one piece. This can be done with stainless steel or solid surface materials. The opportunity to create a uniquely arranged sink configuration, the ability to specify an attached drain board and the ease of maintenance are all advantages to this type of installation.

Rimmed. The sink sits slightly above the countertop with the joint between the sink and the countertop concealed by a metal rim.

Self-Rimming. The sink sits on top of the countertop. A hole is cut in the surface and the fixture is dropped in by the installers. A bead of caulking is applied between the sink and countertop forming a seal.

Under-Mounted. The sink is installed underneath the countertop. This works particularly well with solid surface and stone countertops.

If you are under-mounting a cast iron sink, always order it with a glazed rim. Make sure your client understands there will be a joint where the sink and the countertop meet for sinks that are of dissimilar materials.

A traditional under-mount sink has a square countertop lip extending down to the curved top edge of the sink. A second type of installation can be specified if the sink has a square edge so the joint contour is minimized. With solid surfacing, a seamed under-mount can create a flush joint between the bowl with the square top edge and the similar countertop material.

Figure 4.2 *Fixture Design: A Gallery of Kitchen Sink Installations* A top-mount sink. (Courtesy of Kohler Company)

Figure 4.3 *Fixture Design: A Gallery of Kitchen Sink Installations*
An integrated sink flush with the countertop. (Courtesy of DuPont Surfaces)

Figure 4.4 *Fixture Design: A Gallery of Kitchen Sink Installations*
An under-mounted stainless sink in a stone countertop. (Courtesy of Dura Supreme Cabinetry)

Figure 4.5 *Fixture Design: A Gallery of Kitchen Sink Installations*
A stainless steel countertop section which includes the integral sink. (Courtesy of Robin Siegerman, CKD – Toronto, Ontario, Canada)

Figure 4.6 *Fixture Design: A Gallery of Bathroom Lavatory Installations*
A top-mounted shaped lavatory coordinates with the curved cabinet toekick. (Courtesy of Kaye Hathaway, CKD, ASID – Barrington, Illinois)

TOILET FIXTURES

A toilet, or water closet, is designed as the fixture used by both the male and female. The fixture holds human waste and then flushes it out through the waste lines in the home to the city sewer system or to a septic system.

Selecting The Right Name

The term "water closet" comes from a European home design that featured the toilet and a small lavatory in one room separated from a larger room housing the bathtub—an early version of compartmentalizing the bathroom. This design allows one family member to be bathing while another uses the toilet. Therefore, the term "water closet" really refers to the room, not the fixture.

In North America, the term "toilet" is most often used. You and your company will decide if you want to use the trade designation "water closet," or if you prefer to call the fixture a toilet when talking to clients so they are not confused by unfamiliar terms.

Toilet Construction

Nearly all toilets are made of vitreous china—a hard, high-fired, non-porous ceramic material similar to porcelain. Fused to the china's surface is a high-gloss glaze that further adds to its excellent sanitary properties.

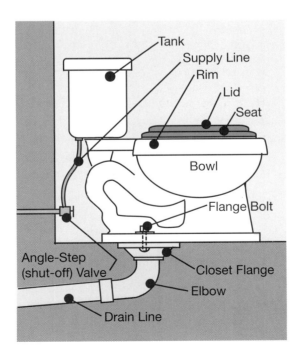

Figure 4.7 *Fixture Design: Typical Toilet Configuration*

Toilet Water Usage

For many years, conventional toilets required more than five gallons per flush (gpf). In the 1980s, the new standard for water saving toilets was reduced to 3.5 gpf (13.25 liters), then to 1.6 gpf (6.1 liters) in the 1990s. Today, toilets flush using as little as 1.4 gpf.

Toilet Styles and Types

FLUSHOMETER

One kind of toilet is a bowl that has no tank. It is fitted with a flushometer valve operating off the main water supply that requires 1" water lines. These bowls, formally confined to commercial and institutional buildings, are available in floor outlet models and in wall outlet models that come with either top inlets or back inlets for the flushometer valves. They are sometimes requested for a residential installation because of the minimal look of the "no tank" fixture and the off-the-floor, easy-care advantage.

TOILETS WITH STORAGE TANKS

More widely used in residential installations are toilets with tanks. These may be one-piece or two-piece toilets. Most two-piece models are close-coupled, the tank being supported by and bolted to the bowl.

While most are floor standing and have a floor outlet, there are models with wall outlets, and they may be either floor-standing or wall-mounted. There are also nostalgic designs with period-style high-level tanks.

TOILET SEATS

There is a wide choice of elongated or round bowls, each accepting standard-size seats. Some luxury toilets are supplied with seats specifically designed for the toilet. Seats are available today with a "soft close" feature, making them close quietly. Kohler Company has a "PeaceKeeper" toilet that will not flush until the user closes the lid!

Figure 4.8 *Fixture Design: One-Piece* One-piece toilets are sleek, seamless and easier to keep clean. (Courtesy of Toto)

Toilet Rough-in Dimensions

A wide variety of floor standing toilets with floor outlets have a 12" rough-in dimension (the distance from the center of the outlet to the finished surface of the wall). There is a limited selection of models with either a 10" or a 14" rough-in, which are sometimes required for retrofit projects.

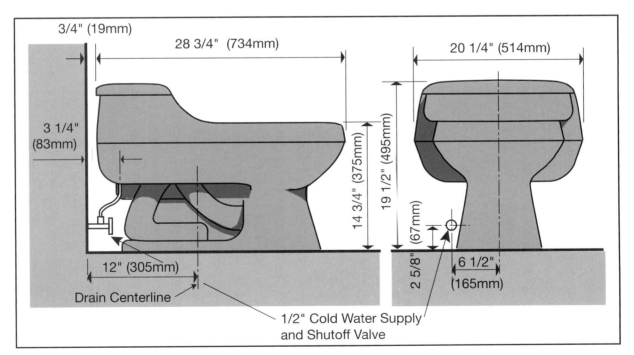

Figure 4.9 *Fixture Design: The Anatomy of a Toilet Installation*

Flushing Methods and Devices

Toilets are flushed either from a tank or directly from the water supply.

Older toilets use 3.5 – 5.0 gpf (13.2 liters) of water to complete the flushing action. The force of gravity alone is employed in this system. Devices incorporated into the tank to provide a gravity flush are a back-flow-protected fill valve (ball cock) and a flush valve.

Water conservation initiatives, as well as extensive re-engineering efforts by leading plumbing fixture manufacturers has led to a wide variety of high-performance toilets that use much less water.

1.6 TOILETS

Gravity Flush. Toilets with 1.6 gpf (6.1 liters) tanks are available either with a gravity flush (for which the flushing devices are similar to those in a 3.5 gpf [13.2 liters] toilet) or with a pressure-assisted flush.

Pressure-assisted Flush. The second type has a pressure vessel in the tank that contains both water and air. The air is compressed by supply system pressure as the refill charges the tank. When the toilet is flushed, the air pushes the water out of the tank at high velocity. The toilet bowl (which has been specially designed to accept this water stream) is quickly emptied. This type of flushing system is noisy.

FLUSHOMETER TOILETS

Toilets without tanks can only be used where large diameter pipes make an adequate flow rate (over 25 gpm) available. The flush is controlled by a flushometer valve, which may be an exposed fitting connected to the top of the toilet bowl or a fitting concealed in the wall and connected to the back of the bowl. Flush valves are available with a hand-operated level or with a no-touch infrared or proximity activator.

Flushing Action of Bowls

There are several basic approaches to designing the flushing action, each with its own unique performance characteristics. In addition to performance considerations, factors to consider in design include:

- Water surface, depth and area provided in the bowl. The larger the water surface, the easier it is to keep the bowl clean, reduce odor and minimize urine splash.

- Trapway size (The actual dimensional measurement of the passageway.) It is based on standards of performance involving the passage of balls of varying diameters.

- Extent of glazing in trapway. A completely glazed trapway provides a smooth, minimal resistant passage for waste materials.

- Boxed or open rim.

Siphon Vortex. This flushing action is based on diagonal rim outlets that cause a swirling or "whirlpool" action. The resulting rapid filling of the trap triggers the siphoning of the bowl contents. Vortex designs are known for their large water surface area and extremely quiet operation. This swirling water action also leads to a "self-cleaning" toilet bowl as the water rinses the surface.

Siphon Wash. This is one of two designs that do not incorporate a jet to develop a siphoning action. It relies entirely on the incoming rush of water from the rim. The resulting rapid filling of the trap triggers the siphoning of the bowl contents. Its small water surface makes it more vulnerable to soiling and staining.

Siphon Jet. Similar in basic concept to the siphon action reverse trap design, this style is more advanced in efficiency. The jet, in this case, delivers flow with such a volume as to begin the siphoning action instantly, without any rise in the level of water in the bowl before the contents are drawn through the outlet. In addition to quiet operation, siphon jet designs also provide a larger water surface area.

Blowout (Compression). This is the one design in the group that does not incorporate a siphoning action. Instead, it relies entirely on the driving force of a jet action. Because of the water capacity required to accomplish this, blowout designs are used in tankless installations only, in combination with a flush valve. Such designs are known for their generous trapway size and large water surface area.

Toilet Planning Tips From Bathroom Pros

Specify the Actuator Finish. Always check the tank lever or push button actuator finish against other fitting finishes if you wish all to blend together. The tank lever can be a button at the top of the tank, a valve on the side of the tank, or a valve on the front of the tank. Decorative actuators are generally the most effective for toilets with the actuator on the front of the tank.

225

Verify the Floor Outlet Rough-in. If you are working in a house that is fifty years old or older, double-check the drain outlet dimension by measuring from the finished wall surface to the center of the bolts on each side of the existing toilet. The 10" and 14" rough-in dimension toilets were used in many cases in the old days. You may need to order a fixture that is available in one of these older rough-ins. This approach will severely limit the models you have to choose from. Alternatively, you may select to use an offset flange (ring) to modify the old outlet center dimension to today's more standard 12". The ring lets you offset the fixture outlet by up to 2".

Measure from Finished Wall. Remember, the rough-in dimension is always from the finished wall surface to the center of the drain. If you are installing a tile wainscoting around the room, and planning on a "mud" tile installation, you may need to rough-in the toilet at 13-1/2" from the drywall surface so you truly have a 12" finished rough-in from the finished tile surface to the center of the floor outlet.

Realize the PSI Will Vary. All toilets recommend a particular Pounds Per Square Inch (psi) of pressure available at the fixture so it can clean the bowl with one flush. However, remember that the time of year, the household activities and the neighborhood activities will affect the available water pressure. This is discussed in *Kitchen & Bath Systems*.

Think About Cleanability. Some toilets are easier to clean than others. If this is a major concern of your client, look for a one-piece toilet and, in particular, one with straight sides which conceal the caps that cover the bolts holding the toilet above the floor outlet.

Remember Fixture Sizes Vary. One European toilet is only 14-7/8" wide. Typical North American products are from 20" to 24" wide. The standard seat height is 14" to 15" high. Fixtures with 18" high seats are also available and are the most comfortable to use by adults and individuals with physical limitations affecting their mobility.

Understand that Different Supply Lines and Rough-ins Are Specified for Different Toilets. A low-profile toilet requires 1/2" rigid water supply lines—not the 3/8" lines typically called for with a two-piece toilet.

Additionally, the height of the supply lines for a one-piece toilet is generally lower than for a two-piece toilet. Check each manufacturer's specification sheet before specifying the supply line pipe diameter/type and/or pipe. Make sure you identify this dimension before you specify the finish baseboard material. There is nothing more unsightly than a 4-1/2" ceramic tile baseboard with 1/4" round trim that is interrupted by a supply line, which is half in/half out of the baseboard dimension.

Make Sure the Client Is Prepared for the Noise Associated with 1.6 (6.1 Liter) Pressure-assisted Toilets. Pressure-assisted 1.6 gpf (6.1 liter) systems cost more than gravity flow units and they are noisier. Although the noise is only heard for an instant, as the pressure moves the water through the system, this may be unacceptable in a powder room adjacent to an entertaining area, or in the middle of the night in the master suite. To minimize the transmission of this noise, try to avoid placing a pressure tank toilet on a common wall separating the fixture from spaces inhabited by guests or other sleeping family members.

BIDET FIXTURES

The book *Bath Planning* from the National Kitchen & Bath Association explains in detail how a bidet is used. Please read that information before proceeding if you are not familiar with how the bidet fixture is used. This book describes how the fixture is designed.

Three different types of bidets are available from fixture manufacturers.

Separate Fixture, Rim-Filled With Vertical Spray

This type of bidet provides an ascending jet spray, as well as a bowl filling mechanism through holes along the rim. A vertical spray delivers water through the outlet in the center of the bowl, allowing the user to direct the spray to the desired area simply by sliding their body forward and backward on the bidet.

This type of bidet requires the following components: individual hot and cold valves, a diverter valve, a pop-up drain control, the spray fitting, and, connections to the waterways. Such bidet fittings come complete from the faucet manufacturer. Specify deck-mount or wall-mount fittings according to the type of bidet chosen. To insure compatibility, some faucet manufacturers will require you to specify the bidet model chosen.

Because the bowl can be filled to a height above the vertical spray, the possibility of contaminated water entering the potable water system exists. This phenomenon is called "back flow." This situation can occur if the city's water supply temporarily has negative pressure (if it sucks instead of pushes), causing a vacuum to be created that would pull contaminated water standing above an inlet into the potable (fresh) water supply.

To prevent such water contamination due to a back flow, a vacuum breaker must be installed behind the bidet. This protective device breaks the back flow, or suction action, by allowing air into the piping system. Check that the vacuum breaker is supplied with the selected bidet fitting. This will insure adaptability between the systems. Alternatively, there are firms who provide "fit-all" vacuum breaker systems that adapt to most faucet lines, and may be more attractive as well.

Separate Fixture, Over-Rim With Horizontal Spray

This bidet has no ascending jet spray in the center of the fixture. It is filled by means of a deck-mounted faucet— like a lavatory faucet— that discharges water over the rim in a horizontal stream. This type of fixture is generally less expensive to purchase and install because both the bidet and the faucet are simpler to produce and a vacuum breaker is not required.

Figure 4.10 *Fixture Design: Bidet Fixtures*
The bidet on the left has a vertical jet. The bidet on the right has an over-the-rim horizontal spray. (Courtesy of American Standard Inc.)

An Alternative To The Bidet: The Bidet Seat

The bidet seat is a toilet seat that is also a bidet. For comfort, these seats have a control panel on the side of the toilet which allows the user to activate a streamlined wand that extends from the back of the seat into the bowl, providing a smooth, warm flow of aerated water for complete cleansing. The nozzle automatically self-cleans before and after use. In addition to water, there is an air dryer and a heated seat. An air purifier is also available.

The bidet seat requires a 120 volt electrical line: a mechanical element not typically associated with toilet installation.

Bidet Planning Tips From Bathroom Pros

The Drain Location. The bidet drain is more like that of a lavatory than that of a toilet. Therefore, there is no fixed rough-in recommendation for the drain outlet. Refer to the selected manufacturer's rough-in book for specifications appropriate for a certain fixture.

Coordinate with the Toilet. Because bidets are installed adjacent to, or across from toilets, fixture manufacturers design suites of products so the rim height is coordinated between the toilet and bidet, as is the shape and configuration of the fixture.

Selection of Faucets. The faucets selected for the bidet must be compatible with the fixture. Not all china products accept valves from other manufacturers. Sometimes, if you order fixtures and fittings from different manufacturers, the hole configuration on the fixture or the shank on the valve and the bidet fitting may not coordinate with one another. (This becomes a particular problem with an American china piece and a European faucet.)

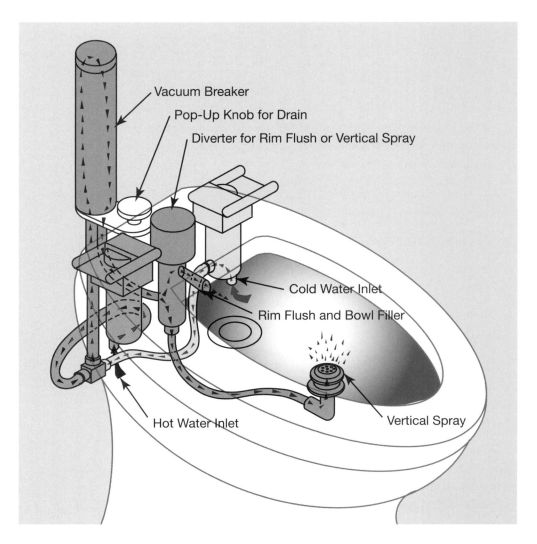

Vacuum Breaker
Pop-Up Knob for Drain
Diverter for Rim Flush or Vertical Spray
Cold Water Inlet
Rim Flush and Bowl Filler
Hot Water Inlet
Vertical Spray

Figure 4.11 *Fixture Design: The Bidet Vacuum Breaker*
The drawing shows how a vacuum breaker is installed behind a bidet that has a vertical spray, and how this backflow prevention device operates.

URINAL FIXTURES

Urinals are available in a wall-hung variety, a stall type that extends from the floor up, and a trough that is mounted horizontally on the wall. Wall-hung units are most widely used. They require the least amount of space, offer the most placement flexibility and, typically, are the most attractive. They are made of vitreous china.

Although it would make sense to install urinals in residential bathrooms, they are rarely seen because most are designed to rely on the building's water pressure and piping system to deliver the necessary water to complete the flushing action and, therefore, do not have a storage tank. They commonly use the flushometer valve discussed on page 224. (Recently, waterless urinals have been installed in large commercial and industrial facilities in an effort to conserve more water.)

Designers also have designed them into home plans. They are ideal in a master suite, where the man has a small room with his toilet and urinal, and the woman has a toilet and a bidet. Other ideal locations are a boy's bathroom and the entry bathroom off the deck, pool or patio area.

BATHTUB FIXTURES

There are a wide variety of bathtubs available today. Although there are many different shapes and sizes, there are four broad categories of bathtubs as defined by the installation method.

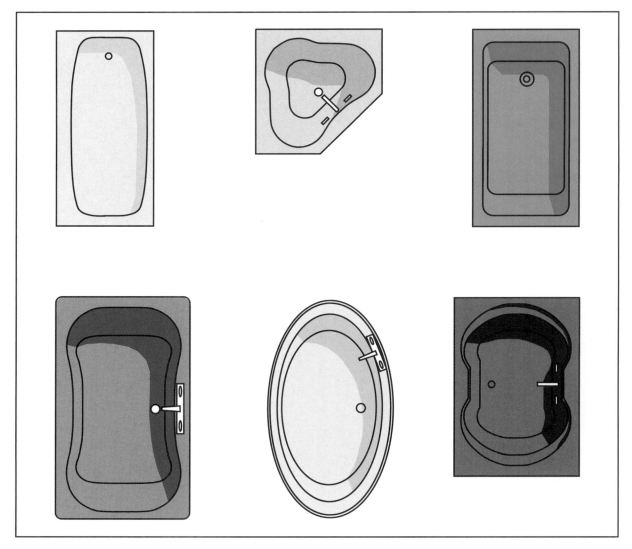

Figure 4.12 *Fixture Design: Typical Bathtub Configurations*

Types of Bathtub Fixtures

CORNER

These units are available in two styles. One type is available in a configuration similar to the standard recessed bathtub. However, in addition to the front being finished, one end has a finished panel, as well. Another type of fixture is designed to fill a corner and features three angled or curved finished sides. Several manufacturers have introduced sculpted bathtub shapes that offer a wider variety of configurations for corner installations.

This second type of corner tub generally requires from 48" to 60" along the back two walls, and extends from 60" to 72" out from the back corner into the center of the room. They are a space-efficient way to plan a whirlpool bath if the available back wall space is limited.

FREE-STANDING

Unique, free-standing bathtubs are also available from several manufacturers. The free-standing bathtub literally stands in the middle of the room. Several manufacturers offer a recreated claw foot bathtub reminiscent of Victorian-style bathrooms. A curved, oblong shaped bathtub attractively trimmed in wood is available. Custom copper bathtubs, as well as sleek, contemporary fixtures are also on the market. Some models are available with a jetted hydromassage system.

As you will read in this section about safety and showering, these free-standing bathtubs should generally not be planned as showering facilities. This is also discussed in *Bath Planning*.

Figure 4.13 *Fixture Design: A Free-standing Bathtub*
(Courtesy of American Standard Inc.)

RECESSED

This type of bathtub comes without finished ends and with one finished side, typically called the "apron." The bathtub is designed to slip between two end walls and against a back wall. You must specify a left or right drain so the drain is in the proper relationship to the finished front. When you are standing in front of the bathtub—about to enter—and the drain is on the left, it is a left hand bathtub. Many bathtubs feature well-engineered, integral backrests and grab bars.

Typical sizes are 30" to 34" wide, 14" to 20" deep, and 60" to 72" long. These tubs generally have an integral tile flange on the two side walls and the back so when the wet wall material is installed, water will not be able to "wick up" behind the surround material and damage drywall or wood studs. Many manufacturers also offer a tile bead kit that allows you to transform a bathtub without such a flange into a recessed unit.

PLATFORM

A popular type of bathtub is a platform bathtub. This bathtub has no finished panels. It is designed to drop into a platform made of another material. Designs are similar regardless of material, but there are some limitations on the cast iron fixture sizes. Because these bathtubs are dropped into a platform, the edge detailing of the bathtub adds to the design statement.

For this type of installation, the designer should be very careful about the relationship of the raised bathtub ledge and any back corners of the platform if the bathtub will also serve as a shower. Water can "pool" in the corners and cause a cleaning problem.

Alternatively, some designers prefer to extend the platform material over the bathtub to create an under-mounted installation. This latter installation may make it uncomfortable for users to rest their head on the bathtub ledge when lounging. It also will significantly increase the cost to change the bathtub if ever necessary.

If a bathtub is a separate fixture from a stall shower, a decorative, protective material is installed, which extends upwards from the bathtub or deck 4" to 12" along the walls that flank the bathtub. This material typically matches or contrasts with the decking material. Where the bathtub doubles as a shower, contrasting material may be specified, the bathtub may have integral walls, or the bathtub and walls may be made out of the same material, but in a four-piece configuration to facilitate moving the bathtub into position in a renovation situation. These types of surround materials will be discussed in more detail when we look at bathtub/shower combination fixtures.

Types of Bathtub Experiences

Consumers today have a wide variety of bathing experiences they can select from. Simply relaxing in a deep, contoured bathtub in warm water is a great way to start the bathing experience. Kohler Company describes them as:

- **The Relax Experience**. Combining the effervescence of an air bath system with a relaxing environment that might be enhanced by chromatherapy. Chromatherapy refers to the tangible effect color has on an individual's body and their feeling of well being: warm colors are stimulating, cool colors are calming. Thermo-massage air jet tubs use a multitude of air jets randomly placed on the floor of the tub, and a circular pattern on the edge of the bathtub, creating a turbulence of water by the injection of air. Since, in reality, there is no water being circulated through a pump, these systems allow the bather to use products such as essential oils to optimize relaxation. This bathing experience can be further expanded with controlled lighting, surround sound systems and televisions that are actually built into tubs.

Figure 4.14 *Fixture Design: A Platform Bathtub*
This surface mounted tub is set into a tile platform. (Courtesy of Jacuzzi)

- **The Spa Experience**. The spa experience combines the effervescence of an air bath system, chromatherapy, and Flexjets. Flexjets are individually adjustable to target specific areas of the body. Most systems have flexjets. Specifically directed back or neck jets are available on other systems.

- **The Massage Experience**. The massage experience is one where there is a specific sequence programmed into the jets to simulate a spa massage, allowing the user to loosen tension up along the back and across the shoulders. Similarly, neck jets are available.

- **The Spa/Massage Experience**. For the true bathing lover, all of these features can be combined and controlled by a lighted keypad on the side of the tub or a floating remote control.

Jetted Bathtubs

Most manufacturers provide a totally integrated whirlpool system and bathtub which has been factory tested before shipment. Although *Bath Planning* discusses the ergonomic planning considerations for this type of fixture, you should also be familiar with the individual mechanical elements of a whirlpool system.

MECHANICAL ELEMENTS

Pump. The pump is at the heart of the system. The size of the pump varies in horsepower rating from 1/2 hp to 1-1/2 hp. However, the horsepower rating is not the only contributing factor to the engineering of the pump and jet system. Therefore, rely on the gallons per minute of water flow pushed through the jets when evaluating the system, rather than simply focusing on the pump horsepower rating. Generally, the whirlpool bathtubs are capable of delivering 5 to 7 gallons (18 to 27 liters) of water per minute, per jet. The system should have UL approved components. Manufacturers typically have the entire system UL-approved for additional safety assurance and for customer satisfaction.

Activator. Older systems may be activated by a timer switch installed on the wall. If used, locate it out of reach of the bather when he or she is in the tub (most codes call for 39" or 60" of distance from the switch to the bathtub) so the chance of an electrical accident is eliminated.

Alternatively, an air switch installed directly on the bathtub may be available. Check the price list—this type of starter may carry an extra charge to you. When an air switch is depressed, it increases the air pressure and a bubble of air travels down a length of tube to an electrical switch at the pump. For both safety and convenience, the air switch is superior to an electrical switch.

A third type of switch is available on luxury bathtubs: called a "capacilance level switch." With this type of switch the sensor operates in a manner similar to a simple capacitor. A high-frequency oscillator is located within the tip of the probe. When the tip of the probe comes in contact with the medium, the frequency of the oscillation reaches a preset point and the protection circuit signals the switch to change state. Therefore, in the bathtub application, the switch senses the electrical differences that occur when a person lightly touches the control panel and turns the system on.

Wiring. Both 120- and 240-volt pumps are available. Generally, whirlpool bathtubs with a 1 hp motor or less will operate off a 120-volt circuit. Whirlpool bathtubs that have a motor larger than 1 hp will generally require a 240-volt circuit. Regardless of the motor size, if an in-line heater is included, a 240-volt circuit may be needed.

Holding the Temperature. An "in-line heater" can be added to keep the hot water temperature constant. These heaters do not raise the water temperature.

Do not confuse the purpose of an in-line heater with that of a storage tank or a tankless water heater. The purpose of the tank or tankless water heater is to heat water before it enters the bathtub at the start of the bath. The in-line heater simply maintains the water temperature in the bathtub during the hydromassage bath.

An in-line heater is a good enhancement for a whirlpool tub that will be used by family members for an extended period of time. Just as the piping and pump require service access, such a heater should be reachable by repairmen in the future. Make sure you have enough electrical power for the 240-volt circuit this heater will require, as well.

MINIMIZING BACTERIA GROWTH IN THE PIPING SYSTEM

New antimicrobial technologies are used by whirlpool bathtub manufacturers today to minimize the growth of bacteria in whirlpool piping. In some cases, the material is applied to the piping as a coating; in other instances, the inhibitor is actually part of the whirlpool piping system. In all cases, the end goal is to inhibit mold, mildew and bacteria growth in the plumbing piping.

PURGING THE PIPING SYSTEMS

Today, manufacturers have designed their whirlpool systems to insure a completed rain of all water in the piping; therefore, no standing water remains between uses. Additionally, some systems have an automatic purge cycle set by the user, which blows warm air through the piping system daily at the same time to further inhibit any moisture remaining in the piping.

Figure 4.15 *Fixture Design: A Typical Whirlpool System*

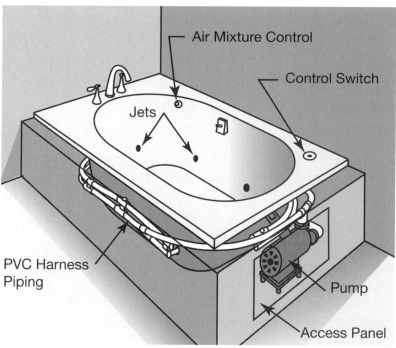

ACCESSIBILITY

The pump must be accessible for future servicing, a requirement often overlooked by inexperienced bathroom designers. Check the manufacturer's literature or find out from your supplier where the pump is in relationship to the overall configuration of the bathtub.

For factory installed systems, the pump fits within the envelope of the bathtub. Some manufacturers do offer alternative pump locations of up to 60" away from the bathtub. Verify such an option by reviewing the fixture literature. If the manufacturer's specifications do allow a remote location, consider concealing the pump in a vanity cabinet adjacent to the bathtub, in a closet space near the bathtub, or behind a concealed access door along the front apron panel of the bathtub. Wherever it is placed, it must be on the same level as the base of the bathtub to provide a complete drain after each use.

NOISE

Be sure to alert your clients to the noise level of all whirlpool systems. The majority of the noise is caused as the large volume of water is pushed through the piping and into the bathtub. Therefore, you cannot design a silent system. However, you can minimize the noise by mounting the pump on a thick rubber block and enclosing it on three sides.

PLACEMENT

For proper performance and safety, the pump/motor assembly must be no higher than the highest jet (which is 2" below the water level) and no lower than the suction fitting. The piping used to connect the system must also be designed to remain rigid through the fixture's years of use. The piping must also be engineered to prevent water from remaining in the lines after use, which can lead to bacterial growth in the standing water. At the jobsite, the installation crew must also be instructed not to pick the bathtub up by the piping.

This pump/jet placement and piping design are required so a 100% drain-out of used bath water will occur every time the bathtub is emptied. If this placement criterion is overlooked, or if the pipe flexes during the bathtub's years of use, the first water to enter the fixture would be contaminated water from the last bath.

THE JETS

Volume/Pressure Relationship

There are two different approaches to whirlpool jet design:

- **Fewer jets with larger outlets that are serviced by bigger water lines.** The jets operate on a high-volume, low-pressure system that provides a comfortable bathing experience for the user as softly pulsating water rolls around the body. They are generally noisier than the next option.

- **More jets with smaller outlets serviced by small water lines.** These jets operate on a low-volume, high-pressure system to bring the water to the numerous jets, which can be individually adjusted for the user's comfort.

Mixing Air with Water

Better systems inject the air into the water, thereby providing a complete mixture of air and water for a more effective massage. This mixture of air and water is called a "venturi" effect. To maximize the flexibility of the system, better bathtubs have jets that are individually controlled for spray direction, volume and air/water mixture. The jets in well-engineered bathtubs are also nearly flush to the bathtub's interior.

However, there is a drawback to mixing air with water: the room's temperature will cool the bath water. Additionally, the jet controls add another visual element to the bathtub. You should think about the overall look your clients hope to achieve as you recommend matching the whirlpool bathtub component parts to the bathtub finish (the most inconspicuous approach) or contrasting the bathtub finish and matching the bathtub fittings to the faucet finish specified elsewhere.

Bathtub Planning Tips From Bathroom Pros

Once the bathtub's equipment has been installed and the bathtub has been placed with the comfort, safety and pleasure of the user in mind, the following special construction constraints must be considered.

Hot Water Requirements. The whirlpool bathtub relies on the hot water system installed in the house to fill the bathtub. Therefore, the existing hot water tank capacity and its recovery rate need to be verified before a bathtub is specified. At an initial filling, you can generally expect about 70% of the hot water tank's capacity to be delivered at the temperature set. Therefore, a 40 gallon hot water tank will deliver about 30 gallons (113.55 liters) of 120° F (48.8° C) water.

The recovery rate of gas hot water tanks is faster than electric tanks; therefore, if the initial drain is not adequate to fill the bathtub, the recovery rate must be taken into account. The manufacturer's literature will tell you how many gallons of water the bathtub will require.

The capacity of whirlpool bathtubs ranges from 50 to 140 gallons (190 to 530 liters) of water. A good rule of thumb would be to size the water heater to provide enough hot water for two-thirds capacity of the bathtub, with the balance being cold water.

If the existing tank is not adequate, you have three options:

- Increase the size of the household water heater, or install two water heaters side-by-side.

- Provide a separate water heater specifically for the whirlpool.

- Specify several tankless water heaters along the supply line.

Generally, the first approach is the best one if other water needs are marginally met by the current system. If you select the third option, be forewarned: the tankless systems are not designed to heat the large volume of water required for these bathtubs. Therefore, you may be required to install a series of 240-volt tankless heaters, which becomes cost prohibitive in most cases.

Water Flow Rate. Regardless of how much hot water is available, if the plumbing supply lines are not large enough and/or if the bathtub filler spout is not adequate, the water will not be able to fill the tub fast enough.

The secret to success is the diameter (size) of the pipe! Normally, 3/4" nominal (inside dimension) hot and cold supply lines service a bathroom with three fixtures. The 1/2" nominal individual branches then bring hot and cold water to the standard bathtub fittings. A 1/2" spout is then used to fill the bathtub.

To provide the increased flow of water needed to fill bigger bathtubs, a 3/4" individual water supply branch line and a 3/4" bath spout and valve should be used to maximize the water flow to the bathtub. Remember, the entire system must be increased in size. If a 3/4" valve is installed with a 1/2" branch line, or the reverse, the water supply will not be adequate. Alternatively, doubling up on the bathtub fillers may help get the water into the bathtub fast enough.

Accessibility. Be sure the bathtub you specify is not too large to get into the house, down the hall and around the corner into the bathroom. In new construction, the bathtub is installed during the framing stage. However, in a renovation situation, a large bathtub may be difficult to maneuver into the bathroom. Find out how much the bathtub weighs. A single tradesman may not be able to lift the bathtub without help.

Supporting the Fixture. Typical North American floor systems are designed to carry 40 pounds (18 kilograms) of weight per square foot. Some large bathtubs may require additional support. Verify the weight of the bathtub when it is filled with water and people. If such information is not available, you can compute the weight as follows: one gallon of water equals 8.33 pounds (3.8 kilograms) and 7.51 gallons (3.5 kilograms) of water equals one cubic foot. Once you know how much the bathtub weighs when filled, determine if the existing floor joist construction is adequate enough to support the bathtub.

SHOWER STALL FIXTURES

Shower stalls are the ideal fixture for the daily showering ritual that is so much a part of the North American life. They come in many sizes and configurations. The book *Bath Planning* from the National Kitchen & Bath Association identifies minimum acceptable sizes and recommended sizes based on human ergonomic studies. The materials that shower pans (the floor and front curb of the shower) and enclosures are made of is the focus of this volume.

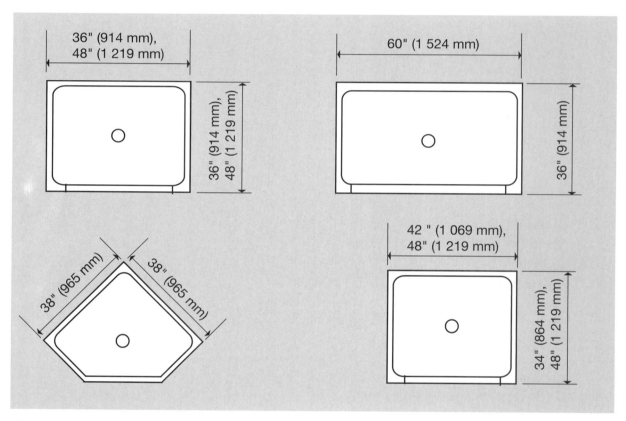

Figure 4.16 *Fixture Design: Typical Stall Shower Configurations*

Types of Custom Pans

Masonry and Stone. Masonry and molded-stone shower pans are available. Masonry pans are of a cement construction with chips of ground stone used as a filler, much like Terrazzo. Terrazzo is a combination of white cement and marble chips.

The mixture is poured into a mold and then subjected to high temperatures and pressure for curing. When removed from the mold, the pan has a smooth finish with a homogeneous wall structure.

Solid Surface. Major manufacturers offer solid surface shower pans in popular sizes. Skilled fabricators can also create custom pans for you.

Plastic. Fiberglass reinforced gel coat, acrylic and ABS plastic shower pans are available. See Chapter 3, "Fixture Materials," for a detailed description of how this material is manufactured.

Cast Polymer. Cast polymer shower pans are also available. The manufacturing process for this material also appears in Chapter 7.

These last three types of pan materials offer an added advantage. The walls in the surround can be made out of the same or similar surfacing. With plastic materials, the enclosure can actually be made in one piece with no seams. These one-piece units can be attractively sculpted to include built-in grab bars, grooming recess areas and reclining seats.

Planning Tips From Bathroom Pros

Make Sure You Can Get it in the House. When selecting a one-piece shower, or a one-piece bathtub/shower combination, you must remember to verify hallway widths and door openings in a remodeling project. Typically, these fixtures are put in-place during the framing stage in new construction. But, in a renovation scenario, the shower must be moved through finished spaces. Therefore, units that feature a separate pan and three walls are more typically specified.

Specify the Drain Location. The drain location of all pre-made pans is determined by the manufacturer. It is typically in the center of square or round enclosures, and off to one side in rectangular units. The location of the drain needs to be clearly specified on the plans to assist the plumber during the rough-in stage. Compare the existing drain in a renovation situation with the specifications for a new pan to make sure they are compatible.

Specify the Curb. All of the man-made material pans are designed with a ledge at the front, which is called a "curb" or a "threshold." Much like a recessed bathtub, the other three sides of the pan have a raised lip or tile flange so the water resistant drywall can sit on a ledge, rather than extending all the way down to the pan. This minimizes the problem of water wicking up behind the drywall and behind the surrounding finished wall surface material.

When you are planning a ceramic tile pan, you have complete flexibility in size and shape of the enclosure. You are also responsible for making sure the pan is watertight.

243

BATHTUB/SHOWER COMBINATION UNIT FIXTURES

As you will learn when you read *Bath Planning*, combination bathtub/shower units do not provide a comfortable bath, nor the safest showering experience. However, the reality of the real design world is that we are often limited to this sort of combination fixture because of space constraints.

Selection Criteria

Bathtubs can be installed with a separate wall surface surrounding them. In this installation, it is always desirable to extend the wet wall surround material past the end of the bathtub and then down to the floor. This protects the wallboard around the bathtub from water damage over the years of use.

Alternatively, the bathtub and wall surface materials can be the same, with the walls available in a separate panel configuration. This option allows the technician to bring the material into a small, difficult-to-reach bathroom and then complete the installation on site.

In room addition work or in new construction, a one-piece combination bathtub/shower can be installed. This last choice provides a fixture that is the easiest to clean, the least susceptible to water damage, and the most flexible in its overall design. Today, manufacturers provide sculpted units with benches and seats in large, oversized showers, fold-down seating areas in bathtub/shower combinations, built-in grab bars, and storage shelves all seamlessly formed.

CHAPTER 5: Fitting Materials and Engineering

After the fixture materials have been selected, you and the client will choose the fittings. Whether they are called the "trim," the "brass," the "fitting" or the "faucet," these water delivering devices are available in a myriad of different materials and finishes for both the kitchen and the bathroom.

Brass

Brass is generally considered an excellent material for faucet construction because it is a strong, durable metal virtually unaffected by prolonged contact with water. Brass is an alloy of copper and zinc, with trace materials such as lead that improve machining, or silicon to improve casting. It varies in color from yellow to red, and can be melted and poured into molds or machined from stock or rods.

Brass faucet bodies may be sand cast, much like a cast iron bathtub. Faucet component parts manufactured this way tend to have the lowest density and can be porous, which can cause pinholes and leaks. Because sand molds cool the brass quickly, this type of brass faucet must have the highest lead content.

Gravity diecasting is another way that brass faucets are manufactured. Molten brass is manually poured or automatically injected into a machined metal form. Waterways and other hollows are either machined or formed through the use of a sand core. This method of casting provides greater density than sand casting, but is still inspected at the factory for pinhole leaks.

Forging is another method of forming faucet bodies from brass. In the forging process, a heated brass "plug" is pressed by extremely high pressure between two machined metal forms, which produces a smooth component part that requires little polishing. Waterways and other hollows are formed through machining. This process results in a fitting with few surface imperfections and a high-quality surface luster.

Lastly, brass stock, bars, rods, tubing or thin sheets can be machined or cold stamped into desired forms and shapes. Again, minimal polishing is required and low lead content brass can be used.

CONSTRUCTION MATERIALS

No matter what manufacturing process is used, brass provides a durable, long-lasting faucet material that stands up well. Even if the finish is damaged, the brass underneath holds up to heavy use. Unfortunately, because it also is a relatively costly raw material and involves complicated manufacturing processes, brass fittings have an initial high purchase price for the client.

Copper

Copper is used for waterways of fabricated fittings and in some valve connections. Because it is softer than brass, copper can be easily shaped and bent. If uncoated, copper is prone to surface corrosion and scratching.

Plastics (ABS, ACETAL, CPVC AND RUBBER)

These are smooth, relatively soft materials commonly used in valve systems and cartridges or the gasket material under the fitting. Some extremely low cost fittings feature plastic bodies or waterways. Plastic materials are inexpensive and not prone to a lime or scale buildup. The smooth, slippery surfaces ease the passage of water and debris, as opposed to rougher surfaces that can catch or slow such material.

Plastic valves can be damaged by line debris, such as sand and silt. Unless the plastic receives special preparation, or is of plating grade, it is not as durable nor as strong as other materials, and is difficult to plate with special finishes. Additionally it can be attacked by certain petroleum-based products.

Color matching plastic components to other components made from metal can be difficult due to the differences in texture, gloss and light reflection.

Stainless Steel

Stainless steel does not need the additional finish that brass faucets do. Stainless steel faucets stand up well to high pressure, high temperatures and potentially corrosive materials in the water supply. Stainless steel is more difficult to work with than brass, though, and is also more expensive.

Stainless steel faucets are oftentimes used in contemporary design and come in both a bright and brushed finish.

Zinc

Zinc is a silvery-white metal that is cast into forms and shapes. It is stronger and more durable than some plastics and smoother than brass. Therefore, it requires less polishing and buffing for a finished product. Zinc must be fully protected from contact with water by plating because it quickly corrodes and disintegrates if unprotected pieces come in contact with water.

FITTING FINISHING OPTIONS

Over the last several years there has been a dramatic increase in the various technical innovations and finishing options available to the designer. While chrome finishes still predominate, modern faucets can be finished in nickel, brass, colored plastics/epoxy, gold, silver, living hand-rubbed finishes and an extremely tough finish developed by NASA, and many more.

Many manufacturers offer a complete line of kitchen and bathroom faucet sets and coordinating accessories. These accessory items will include towel bars, paper holders and other accessories to match their faucet offerings. Occasionally, a client will select specialized equipment that is not part of a "full line" product offering. Or, a client may like one manufacturer's decorative bathtub set and another company's accessories. Although various finishes will blend, if the client is expecting a perfect match, only one manufacturer's product should be specified.

This problem is magnified if the client wants the colored fittings to match fixtures, wet walls and counter surfaces made from other materials. For example, a client may expect the white epoxy coated faucets to match the white solid surface countertop and the white acrylic shower stall. Because of the fixture and surfacing material composition differences, a match cannot be promised. Remember, a bathroom lavatory is china or enamel, the faucets have an epoxy coating, the wet walls/countertop solid surfacing are a blend of polyesters and acrylics, and the tub enclosure is an acrylic fixture. Talk to the client about colors blending with one another, not matching.

To overcome this color match dilemma, consider these solutions:

- Try to use only one surfacing material throughout the project. For example, in a bathroom, use solid surface materials in the shower and on the vanity top. Or, ceramic tile on all surfaces.

- In your showroom, display a setting that is all white. Make sure the whites on the floor, fixture, counter, walls and fittings blend but don't match. This will give you a chance to explain the color variation to a client before the final project specifications are completed.

- Specify fittings that have a colored, chrome or brass escutcheon plate separating them from the counter or wall. Such a color break will help camouflage slight differences in color tones.

Chrome

POLISHED CHROME

Polished chrome is the most popular finish for kitchen and bathroom fittings and hardware. It is extremely hard and does not oxidize in the air as do most other metals, thereby eliminating the need for regular polishing. Chrome is electrochemically deposited over the nickel plated base metal. The nickel provides luster, brilliance and corrosion prevention, while the chrome contributes color and tarnish resistance. It is a very bright and durable finish.

BRUSHED AND MATTE CHROME

A brushed finish is created by using a wire wheel to score the surface of the component part. This can result in a surface with sharp peaks and valleys that does not take the chrome finish quite as well during the plating process because the coating shears away from the peaks and accumulates in the valleys.

A matte finish produces a similar appearance without producing noticeable brush marks or the sharp peaks that are difficult for plating. This process is similar to sand blasting the components with fine glass beads to create a soft matted surface that plates better, to produce a finish as durable as polished chrome.

PVD Finishes

PVD stands for "Physical Vapor Deposition," a process NASA developed for protecting metal. The process is used to apply metallic finishes over chromed brass. The "satin nickel" or "polished brass" finish the faucet wears is deposited on and then bonded to the chrome undercoating.

Differences in the alloys in the vapor deposited on the faucet yield different color finishes. PVD prevents corrosion, tarnish and scratches more effectively than the acrylic-coating process it has replaced.

Typical finishes available are:

- Brushed Bronze, Dark
- Brushed Bronze, Medium
- Brushed Nickel
- Polished Nickel
- Polished Gold
- Polished Brass

Polished And Satin Gold Plate

The highly polished brass product is first nickel plated and then 24 karat gold is applied. Durability depends on the thickness of the gold layer. According to industry standards, plating to a thickness of less than 7 millionths of an inch gold is "gold wash" or "gold flash." Between 8 and 12 millionths is "gold plating," and from 13 to 50 millionths is "heavy gold plating."

All quality gold plated fittings should fall into the latter category. Low quality gold wash or gold flash is not durable and can wear after only 3 to 6 months of normal handling. It is very difficult for the layman to distinguish between high and low quality gold plate. It is important to always purchase fittings from reputable dealers, and never hesitate to ask for data on gold plated parts.

Gold plate is available in either a polished or satin finish. Given a quality plating job, both finishes provide good durability.

Quality gold will not tarnish. Maintenance of a satin gold finish is somewhat easier than polished gold because it hides marks better. The secret to long-lasting gold plate is to clean it only with a soft, damp cloth. NEVER expose gold plate to abrasives or acids as can be found in many commercial cleaners.

Colored Coatings

A tinted epoxy coating is used to create a colored finish. The powder is sprinkled on (or a liquid is sprayed on) to the components and then baked at about 375° F to 425° F (190° C to 218° C) to provide thorough, even coverage and protection.

The coating can be scratched by mild abrasives, which results in an unattractive finish. The key is to clean and dry the faucet frequently after use to avoid the need for heavy cleaning, and to never use an abrasive cleaner.

Living Finishes

Oil-rubbed bronze, weathered copper and real brass are popular in rusticated environments. These finishes change with age. They are not coated in any way, and are not expected to have the finish remain constant. They take continual care and cleaning.

Pewter

This is a dull silvery-gray alloy of tin with brass, copper or lead added during the manufacturing process. Faucets are available in polished and brushed pewter finishes.

FITTING TYPES

At the turn of the century, indoor plumbing systems brought water to the "taps"—one for hot water and one for cold water. The kitchen sink or bathroom lavatory was a bowl with a stopper at the bottom, to allow the user to fill the bowl with hot and cold water mixed from these two separate taps. It is not uncommon to see this type of system still in use around the world, notably in bathrooms.

In North America, hot and cold water is now channeled through a "mixing" faucet, or common outlet or spout. The hot and cold water is regulated by adjusting two separate handles, by turning/pulling/pushing a single handle. In bathroom design, specialty faucets can be turned on by walking up to a faucet that has a proximity sensor, or by touching an electronic pad.

TYPES OF
KITCHEN FAUCETS

Bridge. A horizontal connector (bridge) joins hot and cold water sources, and the bridge is a prominent design feature above the countertop or the deck. These faucets—by definition—are two handle.

Single Hole Faucet. A single handle control that may include a side spray. It requires only one installation hole, the spout may or may not swivel.

Gooseneck. Also called a "high arc" faucet, these deck-mounted faucets feature a tall, arching spout that provides generous clearance underneath. The spout usually swivels.

Pot Filler. These are typically wall mounted, jointed faucets behind the range so that pots can be filled on the range top. There are also deck mounted faucets. Utilizing a pot filler without a sink does not provide any receptor for water other than the pot on the stove.

Pro Style. Over-scaled pull-down faucets that bring a restaurant look into a residence. Typically, they have a long hose or an elongated gooseneck with a spray head that offers choices of spray heights. They are not ideal for islands because they are visually intrusive. The oversized faucet may need to have a support bar holding it in-place to the countertop or wall to provide rigidity.

Pull-Out and Pull-Down. A hose or spray head emerges from the faucet spout and the combination pulls down or out, increasing the faucet's reach. A button, lever or toggle changes the water stream to a spray.

Two-Handle. Before single-lever control faucets arrived 50 years ago, two-handle faucets were the only options. Now they are chosen for their traditional look. Handle choices can strengthen the design message. They are typically deck mounted, but may also be wall mounted.

Wall Mounted. Wall mounted faucets can have a decidedly traditional Old World look or be extremely contemporary. In bath design, there are new electronic sensors that activate the water when the user puts their hand underneath it. New technology is suggesting ways in these faucets that an LCD light source will change from blue (cold water) to red (hot water) when the faucet is in use.

Figure 5.1 *Fitting Types: An Example of a Single Handle Kitchen Faucet* (Courtesy of GROHE America Inc.)

Figure 5.2 *Fitting Types: A Kitchen Bridge Faucet* (Courtesy of ShowHouse by Moen)

Figure 5.3 *Fitting Types: A Kitchen "Pot Filler" Water Source*
Pot fillers (above) can be mounted on the counter or on the backsplash (right) in the cooking area. (Courtesy of Kohler Company and KWC America)

Figure 5.4 *Fitting Types: Single Handle Faucet Installation with Pull-Out Spray Head*
A curved double custom stainless steel sink center features single handle faucets with a pull-out spray head. (Courtesy of Lisa Cortese, CKD – Santa Cruz, California and Co-designer Dan Giffin – Mountain View, California)

ATTACHMENTS AND ACCESSORIES

Figure 5.5 *Fitting Types: A Kitchen Single-Handle Faucet with Side Control* (Courtesy of Elkay)

In addition to the sink having a variety of accessories available, there are special attachments and/or enhancements available for the faucet.

SPOUT SHAPES

The shape of the spout also affects the functionality of the sink. A "goose neck" spout has a high arc and is ideally suited for a family that engages in quantity cooking or a lot of canning. One manufacturer offers a faucet spout that raises up and down so the spout stays in a normal position most of the time, and then rises up to a higher position when needed.

Standard spouts are generally available in 10", 12" and 14" lengths. Longer spouts are needed for corner sinks, or if you are installing integral sinks in a countertop in a custom arrangement and separating them a bit further than is the norm.

SPRAY ATTACHMENTS

Special purpose lavatory faucets are also available. For example, hand-held sprays are available as part of a pull-out spray faucet, or as a separate hand-held faucet.

Integral sprays offer a conventional spray device at the end of a flexible hose. A separate spray is connected to the water line underneath the sink. You must provide an acceptable back-flow preventing device when using such a spray. Some municipalities require that a vacuum breaker be installed if you specify a pull-out, integrated spray faucet. Alternatively, a faucet with check valves should also satisfy the inspector. Either of these protections is required because of the functional differences between the two types of sprays.

DRINKING FOUNTAIN

Several manufacturers offer a spout that can be turned so it is comfortable to use as a drinking fountain. This might be an ideal faucet design for a family where the bathroom users wake up during the night for a drink of water. It is also a useful feature to use when brushing one's teeth.

Also on the market today are cold water taps which are ideal for drinking water taps at secondary locations. These systems can be connected to a filtration system if your client has requested one.

HOT WATER DISPENSER

This accessory has a faucet that is connected to a small storage tank mounted blow the sink. The tank is connected to the cold water supply line and a 120 volt household current. The dispenser tank stores enough hot water for instant coffee, soups or tea; therefore, eliminating the need to heat water in the microwave or boil water at the range top.

LOTION/SOAP DISPENSER

Installed on the sink ledge or in a countertop, these units have a plastic bottle below the sink and a "pump handle" above the deck. Hand lotion or liquid soap then can be conveniently available at the sink without unsightly bottles of jars sitting on top of the countertop.

AERATOR

Most faucets include an aerator at the end of the spout that mixes air with water so splash-back is minimized. When a project is finished it is not uncommon for the client to complain that the water volume is not as high as it should be. Advise the client to unscrew the aerator and remove the sediment from the screen on a regular basis.

AIR GAP

Many codes require a dishwasher to have an air gap installed at the sink to prevent any back-up of water in the dishwasher. The air gap is a metal or plastic cap that sits on the sink and is connected to a hose that leads to the dishwasher. A second hose leads to the knock-out on the side of the food waste disposer.

The dishwasher drains through the tubing below the air gap. There are small openings on the air gap, so an overflow will drain into the sink. Warn the client not to be surprised if there is a "gurgling" sound as the dishwasher drains in their new kitchen with an air gap.

The food waste disposer should be cleared after every use because the dishwasher will drain through the disposer.

POP-UP ASSEMBLY

A "pop-up" assembly allows the user to close the drain when filling the bowl with water. Almost all assemblies are part of the faucet. However, faucets are also available without this feature, so make sure you specify the right model number.

This lavatory drain fitting consists of a brass or plastic waste outlet into which a sliding metal or plastic stopper is fitted. A lever that passes out the side of the drain fitting is connected to a lift rod on top of the lavatory faucet. This rod is lifted to lower the stopper and allow the lavatory to be filled. It is depressed to raise the stopper and drain the lavatory. The stopper should be periodically removed and cleaned to make sure it does not become coated with soap film and/or other debris.

SHUTOFF (ANGLE STOP) VALVE

Hot and cold water is supplied through supply lines that are either inside the cabinetry below the lavatory or sink or exposed behind a pedestal or wall-hung lavatory. Individual shut-off valves should be installed at each supply line. The drain line from the lavatory or sink connects to a waste line with a trap providing a water seal, as is common in all plumbing fixtures.

WATER TREATMENT SYSTEM

In some areas of the country it may be important for you to be familiar with water purification systems. The water quality of a home can be improved as it enters the house, or it can be improved at a point of use within the house (one of the faucets).

The issue of water quality and what equipment is recommended at the sink is covered in the book *Kitchen & Bath Systems*, from the National Kitchen & Bath Association.

There are three broad categories of systems you should be familiar with. One includes installing a filter on the cold water line that leads to a faucet. The second focuses on mounting a filter on the faucet itself. The third method mounts a filter on the line that diverts cold water to a separate faucet.

The first two methods do not affect the overall equipment at the sink, but the last option does require a third and separate faucet. Make sure you know what type of equipment may need to be installed inside the sink cabinet—it may affect a tilt-down drawer head front, a pull-out towel bar, or a lower roll-out shelf you are planning. Also, find out what electrical requirements and/or plumbing connections you need to specify.

Helpful Hints From The Pros

- **Positioning the Sink Holes.** Locate faucet holes along the ledge of an under-mounted sink carefully: they need to clear the sink rim edge. For top-mounted sinks, lay out the hole drilling carefully, with the faucet on-site. Check hole spacing if using a two-handle faucet to insure clearance.

- **Overall Depth of Countertops.** Make sure you have enough room behind the sink for some of the oversized "pro," more elaborate faucets. Faucets with controls behind the spout are particularly problematic, and might be better placed diagonally to the side of the sink.

- **Extra Thick Countertops.** Special planning may be needed for oversized, thick countertops: the shank length of the faucet needs to accommodate the counter thickness.

- **Oversized Sinks.** If the faucet does not have a pull-down spray or a side spray, verify that the spout swivel has a wide enough arc to reach all the sink bowls. Two-handle faucets—including bridge-style faucets—may not work with some double bowl sinks.

Faucet Engineering

The faucet engineering will affect its performance over its years of use. In addition to the design of the faucet, the professional kitchen and bathroom design specialist must understand how faucets operate. All faucets feature either a washer or a washerless design. Each manufacturer has detailed training material available to introduce you to your range of choices.

Figure 5.6 *Fitting Types: An Example of a Wall-Mounted Bathroom Faucet* (Courtesy of Villeroy & Boch)

TYPES OF
BATHROOM FAUCETS

Single Handle Faucet

Single-handle controls are located above the spout or to the side of the spout. Single-handle bathroom faucets are available with different length spouts. Therefore, be sure you specify the proper length for the planned use. Longer spouts are required when used in conjunction with vessel sinks.

The control is turned left or right, pulled up or down, or pushed front to back. These controls are sometimes confusing to individuals not familiar with their operation.

When evaluating the function of single handle faucets—at the lavatory or any other fixture—there are two key factors: the faucet's comfort zone swing and the volume control swing or lift. The typical faucet must be adjusted for both of these factors with use. Some faucets may be turned off leaving the control in a memory position. This allows the user to leave the faucet preset at a comfortable temperature setting for the next use.

Four-inch Center Faucet Set

Small faucets are available where the spout and two separate handles require three holes and are laced along a single escutcheon plate. The drilling is generally 4" on center for this type of faucet. Although this is generally an economical faucet, because the handles are very close to the spout, it may be difficult to clean. Unless it has lever handles, some people may also find it difficult to use.

Widespread Faucet Set

Some decorative faucets eliminate the escutcheon plate and separately mount the spout and two handles. The spacing is flexible and may be anywhere from 8" to 12".

These faucets are usually more attractive and are easier to use and to clean. Lavatories with a standard platform mounting offer an 8" spread. Lavatories which are designed to be used with counter-mounted faucets can feature a spread from 6" to 12".

Figure 5.7 *Fitting Types: Special Faucets*
Special faucets have been designed for "vessel" or above-countertop bathroom lavatories. The faucet may be installed behind or to the side of the fixture, or may come through the wall. (Above: Courtesy of Peter Ross Salerno, CMKBD – Wyckoff, New Jersey. Right: Courtesy of Charles R. Schwartzapfel – New York, New York)

Comfort Zone

Human beings are comfortable using water that ranges from 95° F – 105° F (35° C – 40.5° C). The distance of the fitting swing within this comfort zone determines how much adjustability is offered to the user. The total distance of travel from cold to hot should be as great as possible. A handle with a 120 degree arc from the hottest setting to the coldest, and with a 40 degree arc within the comfort zone from 95° F – 105° F (35° C – 40.5° C) is a functional, safe fitting design.

Volume Control

Most single-handle faucets have a 15 degree lift from the off to the fully on position. Some faucets offer a 20 degree lift. This lift range starts with the valve in a closed position and at the top of the scale the valve is completely open. The ideal faucet design allows the water flow rate to be increased gradually as the faucet valve is opened with a lift/twist/turn action. The water flow should begin at 1 degree off the lift and continue in a gradual increase that is in proportion with the degree of movement. This type of "fine tuning" offers the user a faucet that is safe and easy to use. Unfortunately, some single-handle faucet designs do not allow the water flow to begin until the faucet reaches approximately 7 degrees of the movement. With this type of fitting, the range of control for the user is dramatically increased.

Electronically Controlled In The Bathroom

One of the newest innovations in plumbing fittings is the electronic water control. There are two versions: proximity and touch pad.

Commercial use of proximity products is widely accepted. For example, public restroom lavatory faucets that deliver water at a set temperature and volume are activated when the user's hands are placed underneath the spout or as the individual approaches the lavatory. This type of operation is not as successful residentially because clients want to be able to control the on/off capability, the water temperature and the volume of the water flow. Consequently, touch pad controls are more popular residentially.

Touch pad controls contain several functions: hot and cold water variations; incremental volume increases; a digital read out; and, memorizing the ideal setting of temperature and flow rate for up to five persons. These controls may be installed flush with the countertop or as part of a faucet.

CHAPTER 6: Bathroom Fitting Design and Engineering

BATHTUB FITTINGS

Bathtub fittings include the valve, the spout and (as a separate component) a waste/over-flow. A separate hand-held personal shower may also be included for the bathtub.

Mounting The Fitting On The Bathtub Rim or On The Platform

In addition to making sure the supply line, valve and spout are correctly sized to fill the bathtub in a reasonable amount of time, be sure the spout and valves can be properly connected on the fixture rim or on the bathtub deck.

Most deck-mounted fittings will require connection from underneath the finished deck. This means you must also plan access for future servicing. Some manufacturers now provide "quick connect" systems which allow you to attach the deck-mounted spout more easily than in the past.

Make sure the overall deck ledge depth is less than the overall dimension of the spout outlet. Alternatively, the spout might actually be part of the bathtub.

The Waste and Overflow

The last element in a bathtub is the waste and overflow. The waste is the drain in the bottom of the bathtub. Generally, the overflow fitting is along the end wall of the fixture. It limits the overall amount of water in the bathtub. Because the distance from the bottom of the bathtub to the waste overflow varies between fixture models, make sure you order the correct waste and overflow to fit the bathtub you have specified.

POP-UP AND TRIP LEVER DRAIN

The standard North American pop-up or trip-lever type waste and overflow are economical and fit most bathtubs. The trip lever version has a stopper below the perforated drain. The pop-up version has a lift-up mechanism in the open drain. Either is activated when a lever is "tripped" or a rotary knob is turned.

CABLE DRAIN

An alternative is a cable drain that places no mechanical components in the tubular passageway of the system. Rather, a cable runs outside the system, connects the handle of the overflow to a plug-lift mechanism just below the outlet's flange. It is important to provide access to the plumbing wall behind the bathtub when specifying a cable drain because the mechanism is not accessible from inside the bathtub.

A Hand-Held Shower at The Bathtub

A hand-held shower is one of the most useful fittings you can suggest for a client. It makes washing hair in the tub, or rinsing off, much more pleasant. It is extremely useful when bathing children or pets. And it makes cleaning the bathtub much easier.

There are several systems for you to choose from. The typical installation requires the use of a bathtub filler and a diverter valve to channel the water from the bathtub spout outlet to the hand-held spray. The diverter category offers two mechanical options: a rotary action valve or a spring-loaded push or lift type valve.

Some codes consider the spring-loaded diverter as an acceptable back-flow prevention, therefore no vacuum breaker is required. This is because the spring-loaded push or life type diverter opens the secondary channel, the spout, to the atmosphere in the event of negative pressure.

The second option, a rotary action valve, does not provide back-flow prevention protection. This type of installation, as well as the deck-mounted, single-lever feed, requires a vacuum breaker be placed well above the bathtub along the wall. To avoid this being unsightly, install the vacuum breaker inside a closet or on the other side of the wall.

Figure 6.1 *Bathroom Fitting Design: A Contemporary Hand-held Shower* (Courtesy of KWC America)

Figure 6.2 *Bathroom Fitting Design: A Traditional Hand-held Shower at the Bathtub*
(Courtesy of Barclay Products)

BATHTUB/SHOWER COMBINATION FITTINGS

The bathtub may also serve as a combination shower. In this installation, the fittings include the bathtub filler/spout, a diverter valve that allows the water to be directed down to the bathtub spout or up to the showerhead and the showerhead itself. These three are typically installed on one common wall in a straight line. However, installations can be more elaborate with the addition of a hand shower.

Figure 6.3 *Bathroom Fitting Design: Example of a Combination Bathtub/Shower* (Courtesy of Kohler Company)

Figure 6.4 *Bathroom Fitting Design:*
A Shower Opposite the Bathtub
(Courtesy of Kohler Company)

Figure 6.5 *Bathroom Fitting Design:*
A Shower Adjacent to the Bathtub
(Courtesy of Kohler Company)

Access to The Pipes

In all installations, the supply lines are serviced by shutoff valves. In many installations, an access panel is included so these shutoff valves are accessible in a closet behind the bathtub, or through an access panel in the wall that is camouflaged behind a piece of furniture. Alternatively, some have shut-off valves that are accessible from underneath the escutcheon plate. This feature eliminates the need for an access panel.

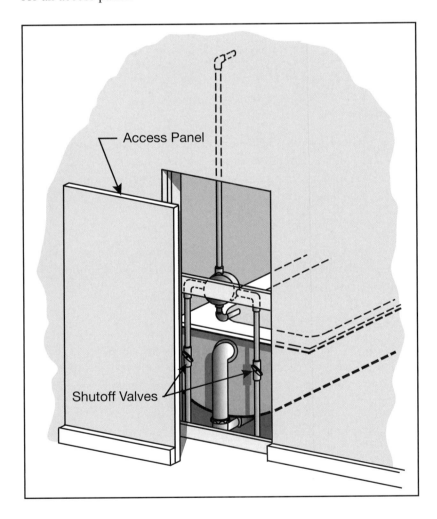

Figure 6.6 *Bathroom Fitting Design: Bathtub/Shower Piping*
Provide access to the bathtub/shower piping in a wall at the end of the fixture.

Figure 6.7 *Bathroom Fitting Design: Removable Bathtub Aprons*
Some bathtub fixtures have a removable front or end apron.

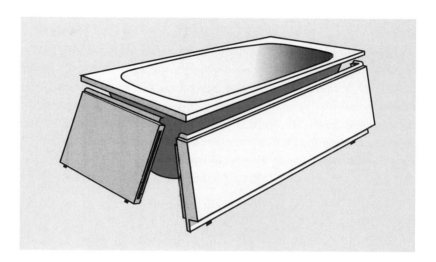

The Diverter

The diverter for a bathtub/shower combination can be a knob you pull on top of the bathtub spout, it can be a handle diverter placed between the hot and cold valve on the wall that you either push or turn, or it can be a button diverter on a single-handle shower control.

SHOWER FITTINGS

Following is a more detailed discussion of shower fittings that are appropriate either for a separate, stand-alone configuration or a bathtub/shower combination.

Safety In The Shower

Before we discuss shower valve or head placement, let's return to the issue of safety in the bathroom. The bathrooms you design must be functionally and ergonomically correct, and they must be safe.

The bathroom is one of the most dangerous rooms in the house. One source puts the number of scalding injuries alone in North America at more than 150,000 each year. Remember, children have thinner skin than adults and are therefore more easily burned in less time and by lower temperature water. Additionally, showers and bathtubs ranked third among products associated with death among people 50 years of age or older due to slipping or falling.

Scald Protection Devices

Scalding accidents can be eliminated. Scald protection valves are available. Currently there are four broad categories of fittings that offer such protection.

TYPES OF SCALD PROTECTION DEVICES

Pressure Balancing Valve. A pressure balancing valve adjusts the mix of the hot and cold water in response to changes in relative supply inlet pressures. The valve compensates for the reduction of pressure in one supply line by increasing the flow coming from the supply and/or reducing the flow coming from the other supply. This type of valve does not compensate for changes in the temperature of hot and cold supplies. Therefore, the valve would not react to water temperature changes that occur because of a diminishing hot water supply.

Thermostatic Valve. This system adjusts the mix of hot and cold water in response to changes in temperature. It automatically adjusts the flow of hot and cold water to maintain a relatively constant temperature. It can be slow to respond or it can briefly overcompensate for changes in supply pressures. This means you may have one to two seconds of a noticeable temperature change as the water supply cuts off or as the valve adjusts. This valve will supply a constant temperature shower because it will adjust the cold water supply as a reaction to a diminishing hot water supply.

Combination Valve. A combination of pressure balancing and thermostatic control. This system compensates for both temperature and pressure fluctuations of supply inlets.

Temperature Limiting Valve. A high temperature limit stop that is adjustable by the installer or a family member. The high-temperature limit stop prevents scalding by limiting the temperature of the water that can pass through the valve. The device is located under the lever and escutcheon of single-handle faucets and requires a simple screwdriver for access. A limit can be set for the hot water temperature delivered at the faucet, which is changeable as the family's life-stage and safety standards change.

All of these systems are designed to be used with a showerhead minimum flow rating of 2.5 gpm (9.5 liters). They are designed to perform under supply pressures up to 125 pounds (57 kilograms) per square inch.

Any well-designed bathroom today should include pressure balanced or thermostatically controlled valves at the shower and/or bathtub/shower combination. Check local codes as it may be required in your area.

The Basic Components Of A Shower

THE PAN WITH DRAIN

The shower will have a prefabricated floor, or pan, made from a formed plastic or solid surface material. Alternatively, the pan may be constructed out of ceramic tile. The pan has a threshold at the entrance and the floor, then slants to the drain.

Figure 6.8 *Bathroom Fitting Design: A Shower Pan and Drain Detail*

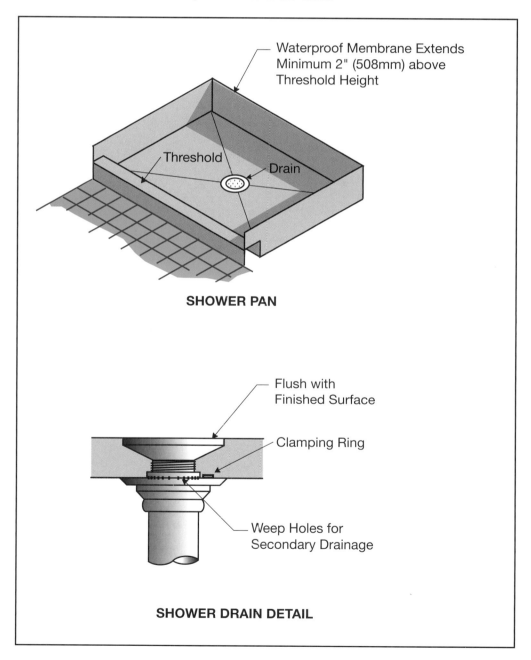

Waterproof Membrane Extends Minimum 2" (508mm) above Threshold Height

Threshold

Drain

SHOWER PAN

Flush with Finished Surface

Clamping Ring

Weep Holes for Secondary Drainage

SHOWER DRAIN DETAIL

THE VALVE

Manual Mixing Valves. Basic mixing valve options for the shower are similar to those previously discussed for the lavatory: two-handle faucets and single-control faucets are available.

Electronic Mixing Valves. The valve acts as an electronic thermostatic valve because it maintains the temperature that has been programmed in by the user. When turned on, the unit always resets and delivers at an initial 98° F (36.6° C). Depressing either the "up" or "down" button shifts the readout display to the "set point mode," causing the numbers to change in the direction of warmer or cooler until released. Once that button is released, the readout reverts to the actual temperature mode so the water temperature begins to move towards the selected setting and stops when it gets there. There is a hot limit device built into the valve, as well as an integral pressure balancing mode.

THE SHOWER HEAD

Flow Rating

The flow rate of a showerhead is measured in gallons per minute (gpm). Currently, some states are in the process of limiting showerheads to 2.50 to 3 gpm (8 to 11 liters). Some manufacturers also offer flow restriction mechanisms that reduce the flow even lower to 1.7 gpm (6.4 liters). Most showerheads on the market fall within the first limit, and have a 2.50 (8 liters) gpm flow rating.

A special note about the lowest flow or 1.7 gpm showerheads. Although they do conserve water, the highly aerated water may not deliver an ideal shower. Because of the increased surface space of the aerated water drops, the water temperature will cool dramatically from the time it leaves the showerhead until it reaches the bather's body. Because humans are sensitive to a temperature drop of 2° F, this type of showerhead may be undesirable.

Types of Showerheads

Ergonomic and usage considerations for showerhead design and placement are discussed in *Bath Planning*. In this chapter, we will identify the different types of showerheads available.

There are numerous showerheads available today. Generally, there are five broad categories of showering options: personal hand-held shower, wall-mounted shower, overhead shower, body spray shower, and body mist shower.

- **Personal Hand-held Shower**. The personal hand-held shower is ideal in showers that will be used by people of varying heights, as well as near a bench in the shower that is out of the stream of water.

  Hand-held showers are also a great addition to a shower that will be used by an elderly person who may need assistance while bathing. Shower cleaning is also much easier with a hand-held shower.

- **Wall-mounted Shower**. The wall-mounted showerhead is the most typical installation.

- **Overhead Shower**. The overhead shower is placed on the ceiling. It may require a great deal of water to operate—check the manufacturer's specifications.

- **Body Spray Shower**. A body spray is a group of individual showerheads, installed in a series of two or three, along opposite walls.

- **Body Mist Shower**. A body mist shower is a series of jets of water in a single bar designed to gently wash the body. When mounted at the right height, both body sprays and body mists are designed to allow a person to take a shower without getting his/her face and/or hair wet.

Water Patterns

When considering any showerhead, some key functions to discuss with your client are:

- **Adjustment**. The basic spray adjusts from fine to coarse: people prefer placing the control on the side of the showerhead as opposed to in the center which forces the user to reach into the stream of water.

- **Spray Pattern**. A full spray pattern is more desirable than one that only delivers water around the perimeter of the head, leaving a hollow in the center.

- **Water Action**. Showerheads can offer a soft, gentle action or a pulsating, invigorating massage.

Designing A Multiple Head Shower Enclosure

When specifying multiple-showerheads in an enclosure, ask a key question: "Is this enclosure designed for one person to use with multiple heads that offer them a variety of shower experiences; or, is it a shower enclosure with multiple heads that will be used by more than one person at the same time?"

DETERMINE HOW THE SHOWER WILL BE USED

If the shower is designed for one person, a diverter system can be designed to offer the user a choice of the various heads. For example, an overhead shampoo showerhead could be used in place of body sprays, rather than concurrently. This type of arrangement is designed with one mixing valve and a diverting device to direct the water to the various heads.

Or, several users may enjoy the shower together. When two or more showerheads operate at the same time, you must pay particular attention to the water pressure, the size of the piping and the flow rate of the showerheads, as well as the mixer and diverter device. Designers should select a multiple head system that has been engineered by the manufacturer and is available with detailed schematic designs and installation requirements.

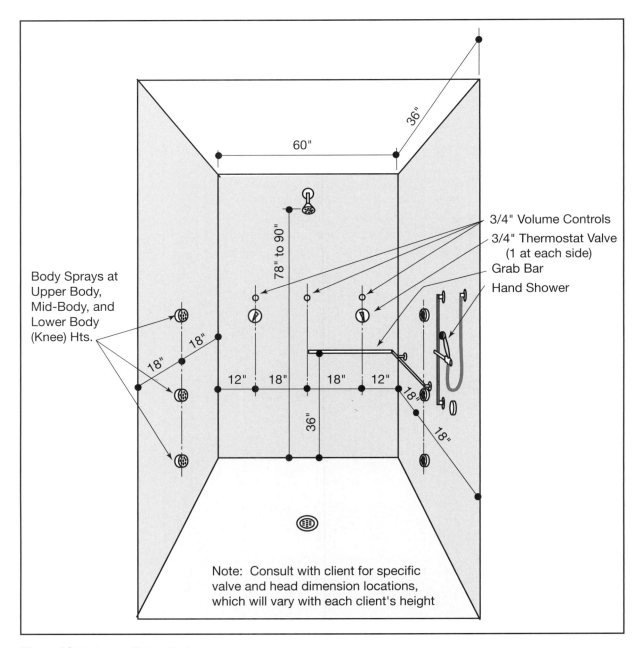

Figure 6.9 *Bathroom Fitting Design: Plumbing Schematic for Multiple-head Shower Enclosure (Imperial)*

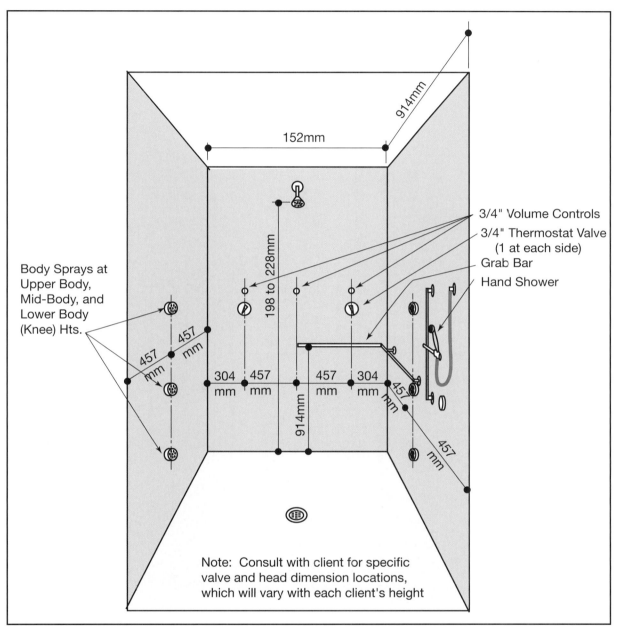

914mm

152mm

198 to 228mm

Body Sprays at
Upper Body,
Mid-Body, and
Lower Body
(Knee) Hts.

3/4" Volume Controls

3/4" Thermostat Valve
(1 at each side)

Grab Bar

Hand Shower

457
mm

457
mm

304
mm

457
mm

457
mm

304
mm

457
mm

914mm

457
mm

Note: Consult with client for specific
valve and head dimension locations,
which will vary with each client's height

Figure 6.10 *Bathroom Fitting Design:
Plumbing Schematic for Multiple-
head Shower Enclosure (Metric)*

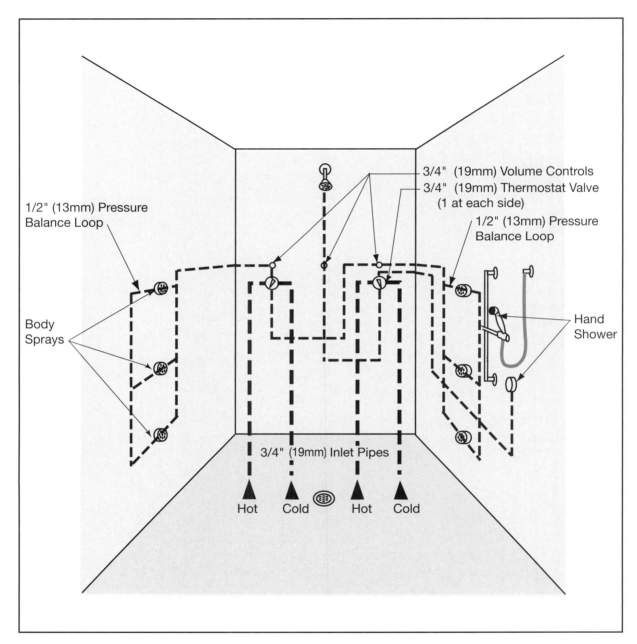

Figure 6.11 *Bathroom Fitting Design: Plumbing Schematic for Multiple-head Shower Enclosure*

SPA BATHS, STEAM SHOWERS AND SAUNAS

We have already discussed the addition of whirlpool jets to a standard bathtub. A steam shower is a marvelous amenity in a standard shower. A sauna is a special addition to a bathroom as well.

Let's consider planning criteria for spa baths, steam showers and saunas.

Spa Bath

There is a growing interest today in larger bath retreats that invite the homeowner to enjoy a spa experience at home—rather than at a secluded club or faraway destination.

Throughout this book we have discussed the various elements of bathroom planning appropriate for a spa bath: the bathing experience—from an invigorating massage to a relaxing soak.

Following we will discuss steam showers and saunas. Earlier we commented on chromatherapy: the use of color to assist the mind and body in finding focus and relaxing.

The spa bath may also include exercise equipment. Designers are wise to measure the consumer's equipment, or partner with a respected sports authority in their community when asked to plan such a special retreat.

A spa bath might also include a small juice counter, water station—or, indeed—a mini-kitchen. A sound system and television equipped to play videos/CDs/DVDs or access the Internet for favorite exercise programs will probably be of interest to the consumer.

Steam Showers

EXPLANATION OF USE

Steam showers are yet another way to provide a relaxing, refreshing experience. A steam bath invigorates the body systems and cleanses the skin by opening the pores and flushing the dirt out. The normal steam bath lasts from 10 to 20 minutes in an enclosed environment with high humidity and temperature levels. It is then followed by a lukewarm shower to relax, or a cold shower to stimulate the body.

In the past, steam rooms were only available at the finest private clubs and spas. Today, including a steam bath as part of a stall shower is an affordable addition to even a modest bathroom space.

The steam bath is energy efficient and does not require any more floor space than the stall shower you are already planning.

ENCLOSURE DESIGN

The following constraints and/or planning concerns must be taken into account when considering a steam bath.

Wet Wall Material

Avoid specifying any material that may be subject to decay because of prolonged exposure to steam or moisture. Verify with the specific manufacturers if their wall surfacing material is acceptable in a high heat, high humidity environment. For example, DuPont currently does not recommend Corian as a wall surface material in any steam room. Also, use a waterproof substrate material behind the decorative surfacing material you do select.

In all applications, use waterproof adhesives or silicone sealants, as well as waterproof or epoxy paint.

Glass

Specify a completely enclosed, vapor-proof door. Fixed or operable transom panels are available as an accessory to standard shower doors to enclose the space to create a steam environment.

Seat Design

Place any permanent or portable benches well away from the steam nozzle. A person sitting in the steam room can be burned by an unexpected burst of steam.

Ceiling Slant

Slanting the steam room ceiling away from the seating area is recommended. A slanted ceiling insures that as steam condenses on the ceiling it runs down the slant, away from the seated user. The ceiling should be 7' high.

Sizing the Generator

Choosing the appropriate generator for the steam room is the most important factor for a functional steam room in the home. A properly sized steam generator should produce a comfortable temperature in 5 to 10 minutes.

The cubic footage of the enclosure determines the size of generator needed. The construction and decorative surfacing materials also affect the size of generator you specify. The surround temperature must also be taken into account.

- Timer. A timer will be included to limit steam generation.

- Wall Material. The porosity level of the material selected affects the cubic footage formula used to determine the generator size. Common surfacing materials and their effect in the cubic footage calculations are as follows.

   All Glass or Glass Block: Add 20% to 40% to the actual cubic footage of the enclosure.

   Ceramic Tile on Water-resistant Sheetrock: Add 15% to the actual cubic footage.

   Ceramic Tile on Cement Board: Add 20% to the actual cubic footage.

   Ceramic Tile on Mortar Bed (Mud) Substrate: Add 25% to the actual cubic footage.

   Ceramic Tile on Cinderblock or Concrete: Add 75% to the actual cubic footage.

   Fiberglass, Acrylic or Cultured Marble: Decrease the actual cubic footage by 20%.

   Natural Stone, Marble, Travertine or Slate: Add 100% to the actual cubic footage.

- Determine Cubic Footage. When calculating the cubic footage of the enclosure, do not deduct for the bench area, since it requires nearly the same surface area. Remember, it is the surface area to which heat is lost in a steam enclosure.

- Surrounding Temperature. Ambient room temperature should be between 68° F and 72° F (20° C and 22° C).

   If the steam room is installed against exterior walls, particularly in a cold climate, the walls should be insulated or the generator will need to be increased in size. Typically, it is recommended you add 10% to the generator size for each exterior wall, whether insulated or not.

- Pipe Run Length. Although the generator can be located in many different places, the closer it is to the steam enclosure, the better. Some manufacturers will tell you it can be as far as 20 feet (6.10 m) away from the enclosure, others say as much as 50 feet (15.24 m). However, the farther the generator is from the enclosure, the longer it takes for steam to get there. Add an additional 15 cubic feet (4.57 m) to the overall shower enclosure size for pipe runs between 15 and 25 feet (4.57 m and 7.62 m).

After you determine the cubic footage of the steam room based on these additional criteria, refer to a specification chart provided by the manufacturer to determine the proper steam generator model.

If the calculated cubic footage capacity falls between two models, always choose the larger unit.

Saunas

EXPLANATION OF USE

Although sauna procedures are as varied as the individual users, most enthusiasts recommend briefly showering, then entering the sauna for 5 to 15 minutes. The individual may sit or lie in the insulated wooden room. The lower bench is always cooler than the higher one. Next, a cool shower, a swim in the pool or a roll in the snow invigorates the body's system. A short 10 to 15 minute rest follows. Finally, a second visit to the sauna for about 20 minutes is enjoyed. During the second visit, a brief whisking of the skin increases circulation.

Ladling water over the hot stones can also add a refreshing burst of humidity during the final moments. A second 20 minute rest is suggested, followed by a final shower and a light snack.

ENCLOSURE DESIGN

Sizing Recommendations

Popular family saunas range in size from 4' x 3' to 6' x 6' shapes. Regardless of the overall shape, a 7' ceiling is recommended to prevent heat from rising into unused space. A 1'-8" to 2'-0" wide door that is 6'-8" high and swings out without any type of locking device is used to minimize heat loss and to maximize safety.

Because showering and resting are an integral part of the sauna experience, this specialty fixture should be located near the bathroom or swimming pool, with a dressing and resting area nearby.

Wall, Floor and Ceiling Materials

The overall sauna enclosure is generally built out of wood. Although the traditional sauna uses aspen wood, kiln-dried, clear, all-heart, A-grade redwood is an adequate substitute for the modern day sauna because of its ability to withstand extreme temperature changes. Redwood acts as an insulator on walls, ceiling and floor. And it diffuses the heat so the surfaces remain warm, but not hot, to the touch.

Ventilation/Lighting

The sauna should feature soft, subdued lighting and good ventilation to prevent people from becoming dizzy. Prefabricated units offer an ideal design solution for sauna planning.

The manufacturer provides you with an easy-to-assemble, well-thought-out system that generally includes the following parts:

- **Intake Vent**. Located near the floor in the wall behind the stove, or installed in the sauna door.

- **Outlet**. For cross ventilation, located at the opposite wall approximately level with, but not below, the intake vent or a few inches from the ceiling.

- **Lighting**. A lighting system that is soft and controlled from the outside of the enclosure.

FUEL SOURCES

A stove used in the sauna may be electric or gas. The proper kilowatt (KW) rating for electric heaters, or British Thermal Unit (Btu) for gas heaters, is based on the size of the sauna, as well as the wall insulation and the location of the sauna in relationship to air-conditioned or non-air-conditioned adjacent spaces.

For example, for a 5' x 7' sauna installed indoors with good insulation, 1 KW of electricity per 40 cubic feet or room space is adequate. 1,000 Btus for a gas heater planned for every 15 cubic feet of floor space will also do the job. (Of course, the traditionalist client may select a wood burning stove with a chimney.)

The sauna must also include a control, located just outside the sauna room.

A Word Of Caution

As you can imagine, indoor whirlpool baths, steam rooms or saunas do offer rest, relaxation and invigoration for your client. However, a word of caution is in order. While these certainly are socializing spaces, care must be taken in their use.

In all three systems, the extreme temperature present stimulates the cardiovascular system. Individuals with high blood pressure, respiratory or heart disease, a circulatory problem or chronic illnesses, such as diabetes or epilepsy, should check with a physician before installing any of these unique relaxation experiences. Pregnant women and individuals under the influence of alcohol or other drugs should also avoid whirlpools, saunas and steam rooms.

Whatever your client's choice—a comfortable, quiet bath, a revitalizing stall shower, a luxurious indoor whirlpool bath, a relaxing steam bath or sauna—it is up to you to carefully question them, and apply thorough product knowledge and in-depth technical knowledge to create a special fixture arrangement for the new bathroom.

CHAPTER 7: Surfacing Materials

In addition to the cabinets and appliances in the kitchen or the fixtures and fittings in the bathroom, another key ingredient of a successful project is the surfacing materials you select for the floors, walls, wet wall surrounds, countertop areas and backsplash verticals.

Before selecting any of these surfaces, you must first understand the importance of a proper substrate material. The book *Residential Construction* covers the basic construction elements of a well-planned kitchen and bathroom. Once the proper substrate has been specified, the functional and decorative surfaces can be selected.

To facilitate this review, the most popular materials are discussed in alphabetical order.

BUTCHER BLOCK: COUNTER SURFACES

Countertops made from laminated wood products are commonly referred to as "butcher block." In addition to full countertops, insert blocks are often installed in the kitchen work surface.

The insert blocks are available in a variety of sizes and finishes. Both edge and end grain laminations are popular. In laminate countertops, an installation ring secures the wood section in-place. A lip in the block can provide stability for a drop-in-place installation.

Unique kitchens will often feature the entire countertop in butcher block. When this type of surface is planned, the designer must specify what type of wood will be used, what type of finish the block will have, and what water and heat protection the block will receive.

Several types of woods are available from different manufacturers:

- **Eastern Hard Rock Sugar Maple**. This wood is considered the hardest, thus cutting or scratching damage will be minimized.

- **Western Maple; Western Alder**. This wood is not as hard as Eastern Maple and will be more susceptible to wear through, cutting or scratching.

- **Walnut, Cherry or Other Specialty Hardwoods.** These woods are sometimes specified in focal point areas which will not receive excessive use.

  Grain patterns with the laminations will vary according to the fabrication procedure used.

- **Full length edge grain laminations** feature long, unbroken strips of the wood laminated together. The edge widths remain constant.

- **Butt-joined edge grain laminations** feature various strips within the overall length of the top. The edge widths remain constant.

- **End grain laminations** feature a checkerboard effect of small squares of wood. This type of fabrication is normally limited to counter inserts.

The wood tops may be finished in several ways. The intended use of the block should determine the finish selection.

Unfinished Wood

The finish will consist of oiling wood throughout the counter surface life span on a four to six week maintenance schedule. This method is most desirable if the entire counter surface will be wood and local fabrication of seams or miters is required. The prefinished tops hinder proper adhesion of seams and must be refinished if any sanding will be done.

Prefinished Wood

The factory finish will include a penetrating sealer and a non-toxic lacquer finish. The combination of sealer and varnish prevents moisture penetration. No oiling is necessary and a damp cloth may be used to wipe the board clean. Chopping on the surface may not damage the finish. This type of finish is appropriate for countertop sections, such as island tops or sandwich centers.

Wood Sealed With Polyurethane

This sealer is used on unfinished wood tops which will not be used as a chopping surface and will not come in contact with food. The finish is very good on tops which will be exposed to moisture and liquids.

Figure 7.1 *Surfacing Materials: Wood*
Butcher block surfaces can be either
rustic or Old World depending on how
they are used. (Courtesy of John Boos,
above, and Craft-Art Company, right)

Figure 7.2 *Surfacing Materials: Wood*
A butcher block prep area is set into an
island with honed granite countertop.
(Courtesy of Karen Williams–New
York, New York)

CAST POLYMERS: COUNTER SURFACES AND WET WALL SURFACES

Cast polymers are used for bathtub fixtures, one-piece shower enclosures and vanity surfaces, often with an integrated lavatory. In slab form, cast polymers can be used in bathtub and/or shower enclosures, as well as for slab vanity tops. They are available in marbleized patterns, granite-like textured patterns, or solid colors.

Cultured marble, cultured onyx, cultured granite and solid-colored polymer-based materials are all used for cast mineral filled polymer fixtures. Although generally referred to as "cultured marble," a better term for you to use when describing all of these materials is "cast polymer." The term is recommended so you can discuss this potential fixture and surfacing material without limiting yourself to describing a product that looks like synthetic marble.

Regardless of the use, cast polymer surfaces are created by pouring a mixture of ground minerals and polyester resin into a treated mold, where the curing process takes place at room temperature or in a curing oven.

Gel Coat Application

The process begins by spraying a gel coat onto a mold. Because most residential fixtures are sprayed by hand, the gel coat thickness ranges from 12 to 20 mil (1 mil = 1/1000th of an inch). Industry research has proven a 12 mil gel coat is the minimum acceptable gel coat thickness. A 20 mil gel coat is more durable. However, gel coats thicker than 20 mil do not add wearability. Quite the opposite—thicker gel coats that are applied unevenly lead to a common problem associated with cast polymer fixtures called "crazing." Crazing is the presence of tiny fractures within the gel coat resulting from the thermal shock caused by repeated exposure of the material to alternating hot and cold water. This problem typically shows up around the drain in a lavatory if the gel coat is not thick enough, if the fixture is improperly installed by the plumber, if water stands in the lavatory, or if the incorrect cleaner is used.

A Molding Process

The gel coat is first allowed to cure. A semi-liquid material which consists of polymer resins, a catalyst to promote curing, and highly filled inorganic particulates of pulverized calcium carbonate, hydrated alumina and, in some instances glass bubbles, are then poured into the mold.

If the cast polymer material will have a solid color, no further steps are taken. If the material will have a marbleized pattern throughout, the second color is swirled into the mixture. The mixture is then allowed to cure, after which it is removed from the mold, inspected, finished, boxed and shipped.

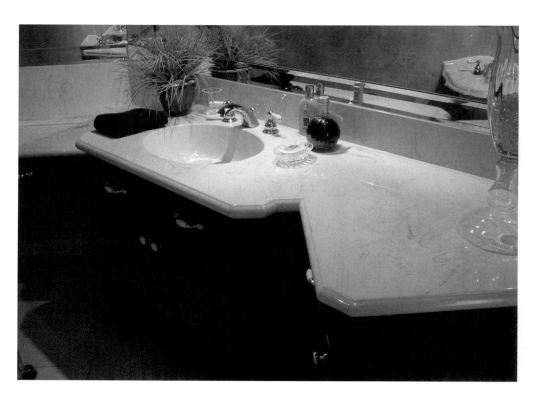

Figure 7.3 *Surfacing Materials: Cast Polymers*
Cast polymers are a frequently used material for bathroom vanity tops, showers and tubs. (Courtesy of Accent Marble – Houston, Texas; and the International Cast Polymer Alliance)

CERAMIC TILE:
ALL SURFACES

Ceramic tile is a favorite surface product for many kitchen and bathroom designers. A beautifully natural material, it also offers wide design flexibility. However, without a solid understanding of the product, installation methods and care recommendations, a profitable job and a pleased client may elude you.

Tile is composed of clays, shales, porcelain or baked earth. These raw products are pressed or extruded into shapes and then fired in a kiln, baked in an oven or cured in the sun. The differences among raw materials, manufacturing methods and surface finishes make some types of tile more durable in heavy use areas than others. The firing method will also affect the moisture absorption rate of different body types of tile, which is an important consideration in exterior tile installations.

Tile specified by designers for any surface other than decorative vertical areas should be selected after careful investigation into its appropriateness for the planned installation. As you consider a tile for a specific installation, first refer to the manufacturer's literature for usage recommendations. Secondly, check the porosity of the tile. Thirdly, check the availability of trim (curved shapes for smooth corners, edges and coves). Fourth, think through your grout selection. And, finally, make sure you have specified the recommended installation method for the tile you have selected.

Types of Tile Available

DECORATIVE TILE

Within the family of glazed ceramic tile, there is a sub-category often called "Decos." These attractive accent pieces may include a raised or recessed relief pattern or feature a painted or silk-screened design. Generally the relief designs are planned for vertical use only because the three-dimensional tiles are difficult to clean on a counter surface or floor area. Some of the hand-painted tiles may be so delicate that general countertop or floor cleaning will damage the pattern; but they are popular for walls and as inserts in backsplashes.

Some decorative tiles create a design which flows from tile to tile to give designers great flexibility for a unique, one-of-a-kind wall, border or backsplash. Others are one-of-a-kind art pieces that should be showcased within the field of plain tile.

In addition to relief-type "Deco" tiles and hand-painted tiles, long, slender tiles called "liners" are considered as "Decos." Additionally, metallic tiles are oftentimes used as a decorative element. These tile pieces have different names and come in many sizes and thicknesses from different manufacturers. The designer needs to become familiar with the manufacturer before they can identify the specific accent tile they are considering.

Figure 7.4 *Surfacing Materials: Ceramic Tile*
Pillowed tiles are used in a surface area. (Courtesy of Walker Zanger)

GLAZED TILE

A coating of glass-forming minerals and ceramic stains is called the glaze. The glaze is sprayed onto the body of the tile (known as the bisque) before firing. The finished surface may have a shiny luster. Some glazed surfaces can be slippery to certain footwear, especially when the footwear or surface is wet. Glazed tiles are available in 4" x 4", 3" x 6", 4" x 8", 6" x 6', 12" x 12", 18" x 18" and 24" x 24" general sizes, as well as a variety of special application accent sizes and shapes.

Glazed tiles are also available in a variety of finishes; some have a slip-resistant glazed texture. Various thicknesses are available. Shiny, high-gloss glazed tiles may dull slightly with wear over a period of time with continued use. Black or dark-colored glazed tiles will show wear more rapidly than lighter colors. The type of glaze often determines the recommended end use of the tile (i.e., walls, floors and counters).

Figure 7.5 *Surfacing Materials: Glazed Tile*
Naturally textured tiles in beige and green are used at the floor and wainscoting. Note decorative tile creates the wainscot cap. (Courtesy of Charles R. Schwartzapfel – New York, New York)

GLASS TILE

Decorative glass tiles—the roots of which go back to Mesopotamia more than 4500 years ago—are a popular alternative today as manufacturers and artisans experiment with colors, materials and techniques. One of the main attractions of glass tile is the way light reflects off of them, drawing the eye to their sleek surfaces. Glass tiles come in textures from mirror-slick to rough, and in a variety of colors from deep and muted to multi-colored with iridescent options. Glass tiles are available in clear glass all the way through or with a backing finish designed to camouflage the rough wall surface.

A variety of sizes are available. Custom mosaic patterns are possible with 1" x 1", 2" x 2" and 4" x 4" tiles. Mosaics 1/2" x 1/2" to 2" x 2" are mounted in 12" x 12" sheets with a mat backing or paper overlay on the face of the tiles. This is removed after the tiles have been mounted. Individual tiles and field tiles come in basic geometric (square, rectangles, octagons) and specialty shapes.

Glass tile installations require special expertise. Because of the translucency of many tiles, manufacturers recommend setting glass tiles in white adhesive that should be smoothed carefully to prevent notched trowel lines from showing through. Additionally, a typical tile saw will not cut glass tile: a diamond wet saw will be required for cutting. Although glass tiles are more difficult to work with, they are extremely durable because they are hard and non-porous. Some can actually be installed in exterior environments. Because they can scratch easily, they are not recommended for kitchen counters or floors unless they are etched and embossed with a textured surface.

Glass tiles are typically manufactured in one of two ways:

- *Slumped or Heat Molded*. Sheets of glass are heated to the point where they soften and sink into molds that give the glass distinctive 3-D patterning or texture. It is in this manufacturing process that color can be added to the mix or fused to the back.

- *Cast or Poured*. The oldest method of making tiles is to pour molten glass into forms. Glass can be colored by adding pigmenting oxides or pieces of different colored glass into the mix. Once again, fusing colorful glass to the back of the tile can add to the depth and make it an opaque finish.

LIMESTONE TILE: See Stone – Limestone, page 336.

MARBLE TILE: See Stone – Marble, page 338.

MOSAIC TILE

Mosaic tiles are distinguished from other kinds of tile by their small size, which must not exceed 6 sq. in. (2.45" x 2.45" if square shaped). The most common types are natural clay and porcelain in which the color is throughout the tile, rather than having it applied on the surface such as a glaze. However, glazes may be applied as well. Porcelain ceramic mosaic tiles are always vitreous (natural clay) or impervious (porcelain). Therefore, they have a very low water absorption rate, less than 0.5%. They have a harder, denser body than non-vitreous wall tile. Glass mosaic tiles are also available.

Mosaics are usually sold face-mounted with paper, back-mounted with a mesh or plastic tab backing, or mesh-backed in 12" x 12" or 12" x 24" sheets. Mounted sheets facilitate installation and control the evenness of spacing.

When combined with the appropriate trim, the small-size units allow contour design applications in bathroom layouts. They are also very effective in kitchen backsplash designs.

Figure 7.6 *Surfacing Materials: Mosaic Tile*
Mosaic tiles are used to create a patterned design at the kitchen backsplash area around the hood. (Courtesy of Ellen Cheever, CMKBD – Wilmington, Delaware)

QUARRY TILE

Quarry tile is made from shale, clays or earth extruded to produce an unglazed product which has color throughout the tile body. There are a great variety of quality levels within the broad term "quarry tile." The earthen clay tiles may be very soft and irregular in shape. Other types of quarry tile are so porous they require a penetrating sealer to protect the surface. Before such a sealer is applied, the tile and grout must be allowed to cure. New sealer products have been formulated to minimize the cure time. Depending on the product used, this curing process can take as little as 48 hours, or as long as two weeks.

Other so-called quarry tiles must be stained and sealed. If such extra steps in the installation process must be completed, the designer should include the extra costs incurred in the estimate.

Certain manufacturers' quarry tiles meet the ANSI standards and are considered stain-resistant, although not stain-proof. Thus, application and renewal of a sealer is optional. To achieve the subtle patina or rich glow of natural quarry clay, seasoning the tile with oil-based cleaners (e.g., Murphy's Oil Soap or Lestoil) is preferred to sealing.

Quarry tile is suitable for interior residential and commercial floors, walls and fireplace facings. Quarry tile may be used on exterior surfaces when proper installation methods are followed.

SLATE TILE: See Stone – Slate, page 341.

TUMBLED MARBLE TILE: See Stone – Marble, page 338.

SELECT GLAZED OR UNGLAZED SURFACES

The glaze finish is an important criterion to consider. Tiles are available in a variety of glazes:

- Semi-gloss

- High-gloss

- Matte

- Two-tone – or a combination of gloss and matte.

Gloss finishes can dull with heavy use. With a matte glaze, wear is not nearly as noticeable. Both tiles have the same degree of hardness. For floors, matte or unglazed porcelain are recommended.

Glazed tile, smooth to the touch, can be slip-resistant due to a special manufacturing process. Textured glazes with a noticeably rough surface are also slip-resistant. Varying degrees of slip resistance are needed for a variety of end uses. Safe bathroom and kitchen designs demand slip-resistant tiles be specified for floor applications.

SELECT THE CORRECT SURFACE TRIM

Just as important as the tile shapes is the availability of trim shapes. While the floor can be installed with nothing more than a plain or field tile edge (tile without any finished or shaped edge), the countertop, bathtub enclosure, shower stall, floor baseboard treatment or vanity top calls for specially designed pieces to complete the installation.

Trim shapes are available with 3/4" radius for conventional mortar installations, and 1/4" radius for organic adhesive installations. These trim shapes are generally more expensive than the square footage price of the field tile because of the cost of production. The color and texture match is generally good between field tile and trim shapes, but there may be a slight or pronounced texture difference in some selections. When you are using ceramic tile for the first time, visually compare a field tile and trim shapes before the order is placed. If there is any variation, the client should approve the difference before the order is placed.

Figure **7.7** *Surfacing Materials:*
Shapes of Tile Trim

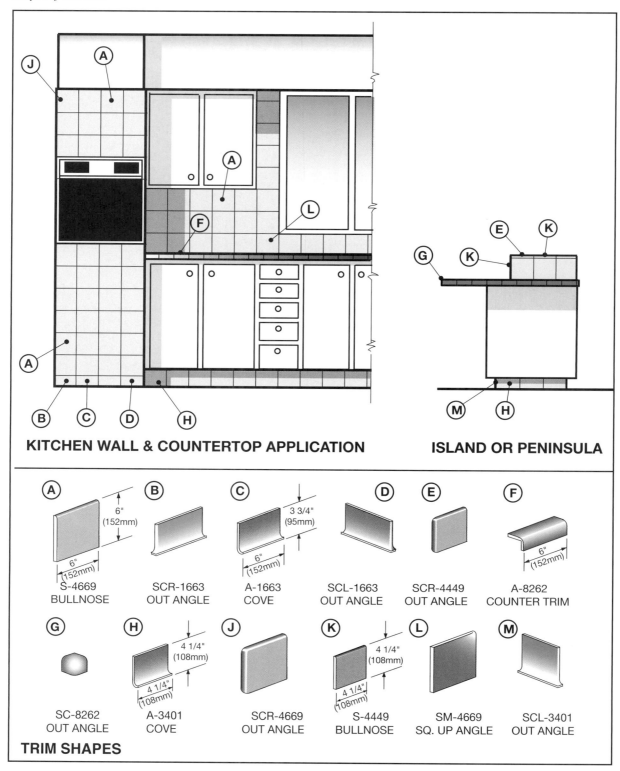

KITCHEN WALL & COUNTERTOP APPLICATION

ISLAND OR PENINSULA

A 6" (152mm) 6" (152mm)
S-4669
BULLNOSE

B SCR-1663
OUT ANGLE

C 3 3/4" (95mm) 6" (152mm)
A-1663
COVE

D SCL-1663
OUT ANGLE

E SCR-4449
OUT ANGLE

F 6" (152mm)
A-8262
COUNTER TRIM

G SC-8262
OUT ANGLE

H 4 1/4" (108mm) 4 1/4" (108mm)
A-3401
COVE

J SCR-4669
OUT ANGLE

K 4 1/4" (108mm) 4 1/4" (108mm)
S-4449
BULLNOSE

L SM-4669
SQ. UP ANGLE

M SCL-3401
OUT ANGLE

TRIM SHAPES

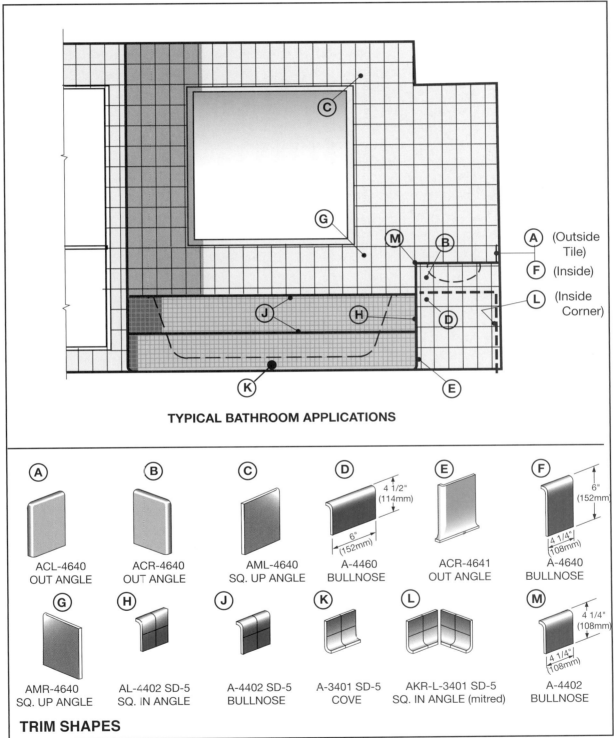

Figure 7.8 *Surfacing Materials: Shapes of Tile Trim*

TYPICAL BATHROOM APPLICATIONS

(A) (Outside Tile)
(F) (Inside)
(L) (Inside Corner)

TRIM SHAPES

A — ACL-4640 OUT ANGLE
B — ACR-4640 OUT ANGLE
C — AML-4640 SQ. UP ANGLE
D — A-4460 BULLNOSE — 4 1/2" (114mm), 6" (152mm)
E — ACR-4641 OUT ANGLE
F — A-4640 BULLNOSE — 6" (152mm), 4 1/4" (108mm)
G — AMR-4640 SQ. UP ANGLE
H — AL-4402 SD-5 SQ. IN ANGLE
J — A-4402 SD-5 BULLNOSE
K — A-3401 SD-5 COVE
L — AKR-L-3401 SD-5 SQ. IN ANGLE (mitred)
M — A-4402 BULLNOSE — 4 1/4" (108mm), 4 1/4" (108mm)

LAY-OUT ACCENT TILES ALONG WITH THE ELECTRICAL OUTLET DETAIL

Codes require a specific spacing of electrical outlets along a backsplash. Task light switching, as well as the switch for the food waste disposal will also be located along the backsplash. The backsplash light, as well as the backsplash design details must be coordinated with the electrical lay-out so outlets or switches do not interfere with the backsplash itself or decorative elements of the space between the base cabinets and the wall cabinets.

Grouts

Different types of grout are available, each designed for a particular kind of installation and to be used with specific tile sizes and shapes. Definitions of various grout types may be found in the Tile Council of America Inc. "*Handbook for Ceramic Tile Installation*" (P. O. Box 326, Princeton, New Jersey 08540).

Generally, three broad categories of grout will be specified by the kitchen and bathroom designer:

EPOXY

Epoxy grouts, in many colors, are used when superior strength and chemical resistance are desired. They dry to nearly flush joints and are effective in vertical joints such as backsplashes and cove base trim, as well as horizontal joints in floors and counters. Epoxy grouts are more expensive than other types of grout.

NON-SANDED

Non-sanded grouts, in white or colors, are suited for grout joints not exceeding 1/8" in width.

SANDED

Sanded grouts, in whites and colors, are used for grout joints up to 3/8" in width. The sand is added to the grout to insure proper strength of the wider joint. Most often they are used for floors and ceramic mosaics.

Both dry-set and sanded grouts have been enhanced by the addition of a latex additive in the product mix. The latex additive increases the bonding strength and provides a better cure. Also, you can expect less water absorption, so use latex for wet areas (showers, bathtub surrounds or sink counters).

Method Of Installation

Three methods of installation are used for ceramic tile projects.

CONVENTIONAL MORTAR BED (MUD)

In this method, the tile is installed on a bed of mortar 3/4" to 2" thick. Two systems are popular in North America. In one, the tile is set on a mortar bed while it is still soft. In the other, tile is set on a cured mortar bed.

MASTIC (ORGANIC ADHESIVE)

In this method, tile is directly applied to the countertop, decking or cement surface with troweled-on mastic. When this method is used, the finished floor will only be raised the thickness of the tile. Manufacturers state that a mastic installation may use any of the following base surfaces: existing tile, fiberglass, wood paneling, brick, masonry, concrete, plywood or vinyl. The surface must be dry, flat and free of dirt and grease.

Any existing structural problems cannot be camouflaged by the tile installation. If there is a bow in the floor before the tile is installed, it will be there after the tile is installed.

THIN SET OVER BACKERBOARD

A glass mesh concrete backerboard may take the place of a conventional mortar bed. It is unaffected by moisture and has one of the lowest coefficients of expansion of all building panels. Additionally, the boards are only one-half the weight of conventional mortar installations. In non-wet areas, exterior grade plywood can be substituted for backerboard.

CONVENTIONAL MORTAR (MUD) OR THIN SET OVER BACKERBOARD SPECIAL CONSIDERATIONS

In either conventional mortar bed or thin set over backerboard installations, the floor or vanity height will be raised the thickness of the tile and the mortar bed or glass mesh concrete backerboard. This height difference may require special floor preparation. In new construction, the subfloor can be recessed to accommodate a tile floor. In renovation projects, a transition method between the new higher tile floor and adjoining floors must be specified. Special toekick heights must also be detailed so the industry standard of 4" high kick space is maintained.

Figure 7.9 *Surfacing Materials: Tile Details*
Detail how you want the tile to be finished around the windows in your elevation drawing.

Most tile setters recommend the mortar installation be used over wood subfloors. The advantage to this type of installation is the tile (installed with a cleavage membrane) will "float" on top of the wood. Normal wood expansion and contraction will not cause cracks in tile or grout. The mortar installation is also more desirable when there is heavy traffic.

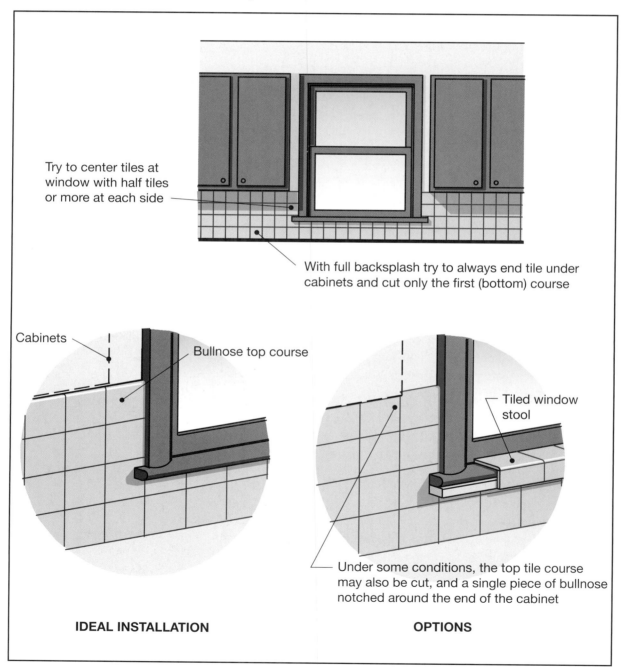

Try to center tiles at window with half tiles or more at each side

With full backsplash try to always end tile under cabinets and cut only the first (bottom) course

Cabinets

Bullnose top course

Tiled window stool

Under some conditions, the top tile course may also be cut, and a single piece of bullnose notched around the end of the cabinet

IDEAL INSTALLATION

OPTIONS

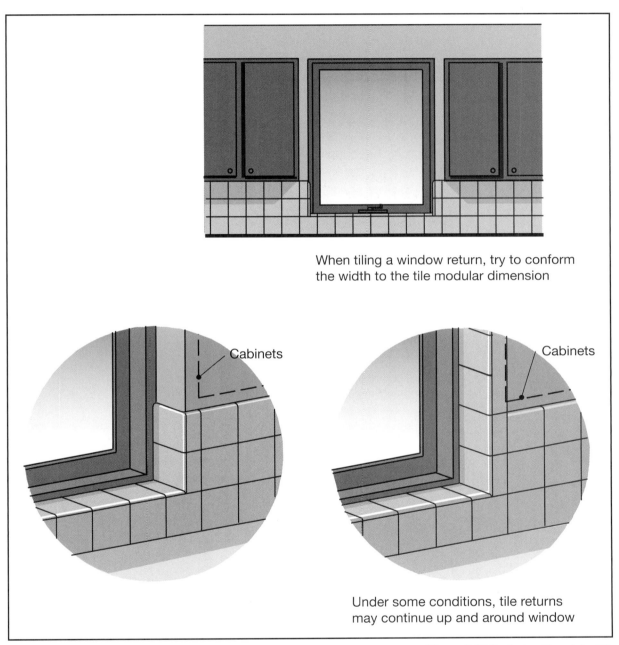

When tiling a window return, try to conform
the width to the tile modular dimension

Cabinets

Cabinets

Under some conditions, tile returns
may continue up and around window

Figure 7.10 *Surfacing Materials: Tile
at Windows with Sheetrock Returns*
Include details of finished windows in
your elevations.

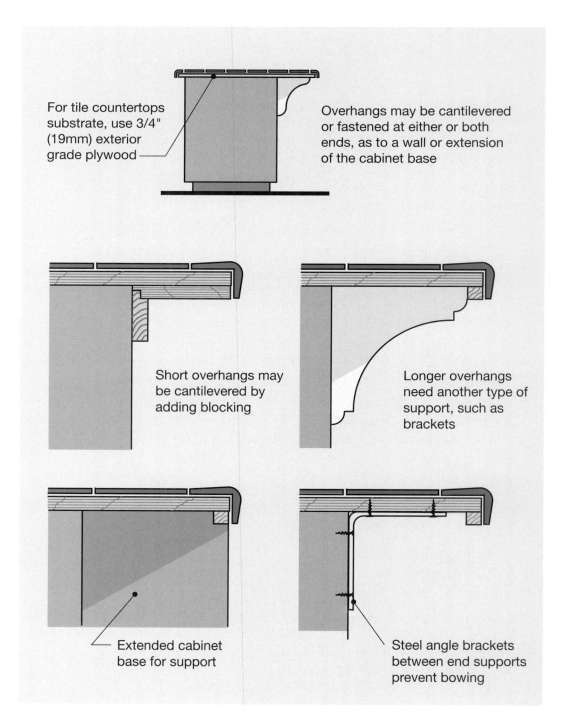

For tile countertops substrate, use 3/4" (19mm) exterior grade plywood

Overhangs may be cantilevered or fastened at either or both ends, as to a wall or extension of the cabinet base

Short overhangs may be cantilevered by adding blocking

Longer overhangs need another type of support, such as brackets

Extended cabinet base for support

Steel angle brackets between end supports prevent bowing

Figure 7.11 *Surfacing Materials: Support Tile Overhangs*
The tile overhang must be supported so the surface does not flex, causing tile or grout to crack.

Tips From The Pros

FLOORS

- **In renovation jobs, removing the existing floor covering is recommended**. Generally, this is necessary if vinyl tiles or cushioned vinyl floors are installed over a slab or wood foundation. In many parts of the country, tile is installed directly over old non-cushioned sheet vinyl.

- **Doors may require modification** to accommodate a tile floor. With a mastic installation, the designer is only concerned with the thickness of the tile. When a conventional mortar installation is planned, the designer must allow clearance for a 3/4" to 1-1/4" thick mortar bed, plus the thickness of the tile. A glass mesh concrete board installation will require a clearance dimension equal to the thickness of the board, plus the tile.

- **Allow enough time for the door modification**. Interior hollow-core or solid-core doors are easy to cut down. Pocket doors must be the type that can be removed from the pocket.

- If the new tile floor will be higher than the finished flooring of an adjacent room, **the tile selected must have trim pieces or a threshold must be planned**. Thresholds are generally marble or wood. Solid surface material can also be used as a threshold.

Figure 7.12 *Surfacing Materials: Carefully Plan a Tile Floor*
A tile floor must be carefully planned so it meets the threshold or weather stripping at an exterior door.

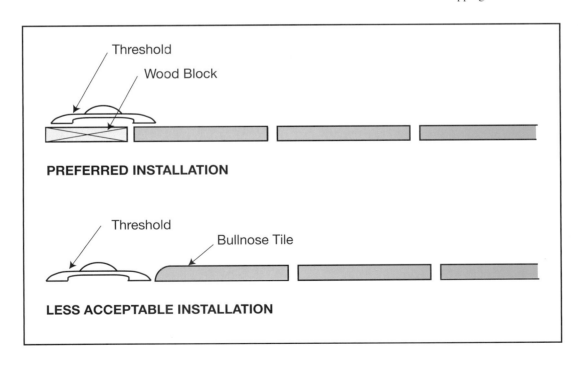

PREFERRED INSTALLATION

LESS ACCEPTABLE INSTALLATION

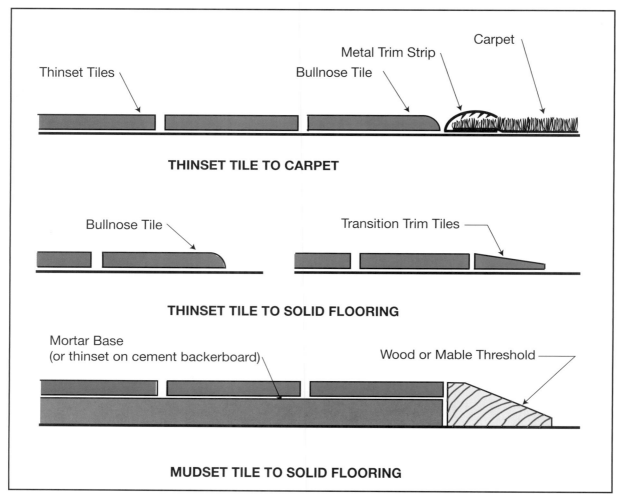

THINSET TILE TO CARPET

THINSET TILE TO SOLID FLOORING

MUDSET TILE TO SOLID FLOORING

Figure 7.13 *Surfacing Materials: Tile Floor Transition Methods* Transition methods from a tile floor to other interior floor surfaces.

- Make sure the distance from the finished tile floor to the underside of the kitchen countertop leaves enough room for a built-in dishwasher, and extend the flooring under the dishwasher.

- Make sure a tile backerboard does not interfere with the toilet supply line escutcheon plate.

BATHROOM WALLS

- **Run the tile to the floor.** When planning a tile enclosure around a bathtub, make sure the tile extends past the tub and runs down to the floor. This extra tile width will protect the drywall surface underneath from moisture damage over years of use.

- **Coordinate wainscot height with vanity backsplash.** When planning a tile wainscot in a bathroom, specify the height so it has some relationship with the vanity and its backsplash. You may eliminate the backsplash completely and run the trim or molding at the top of the wainscoting in place of a backsplash. Alternatively, you can step the wainscoting up so it ties in at the same elevation as the backsplash.

- **Tile a small wall next to the toilet.** When planning a 36" high tiled privacy wall that shields the toilet area from view, plan to tile the entire wall if the floor in the room is also tiled. This small wall section can be quite awkward if it has a tile baseboard at the bottom of it and a tile cap at the top, but no tile in between.

- **Determine finished wall dimensions.** If you are going to be tiling the wall area around the toilet, make sure you take the added dimension of the installation method and tile thickness into account when you determine finished wall dimensions. For example, if you are going to tile three walls around a toilet with a conventional mortar installation, you need to maintain a minimum clearance between your drywall of 33" to 35" to make sure the job meets the code requirement of 30" between the finished side walls. Another typical error occurs when a tile wainscoting finish is applied to the wall behind the toilet, which then reduces the actual finished floor distance from the wall to the toilet's floor outlet. That 12" rough-in dimension must be from the center of the floor outlet to the finished surface on the wall, not the drywall behind the tile.

- **Plan the grout lines.** If you are planning to tile all four walls in a room, plus the ceiling, decide where it is most important to have grout lines on the wall line up with the grout lines on the ceiling. Generally, as you stand at the doorway, the wall at the far end of the room, or the most important wall will be the focal point. Therefore, this wall should be where the tile setters start running the tile up the wall and then across the ceiling. If the room is square, the grout lines will run down the wall on the opposite side. However, in renovation situations this rarely occurs.

- **Specify the accessory placement.** If you are tiling a wall surface, remember to decide where you are going to install the accessories (the toilet paper holder, towel bars and robe hooks) and make sure you determine how you are going to install the accessories on the new tile surface.

CONCRETE

Concrete is a specialized countertop surfacing material. Molded into shape, it is seamless: concrete can also be dyed just about any color. While it has a rougher appearance than granite or solid surfacing, with hairline cracks (called "crazing") and surface imperfections, these qualities make it appealing to many. Like granite and other natural stone materials, upkeep is minimal, but it must be sealed to prevent stains.

One major consideration for the kitchen planner is the weight of the countertop. Open spans must be engineered and some cabinets will require reinforcing. An excellent resource for information around custom concrete countertops is *"Concrete Countertops: Design, Form and Finishes for the New Kitchen and Bath"* by Fu-Tung Cheng with Eric Olsen, 2002 (Taunton Press, 63 South Main Street, Newton, CT 06470-5506).

Figure 7.14 *Surfacing Materials: Concrete Countertop*
A kitchen featuring a concrete countertop. (Courtesy of Beverly Leigh Binns and Co-designer Anthony Binns, CKD, CBD – Pickering, Ontario)

Figure 7.15 *Surfacing Materials: Concrete*
A bathroom featuring concrete on the back wall and on part of the countertop. (Courtesy of Fu-Tung Cheng and Co-Designers Milton Tong and Frank Lee – Berkeley, California)

CORK FLOORING

Cork comes from the bark of special oak trees in Spain and Portugal. The wood product comes from a renewable process where 6" to 9" of bark is cut from the trunk. It takes 5 to 7 years to grow back after harvesting.

Cork is a soft-hard surface! It is soft, warm and quiet. It also may be helpful to homeowners with allergies. A variety of patterns are available which are achieved by different peeling techniques: some look like a cork stopper, some like a bulletin board or burled wood. The most popular finish is natural—similar to natural oak. Cork is also available in different stains, including brown, deep reds and a white washed tint.

Quality levels do vary in cork products—the thicker the top veneer, the more cushioning and the better wear and performance. Therefore, price varies on the density and thickness of the cork veneer, as well as the padding underlayment. The number of urethane coats on the veneer (between 2 to 5) determines the wear.

Similar to laminate, floating floor planks snap together and can be installed over concrete or wood. Cork can be installed anywhere wood flooring can be placed, however most experts caution against using it in high moisture areas such as the bathroom.

GLASS BLOCK

Glass block is enjoying a rekindled interest among designers. While popular in the 1930s and 1940s, the use of glass block came to a standstill in the 1970s. These translucent hollow blocks of glass are ideal for kitchen and bathroom use. They transmit light, yet provide privacy. When used in exterior wall installations, they deaden outside noise and offer insulating qualities similar to thermal-pane windows. Available in a variety of shapes, sizes, textures and colors, glass block offers great design flexibility.

However, installation is not easy and should not be attempted by anyone other than a skilled mason. The blocks are non-porous, slick and heavy, and require a footing because of their weight. During installation, they are slippery and difficult to align.

Alternatives to glass block are decorative glass-looking products that are made out of plastic materials. These substitutes are very strong, as well as being lightweight, and do not need a footing. Assembly is generally quicker with these types of acrylic and proprietary polymer blocks because they have an engineered inner locking system that fastens them together. Therefore, traditional mortar joints are not required. Some manufacturers have available a preformed, weather-resistant sealant that looks like a mortar joint to complete the finished product.

HARDWOOD FLOORING

Throughout the house, wood floors are in great demand today, and wood is a viable flooring material for kitchen and bathroom projects. Hardwoods, renewable woods such as bamboo, and laminated wood floors are all possible choices.

Natural Wood Floors

Woods used for floors are mostly cold weather hardwoods. The slow growth in cold temperatures provides the most durable wood possible. Pine flooring is the exception.

Oak is the most popular wood flooring in residential use because of its beautiful grain and durability. Cherry is also often specified. Antique reclaimed pine, oak, hickory and cherry woods are available for rustic interiors.

Awaiting the homeowner seeking broader horizons are exotic woods in either manufactured or custom floors, starting at roughly twice the price of oak. These woods range from the unusually beautiful rose wood to the exceptionally rugged iron wood, to pecan, teak and the darkest ebony.

Wood floors are graded according to standards that measure color, grain and imperfections. Clear or Select grades are generally specified for a formal look and for lighter finishes. Select and #1 Common grades are used for traditional and light-to-medium stained floors. For rustic and specialty areas, specify #2 Common, which features wide color variations and character marks like knots, streaks and worm holes.

LAMINATED WOOD FLOORING

Prefinished laminated hardwood-looking floors are very functional for a kitchen or bathroom application. Available in tile and plank patterns, the durable laminated finish wears well in a high traffic or high use area. In the past, these floors were, oftentimes, very noisy: manufacturers have gone to great lengths to sound-deaden the surfaces of these floors.

RENEWABLE BAMBOO FLOORING

Bamboo is a renewable grass product. The product used to make floors is up to 12" in diameter and 30' high. After harvesting, a 4' stump remains which regenerates in 5 years.

The product comes in tongue-and-groove boards that can be glued or nailed. While comparable in price to 3/4" solid wood flooring it is 30% harder than oak. The natural color of bamboo is light, resembling maple—and offers a clean, contemporary look. It is also available in a darker brown finish, as well. Darker woods, because the color goes all the way through, can be sanded and refinished.

Bamboo can be installed anywhere an engineered wood product can be used provided there is not too much moisture from the slab. A key ingredient to a successful bamboo installation is acclimation: the product should be delivered at least 48 hours before installation and allowed to sit in the environment where it will be installed, adjusting to the humidity level in the room so it will not shift after installation. This means bamboo floors should only be installed in conditioned spaces—not before the heating/air conditioning is turned on.

Floor Styles

There are several styles of flooring currently being used.

PARQUET FLOORING.

Simulated 12" x 12" tiles or actual individual pieces of wood, it is interlocking, and blind-nailed. Parquet is sold by square footage. Allow for waste and cutting.

PLANK FLOORING.

Interlocking flooring which is blind-nailed. Generally, random lengths of 9" to 96" are used, as well as random widths. The width combinations are:

> 3" and 4"
>
> 3", 4" and 6"
>
> 3", 5" and 7"
>
> 4", 6" and 8"

The plank flooring is generally sold in bundles. In this case, random lengths and widths cannot be varied. Allow for waste and cutting.

STRIP FLOORING.

Butt flooring which is top-nailed. All boards are the same width (2" and 2-1/4") and random lengths. Both plank and strip flooring is sold by board feet. Provide allowance for waste and cutting.

Finishing

To jobsite finish or to spec prefinish—to wax or not—the great debate between finishing techniques and materials rages on.

FINISH FOR DYE-STAINED OR NATURAL FLOORS

Tung oil and wax is a nearly forgotten, but beautiful way to protect new or resurfaced floors. It can be renewed indefinitely by waxing as required. Two coats of a name-brand polyurethane is a great way to protect floors too, but eventually it will wear and need to be recoated. This requires resanding since cured urethanes are so hard that a new coat does not adhere well to the old one. Patching worn areas that had been protected by polyurethane is rarely successful.

WAX MAINTENANCE

Waxing the surface remains a time-honored finishing option. Most people think they will continually be on their knees with a polishing rag. Actually, a waxed floor might need rewaxing once a year—and it can be done with a small buffing machine that homeowners can buy or rent. New finishing innovations offer the consumer a waxed finish that eliminates re-waxing. It is really a choice between periodic maintenance, or sanding and recoating your floors with polyurethane every five or six years. Penetrating oil and wax is the way it was done for years. The soft look of it is incomparable.

WHITE-WASH FLOORING

The white-gray stain is called a pigmented stain. It creates color by causing finely ground particles to adhere to the floor's surface. Unlike a dye-based stain that penetrates the wood, a pigmented stain floats mostly on the floor's surface like paint. The particles and resins of the pigmented stain limit penetration by the tung oil and, hence, make good adhesion difficult. Besides, tung oil or polyurethane would well give the floors an amber tone. A clear, non-yellowing varnish with an alcohol, toluene, oraliphatic-resin base is best; they're available through suppliers to professional floor finishers.

Prefinished Wood Floors

Modern prefinished floors have a durable penetrating sealer finish applied at the factory. A lovely finish that increases in beauty as one walks on it, if it is waxed there are several major disadvantages.

First, the wax will be affected by water. The factory finish will not accept an additional protective coat of urethane. The installer must completely sand the floor, remove the factory finish and start from scratch if the water-resistant properties of a urethane are required.

Second, the prefinished floor does not allow the installer the opportunity to sand the entire surface after installation to insure a perfectly even surface.

Lastly, the prefinished tiles or planks do not provide a completely sealed top surface. Therefore, moisture from kitchen or bathroom spills can get down between and under the wood floor.

Unfinished Wood Floors

Another approach in a kitchen or bathroom is to install an unfinished floor. The urethane finish, which is impervious to stains and moisture, can then be installed after the unfinished wood has been sanded smooth. The multiple coats provide a sealed top surface for a kitchen or bathroom environment.

Once finished, the floors should be inspected from a standing position. Flooring is not furniture; a finish similar to the one on a grand piano should not be expected. However, small particles of debris in the finish, a wavy look or feel along the strips, deep swirls or sander marks, and splotchy areas are indications of inadequate finishing or cleaning. A quality finish may include some of these problems, but they should not appear over the entire floor.

LAMINATES

Laminate surfaces are found on countertops, as well as cabinet interiors and exteriors, bathroom wall areas and bathtub platforms. The following information describes the different types of laminates available.

Laminate Flooring

The newest floorcovering on the market is laminate. It consists of several layers of material bonded together under high pressure, similar to the laminate products used for countertops. A clear melamine top layer protects the design layer. Then follows a plastic resin-impregnated paper layer with wood grain pattern printed on. These are bonded to a structural fiberboard core, backed by a layer of melamine. The clear topmost wear layer is smooth and can be slippery when wet, making laminate flooring a questionable option for baths.

Installing laminate flooring entails applying glue to the tongue-and-groove edges of each piece and pressing it into the abutting piece on the floor, without actually attaching it to the floor. The finish floor then "floats" above the substrate. There are currently two choices of underlayments, a 1/4-inch (13 mm) thick, low-density fiber panel, 24 inch x 30 inch (610 mm x 762 mm), or closed-cell foam cushion, which is shipped in rolls. Laminate flooring installs over concrete slab floors in much the same way as over wood-framed floors, except that a poly vapor barrier is placed over the slab before the underlayment material.

Figure 7.16 *Surfacing Materials: Laminate Countertop*
(Courtesy of Nevamar Company)

Composite Panels

A composite panel is a layer of decorative paper impregnated with either melamine resin or polyester resin, which is thermal-set or thermal-fused (fused with heat and pressure) to a substrate of particleboard, fiberboard or some other material. It is sold as laminate board. This differs from high-pressure laminate, which is sold in sheets to fabricators who apply it to boards themselves. It is sometimes known as thermally fused melamine, low-pressure laminate, short cycle laminate, melamine or MCP.

Composite panels generally have just one print sheet on the surface, although some suppliers offer an overlay sheet. Both front and back of the panels are laminated to avoid warping. Generally, these panels are offered in a limited range of colors and patterns.

Composite panels are used in vertical or light-use horizontal applications, such as shelving. They should not be used for countertops.

Generally, because they are thermal-set, composite panels are joined to the substrate with a stronger bond than high-pressure laminate, paper or other surfaces, which are mechanically fused. It will not delaminate because it becomes part of the substrate surface.

Composite panels have a lower weight than high-pressure laminates, and offer some cost savings. However, composite panels typically offer less impact and abrasion resistance than high-pressure laminates.

High-Pressure Decorative Laminates

High-pressure decorative laminate is typically composed of three types of paper fused under heat and pressure into a single surface. The top coat is a melamine resin-saturated overlay. The second sheet is the decorative paper. It is a melamine resin-saturated paper carrying either a surface color or a gravure print. Under these two levels is a core or body made up of three to nine sheets of phenolic resin-saturated Kraft paper.

The entire assembly is pressed at between 1,000 to 1,200 pounds (454 kilograms to 544.8 kilograms) per square inch for about one hour, at temperatures exceeding 280° F (137.78° C).

High-pressure decorative laminates are divided into forming and non-forming grades. Non-forming laminate is rigid, while forming laminate has been engineered to be more flexible so it can be bent under heat. This process is called "post-forming."

The cabinet industry uses vertical-grade high-pressure decorative laminate which is 0.030" thick and may be formable. Countertop fabricators use a horizontal grade of high-pressure decorative laminate which is .050" thick and is typically not formable. The post-forming countertop grade is .042" thick.

High-pressure decorative laminates are used most frequently on countertop surfaces. They are also used by many cabinet manufacturers for door styles. The high-pressure decorative laminate is generally applied to a particleboard substrate. Occasionally, codes may call for a plywood substrate for a countertop.

Of all the laminates available, high-pressure decorative laminates offer the greatest impact resistance. They are available in a wide range of colors, patterns, textures and finishes. Some manufacturers offer special fire-resistant, abrasion-resistant and chemical-resistant surfaces. Others fabricate laminate in a grooved tambour form. Generally, all high-pressure decorative laminates have excellent stain, abrasion, scuff and wear resistance. However, because the laminate is applied on a substrate, if a chip occurs, it is not repairable. Smooth glossy finishes show scratches more easily than matte, textured. Solid colors typically show scratches more readily than pattern surfaces.

Figure 7.17 *Surfacing Materials: High-Pressure Decorative Laminates* A Kitchen Featuring High-Pressure Laminate Countertops (Courtesy of Kraft Maid Cabinetry)

PAINT

Painting is one of the finishing steps in a kitchen or bathroom project. Often the designer is not responsible for this activity, but is expected to understand the craft and make recommendations to the client. Therefore, a basic understanding of paints will aid the designer.

Paint Coverage

Paint is designed to bond itself to either a fresh, new surface or an old, uneven one. It should cover and help to protect the surface against the assaults of weather, airborne chemicals and dirt. It should remain flexible enough to stay intact for years while the walls settle, vibrate, expand and contract.

Paint Gloss Choices

The two major types of finishing coats—latex and alkyd paints—come in versions labeled flat, egg shell, satin, semi-gloss and high gloss.

FLAT PAINTS provide a desirable low-glare surface for walls and ceilings that do not need frequent washing.

SEMI-GLOSS PAINTS afford moderate durability with a less obtrusive shine for most woodwork.

HIGH GLOSS PAINTS are the most wear-resistant and moisture-resistant because of their relatively high proportion of resin. The more resin, the heavier and tougher the film. The high resin film of the glossy paints makes them ideal for areas subject to heavy use and frequent washing.

Paint Classification

ALKYD PAINT

This paint has replaced oil-based paints in most cases. It is considered the best type of paint to use in rooms that will receive a great deal of use. Any painted or wallpapered surface or bare wood can be covered with paint made from a synthetic resin called alkyd (often combined with other resins). This type of paint will adhere to bare masonry or plaster, but should not be used on bare wallboard because it will raise a nap on the wallboard's paper covering.

Alkyd is the most durable of the common finishing paints. Most alkyds are sufficiently dry for a second coat in four to six hours. Although some latex paints will not bond well to alkyd, most other paints can be applied over it.

LATEX PAINT

This paint provides simplified cleanup, is practically odor-free and is quick-drying. Water is the solvent for latex paint, which is made of plastic resin and either acrylics or tough polyvinyls. Its water solvency gives latex advantages that have made it the most widely used paint for walls and ceilings in living areas, other than kitchens and bathrooms. Tools, spills and hands can be cleaned with soap and water while the latex is wet. Latex paint is almost free of odor and harmful fumes, and a coat is usually dry in little more than an hour.

Latex adheres to most surfaces painted with flat oil or latex paint; it does not adhere to some alkyds and tends to peel away from any high gloss finish. Latex can be used over unprimed wallboard, bare masonry and fresh plaster patches that have set but are not quite dry.

Its water solvency imposes certain limitations on latex paint. Although it can be applied directly over wallpaper, the water in the paint may soak the paper away from the wall. If latex is applied to raw wood, the water swells the fibers and roughens the surface—a disadvantage where a smooth finish is desirable. Used on bare steel, it rusts the metal.

Flat latex is less resistant to abrasion and washing than either oil or alkyd paint, and the high-gloss latex is less shiny and less durable than comparable alkyds or oils.

Faux Finishes

Faux finishing is the fine art of creating illusions with paint. With combinations of colors, finishes, tools and techniques, painters—or talented homeowners—create unique effects for wall and ceiling surfaces.

Faux techniques can be used to showcase a client's individuality, create dramatic focal points, bring out the strengths of a room, or beautifully hide imperfections.

TROMPE L'OEIL. The term trompe l'oeil is a French one that means "fool the eye." Oftentimes, it is used to describe a three-dimensional mural created on a residential flat wall surface. It typically refers to a painted scene which "fools the eye" into looking like something with depth and distance.

Figure 7.18 *Surfacing Materials: Examples of Faux Finish Techniques* Softly painted faux finishing runs above the tile walls up to the ceiling in this dramatic kitchen. (Courtesy of Robert Schwartz and Karen Williams - New York, New York)

Most major paint companies have faux finish systems and tools designed with well-written instructions for their application for the do-it-yourselfer. Many talented painting professionals are master faux finishers, and will provide samples of their more creative techniques, upon request, for review by the designer and client.

The basic techniques typically seen are as follows.

COLOR WASHING. A decorative paint technique that creates visual texture by layering paint colors, bringing the room to life. Sometimes referred to as a modern-day "fresco" technique.

CRACKLING. Crackling is reflective of the aging process of wood finishes, as well as deterioration of porcelain finishes. Porcelain crackle glazes are very small in pattern; weathered crackle glazes have a much larger overall effect. Many crackle techniques are created with color-on-color and may be best reserved for accent pieces. Some cabinet manufacturers offer crackle on their cabinetry.

DISTRESSED WOOD FINISHES. Recreating the antique appearance of furniture, paneling, trim and accent pieces, this rustic finish softens the look of new wood, creating a vintage finish.

Distressing effects may include physical distressing, which is created with a variety of tools and techniques to age the wood. Additionally, distressed finishes may include wear-through (wearing through the top layer of the finish to the raw wood or base coat), as well as glazing techniques. Glazing techniques are typically defined as burnished, antique or striate.

DRAGGING, COMBING AND STRIATE. A brushing technique that creates a directional pattern with layered colors.

SPONGING AND RAG ROLLING. A multi-colored/layered faux finish is created by dabbing color on with a rag, a roller, or a sponge.

STIPPLING. The stippling technique transforms a flat surface into a finely grained finish, adding dimension to the wall surface.

OTHER SPECIAL EFFECTS. Patterns, stripes, fabric reproductions, basket weaves and metallic finishes and glazing are other special finishes possible.

QUARTZ COMPOSITE

Quartz composite captures the hard durability of stone in a man-made surfacing material. Manufacturers claim it is more resilient than granite and more stain-resistant than solid surfacing. But the feature that is attracting designers and homeowners is the polished elegant look that is attainable with color and pattern consistency.

Quartz composite (also known as engineered stone) is a stone-synthetic composite made of quartz particles mixed with an acrylic or epoxy binder. Since the composites are man-made, they do not have the variations in color and texture of granite or marble. And because they are non-porous, they do not have to be sealed. It is also more stain-resistant than natural stone and resins add a flexibility that prevents chipping. The composites also have a color consistency that saves homeowners from having to carefully choose slabs to assure they match.

The slabs are 3/8" to 1-1/8" thick and 10' long. Widths range from 52" to 55", slightly larger than the European standard of 48". Because United States kitchen counters are typically 25" deep, the increased width allows fabricators to cut two lengths from one slab.

Figure 7.19 *Surfacing Materials: Quartz Composition Kitchen Countertop*
A quartz composition countertop in a country kitchen, right, and a close-up of a quartz top, below. (Courtesy of DuPont Surfaces)

SOLID SURFACING

Introduced more than a quarter of a century ago by DuPont Surfaces, Corian led the way to bringing solid surfacing material to kitchen and bathroom designers. Today, the designer has many solid surfacing materials to choose from.

The designer should compare these new materials against the guidelines detailed in the following review of the major products to ascertain their level of quality and durability. Although the major product offerings vary in composition and breadth of product line, there are some common features.

- All solid surfacing material is stain resistant because it is non-porous, and repairable because the color runs through the material.

- All manufacturers recommend cleaning with a damp cloth or sponge and ordinary household soap or mild cleanser.

- The color-through feature of these materials means severe stains (including cigarette burns) can be removed with a Scotchbrite pad and cleanser. Deeper scratches can be removed with 320 to 400 grit sandpaper, steel wool and/or a buffing pad. Deeper scratches or damage should be repaired by a certified fabricator.

- While most products have excellent resistance to household chemicals, paint removers and oven cleaners can sometimes cause damage.

- All of the manufacturers offer solid surfaces with a factory finish that may be sanded to a matte finish or can be buffed or polished to a high gloss. None of the manufacturers recommend high-gloss finishes on dark colors in heavy use areas, such as countertop surfaces.

- When properly fabricated, the seam between two pieces of all the solid surfacing materials is almost imperceptible. However, you should never promise an invisible seam.

- Solid surfacing is quite "fabricator sensitive" and all manufacturers stress the importance of retaining only qualified and/or certified fabricators.

- Companies offer sheet goods in 1/2" and 3/4" thicknesses. Other thicknesses are available and vary by company. The availability of molded sinks also varies by company.

- Manufacturers recommend that unsupported overhangs should not exceed 12" with 3/4" sheets and 6" with 1/2" sheets.

- Manufacturers recommend the material "float" on the substrate; most recommend perimeter frames and a web support system rather than a full substrate.

- Although solid surfacing is considered more durable than laminates, it is not impervious to heat. Because solid surface materials expand when heated, all manufacturers recommend at least 1/8" clearance on wall-to-wall installation.

- Most manufacturers recommend these materials for interior use only. Potential problems with exterior use of some of the materials include shrinkage and expansion, as well as color changes with exposure to direct sunlight. Some products, like DuPont Corian can be used in exterior applications.

Quality Standards

The National Association of Home Builders Research Center (NAHB RC) has developed a tier to its solid surface material certification. The third-party certification program, which is endorsed by the International Cast Polymer Alliance (ICPA), was developed to verify that products meet or exceed the performance requirements of the American National Standards Institute (ANSI) national consensus standard for solid surface materials (ANSI/ICPA SS-1-2001).

The new ANSI standard establishes the test methods pertaining to the structure, water resistance, colorfastness, stain resistance, cleanability, and other significant properties of solid surface materials, including the ability to be fabricated with inconspicuous seams and to be restored to its original finish. In addition, there are general requirements of materials and workmanship and finish. ANSI/ICPA SS-1-2001 establishes a common set of performance criteria for the benefit of manufacturers, fabricators, architects, specifiers, consumers, and others that manufacture, specify, or use solid surface materials.

For more information about solid surface material certification, visit the NAHB RC's website: www.nahbrc.org.

Figure 7.20 *Surfacing Materials: Solid Surface Bathroom Vanity*
A solid surface shaped vanity top provides an unusual storage area for bathroom linen. (Courtesy of Tony Hunt, CKD – Toronto, Ontario)

Figure 7.21 *Surfacing Materials: Kitchen Featuring Solid Surface Materials* (Courtesy of Brookhaven/Wood-Mode Inc.)

STAINLESS STEEL

Long a mainstay of the commercial kitchen, stainless steel is increasingly finding its way into the home as a countertop material. While it is heat- and stain-proof as well as non-corrosive, its main attraction to homeowners might be that it looks great next to popular upscale stainless steel kitchen appliances and in Contemporary rooms.

Stainless steel is susceptible to dents and scratches; since it shows fingerprints, water marks and smudges, it needs to be cleaned frequently.

Figure 7.22 *Surfacing Materials: Stainless Steel*
A kitchen featuring a stainless steel countertop section. (Melissa Smith, CKD and Co-Designer Carla Taylor, CKD – Nashville, Tennessee)

329

STOME

Flagstone

Flagging is a process whereby stone is split into thin slabs suitable for paving. Although generally identified as "flagstone," bluestone and slate are the most common types of flagging stones used.

Bluestone is a rough sandstone paver, usually buff, blue, green or gray in color. Slate is a smooth, gray, sedimentary stone. The thicker the stones, the less likely cracks will occur over the lifetime of the floor. The weight of the floor must be carefully computed when used over wood foundations.

Both bluestone and slate absorb heat, rather than reflect it, and can get quite hot. Irregularly cut stones are the least expensive pre-cut patterned stone.

Granite

Polished and honed granite countertops are a popular element of up-scale kitchens and bathrooms. A natural stone countertop conveys a sense of beauty and warmth that is combined with a durable work surface that can withstand the expected high use of the new space.

Granite begins as the liquid magma (hot molten stone) in the center of the earth. It is a type of stone called "igneous." Due to extreme pressure within the earth, and the absence of atmosphere, granite is formed very dense with no pores. Granite is really a host of ingredients including common minerals like feldspar, quartz and mica. Feldspar is the major mineral component of granite, comprising 60% to 80% of the stone.

Granite is not as subject to staining as marble is because of an extremely low absorption rate. The stone is less prone than marble to scratching. Its coarse grain also makes it more slip-resistant than marble.

Figure 7.23 *Surfacing Materials: A Granite Island Countertop* (Courtesy of Tom Trzcinski, CMKBD – Pittsburgh, Pennsylvania. Photography by Craig Thompson Photography)

Figure 7.24 *Surfacing Materials: All Kitchen Surfaces Are Granite* (Courtesy of Terry Schwartzman – Scottsdale, Arizona)

Figure 7.25 *Surfacing Materials: Granite*
Granite continues up the backsplash in this installation. (Courtesy of Rick Farrell – Pickering, Ontario)

Figure 7.26 *Surfacing Materials: Granite and Glass Combined* (Courtesy of Beverly Staal, CKD, CBD – Kirkland, Washington and Co-Designers Michele Marquardi and Lucia Pizzio Biroli – Mercer Island, Washington)

Coloration

Granites vary widely in shade, clarity and movement of pattern. There will be variations from slab to slab because of mineral content and veining, which adds to the character of the natural stone. Therefore, most granite selections are made at the stone yard, allowing the client to reserve their stone slabs for the project underway.

Granite is available in three different finishes: a highly polished surface, which is appropriate for most countertop applications; a flamed finish, which has a rough-textured touch; and a honed finish, which provides a matte surface ideal for kitchen and bathroom floor applications.

Figure 7.27 *Surfacing Materials: Shaped Granite Splash Used in Bathroom*
(Courtesy of Gioi Ngoc Tran and Co-Designer Vernon Applegate – San Francisco, California

Fabrication

Granite countertops are templated at the jobsite and fabricated at the yard (stone fabrication facility) before final installation at the jobsite. For some projects, measuring the countertop for installation can be completed when the cabinets are ordered. Working from the design layout and using newly developed measuring techniques to calculate exact dimensions, fabricators can prefabricate and deliver granite tops to the jobsite ready for installation.

Sizing

For most countertops, the optimum thickness is 1-1/4". The difference in cost over more fragile 3/4" slabs is minimal and the added thickness gives more strength for extensions and cutouts, while reducing the risk of breakage during transport and installation. This thickness also eliminates the need for a built-up edge. For example, a 1-1/4" granite slab can support 12" of overhang. Keep in mind the weight of these tops as you schedule the installation crews.

Granite slabs for countertops are available in a variety of sizes. Should more than one piece be necessary, the slabs can be matched to another in the sequence for color and grain consistency and then cut to butt squarely against each other. For this type of installation, locate seams in the most inconspicuous location possible, around cutouts or back corners.

Limestone

Limestone is popular for its earthy tones and its variety of colors and characteristics. Even more easily stained and etched than marble, limestone is not a typical kitchen countertop choice, but it does wear well enough to be used in floors, backsplash areas and bathroom surfaces. To decrease the material's susceptibility to staining, it must be regularly sealed.

Limestone is the result of millions of years of seashells and bones of sea creatures settling as the sediment on an ocean floor. The calcium in the bones and shells combines with the carbon dioxide in the water to form calcium carbonate, which is the basic mineral structure of all limestone and marble. Less than 3% of the stone is the color, which is simply other natural elements present when the stone is formed. Given enough heat and pressure, limestone will crystallize, resulting in marble. Limestone that has not been crystallized will not be able to be polished and will be honed.

Figure 7.28 *Surfacing Materials: Limestone Kitchen Counter*
A kitchen featuring a combination of limestone, marble and butcher block. (Courtesy of Julie Stoner, CKD–Wayne, Pennsylvania and Co-Designer Mari Dolby – Berwyn, Pennsylvania)

Marble

Marble and limestone begin as the same material. Given enough heat and pressure, limestone will crystallize, resulting in marble. The crystal structure allows marble to take a polish that brings out the color of the other trace elements. Italian marble is world renowned. Belgium, Spain, Greece and France are also known for their marble quarries. Many U.S. quarries also produce beautiful stone slabs.

The patterns and color of marble are more varied than those of granite, and they create a softer appearance overall. Like granite, marble fits well in either Contemporary or Traditional settings. But because marble is not as hard as granite, it is more subject to surface damage. For this reason, some experts rule out marble for use on kitchen countertops, unless the work area is subjected to gentle use only. Others suggest using very hard marble to resist wear, and to hide scratches they recommend honed marble. For use on floors, tumbled marble—marble that has been tumbled with water and abrasives to give it a soft, antiqued texture that hides wear and improves traction— is recommended. Unless the finish is etched, honed or pummeled, marble is slippery when wet. Therefore, make sure your clients understand a polished marble floor will be slippery.

7.29 *Surfacing Materials: Marble*
A kitchen featuring a marble counter-top section. (Courtesy of Karen Williams – New York, New York)

Figure 7.30 *Surfacing Materials: Marble*
A bathroom combining marble tiles and marble slabs. (Courtesy of Kohler Company)

Coloration and Durability

Numerous minerals are present which account for the markings and color range associated with marble. Marble is available in a wide color palette. Some marbles feature fluid directional patterns; others offer a general, overall design.

The more colorful and decorative the marble, the more fragile it is. Each vein in a stone is the result of natural discoloration from water. It is like a tiny fracture that, under pressure, can lead to breakage. Marble is rated according to an A-B-C-D classification based on the fragility of the stones. A and B marbles are solid and sound. C and D marbles are the most fragile, but also the most colorful and decorative.

The grade of marble, rarity of the specific type of stone and the demand for the type of material affects pricing. Before specifying marble, advise the client about durability.

Marble is soft and porous. This means it stains easily if not initially sealed with at least two coats of a penetrating seal. And, it must be frequently resealed. White marble is softer and less dense than colored marble, so it is more easily stained. Dark marble shows scratches more easily.

Slate

Durable, elegant and acid- and stain-resistant, slate has a natural cleft, a split face, and a texture similar to split-cedar shingles. New England slate is stronger than granite and marble because it is made of laminated stone. The wide range of colors includes hues that range from earth tones to reds. With its satiny, non-shiny surface, a slate countertop would blend well with matte finish cabinets in Shaker and Victorian style houses, where high-gloss granite might be overwhelming. But beware: tables and chairs may rock on the irregular cleft face of a slate floor.

Slate is a metamorphic rock formed from the low-grade metamorphism of the sedimentary rock shale. Slate, like shale (mudstone), is a very fine-grained rock of mostly microscopic quartz and calcite. Slate can also contain some of the same minerals found in granite, which makes some slate iridescent and/or hard. The alteration of shale by heat and pressure produces the pronounced partings that give slate its layered characteristics. Like limestone and marble, the colors come from trace metals. The vivid colors on most Chinese and Indian slate are the result of splitting the slate along natural layers, which exposes the metals to the atmosphere and causes them to rust.

Unlike granite and marble, slate—because it is nonporous—does not require a penetrating sealer, but a clear surface wax gives slate a wet look and enhances its color. Although slate scratches easily, marks that do not come off with normal cleaning can usually be removed with steel wool.

Figure 7.31 *Surfacing Materials: Slate*
A bathroom featuring slate surfaces. (Courtesy of Tess Giuliani, CKD – Ridgewood, New Jersey)

Soapstone

Soapstone earns kudos as a countertop for its resistance to chemicals and its appealing matte, smooth finish. One disadvantage: the maximum length of a slab of soapstone is 4' to 6' (1.2192 m to 1.8288 m), whereas granite slabs measure from 8' to 12' (2.4384 m to 3.6576 m) long. As for flooring, a low supply of soapstone has kept prices too high for widespread use.

Unlike granite and marble, soapstone—because it is nonporous—does not require a penetrating sealer. Treat soapstone with mineral oil monthly during the first year to speed the natural oxidation from light gray to a rich dark gray. After a year, clean with a standard household solution. Dents in soapstone can be feathered out with a block and sandpaper.

Figure 7.32 *Surfacing Materials: Soapstone*
A soapstone counter can be combined with a custom soapstone sink. (Courtesy of Vermont Soapstone Company)

343

Figure **7.33** *Surfacing Materials:*
Soapstone
A soapstone top sits on a furniture
type vanity. (Courtesy of Joseph
Giorgi, Jr., CKD – Wilmington,
Delaware)

Terrazzo

An alternative to marble is terrazzo—a combination of marble, concrete, and cement that can be formed into a variety of configurations, such as a countertop with an integral sink.

Terrazzo is a slurry mixture of stone chips consisting of marble and cement. This marble aggregate concrete produces a hard and durable flooring surface. It is also used as a wall treatment.

It is available in field tiles of a more solid nature and decorative border tiles in various patterns and colors to match or contrast with the field tiles. Such a combination can provide a dramatic "old world" look.

Travertine

Travertine begins as limestone, which, over time through geological shifting, has found its way deep in the earth. The porous nature of limestone makes it a great reservoir for liquids. Aquifers, which are enormous underground pools of water that feed our wells, are the remnants of Ice Age melting, which sank and were absorbed by limestone. Heated by the earth's inner core, the water rises as steam and hot pressurized water to form geysers. This rising hot water dissolves the limestone and brings with it granules from below, forming mud beds on the surface. If enough time transpires and the mud beds cool, they will crystallize into solid stone called travertine.

Stone Installation Guidelines

To determine the exact measurements necessary for a countertop, installers first create a template on site—once the base cabinets are in-place—that adjusts for dimensional inconsistencies resulting from the settling of cabinetry and walls. Once the template is complete, a stone fabricator uses it to create the slabs, including the necessary cutouts, such as those for a sink. While most of the cutting and finishing is done at the fabricator's workshop, installers make minor cuts on site for a custom fit. The installers then place slabs together as tightly as possible, pack the joints with epoxy and adhesive, allow it to harden, and sand and buff the joints until they are almost invisible.

For flooring, a qualified installer cuts the tile to precise measurements on the jobsite, makes sure the "lippage"—the difference in face plane between tiles—falls within 1/12th of an inch of "true" (perfectly flat), and shuffles similar colors together to create a uniform appearance.

Although stone is many times heavier than man-made materials, it usually requires no special reinforcement of cabinetry or subflooring. Substrates between the joints and the stone floor, in order of preference according to rigidity, are a mortar, or sand cement bed; a backer board of concrete and ash; and wood.

SLAB VS. TILE

Traditionally, stones are used in large slabs. Suppliers differ on the size and thickness of countertops they stock. Many slabs are available 1-1/4" thick. Other suppliers, however, stock 3/4" thick countertops; some carry 1-1/2" thick slabs. The appearance of a 1-1/2" thick counter can be achieved by joining the 3/4" counter to a 3/4" edge treatment. If pieces are glued together the seam will be noticeable. It is better to offset one 3/4" slab from the second 3/4" slab of stone to minimize the joint seam.

An alternative is 6" x 6", 12" x 12" and 24" x 24" tiles that are installed by a tile setter following specifications developed by the Ceramic Tile Institute.

VINYL RESILIENT FLOORING

Better materials and the manufacturers' ability to improve photographic realism have improved the ability of vinyl to mimic natural materials such as wood, marble, slate, granite and ceramic tile. However, the trend today in vinyl floor patterns is towards graphic simplicity that highlights simple, geometric patterns. Vinyl remains one of the easiest floors to maintain.

Vinyl Sheet

Vinyl sheet flooring is available as "inlaid" (the pattern going throughout the wear layer of vinyl) and as "rotogravure" (the pattern is printed on a sheet). Both are then covered with a layer of wearing surface. The thickness of the wear layer does not affect the durability of the floor or the price. Thick vinyl wear layers resist scuff and stains well, but lose their gloss more quickly than a thinner urethane wear layer which maintains a high-gloss surface better and provides a more scuff-resistant surface.

Vinyl sheet floor coverings range from having no cushion at all to a thick cushion beneath the wear layer. Although the thick cushion increases comfort, the vinyl can be dented by heavy objects.

Vinyl Tile

Solid or pure vinyl tiles are homogeneous vinyl that is unbacked and usually has uniform composition throughout. By far, the biggest seller is vinyl composition tile called "vinyl tile."

Both can be installed on suspended wood subfloors or over on-grade and below-grade concrete. They are durable and easily cleaned. Solid vinyl tiles do not have a wear layer top coat. Vinyl tiles do feature this easy maintenance advantage.

WALLPAPER

Within the kitchen and bathroom industry, a perplexing dilemma continually faces the designer—how to combine style with function. Wallcoverings are often the planner's salvation.

Manufacturing Methods

The patterns in wallcoverings are achieved by using two methods: machine prints and hand prints. In machine printing, all the wallpaper rolls are printed in a continuous "run" and are identical in color. Hand prints are printed by a process called "silk screening" and cannot be matched for color as closely as machine prints because each roll is individually hand-screened with slight color or variations occurring from roll to roll. To protect the hand print edges, the rolls are normally manufactured with selvages (untrimmed edges). A color variation will also occur in grass cloths and similar materials. The fibers from which they are made do not respond evenly to dyes; color gradually lightens or darkens from one edge of a strip to the other, and varies along the length of the roll.

Determining Quantities

The following procedure is suggested to determine wallpaper quantities for papers from American sources, which are based on Imperial sizes and generally have 60 square feet of product on each double roll.

- Measure the width of each wall to be prepared. Round the figure up to the next full foot measurement.

- Add the wall dimensions together.

- Multiply this figure by the ceiling height plus 4". Again, round up the figure to the next full foot measurement.

- Do not subtract the wall space covered by windows, doors and appliances from the total square footage to be covered because the fall-off material must be discarded to maintain the match.

- Depending on the pattern match, divide the actual wall space to be covered as follows:

  18" Repeat   = Divide by 30

  19" to 24" Repeat = Divide by 27

  25" Repeat   = Divide by 24

- Always round up to the next full number of rolls.

For papers which are sized metrically, you can assume 28 to 30 square feet per roll. Therefore, you generally need to order twice the amount of product.

Jobsite Considerations

The finished appearance of the wallcovering can only be as good as the wall surface under it. The walls must be clean and smooth. Although foils are notorious for allowing imperfections to telescope through the covering, all wallcoverings will reveal the surface below them to some extent. The walls must be properly sealed. The correct adhesive must be used.

Always open all rolls and inspect them for color match or defects before any installation begins. Because dye-lots vary, it is important to check the material before installation begins. This same concern prohibits the installation of part of the wallcovering before all the material ordered arrives.

Figure 7.34 *Surfacing Materials: Wallpaper*
Wallpaper sets off the cabinetry in this bath. (Courtesy of MasterBath by RSI)

Figure 7.35 *Surfacing Materials: Wallpaper*
Textured wallpaper is used to duplicate a painter's faux finish technique. (Courtesy of Wellborn Cabinet Inc.)

CHAPTER 8: A Closing Comment

The variety of equipment and materials available for the kitchen and bathroom are extensive. You must have a broad base of knowledge to help you differentiate between the major categories. Learning the material in this volume of the NKBA's Professional Resource Library will help you reach this first plateau of product knowledge.

Once you have mastered this information, concentrate your efforts on learning everything you can about the specific products you represent. Visit the manufacturing facilities of your cabinet equipment and appliance companies. Spend time with your distributor learning all the benefits of a particular brand. Visit with your fabricators and installation experts as well.

Next, commit yourself to faithfully reading the trade journals and attending local, regional and product exhibitions so your bank of product knowledge will be expanded each year you are a practicing kitchen and bathroom designer.

Knowing all that is available is still not enough. You must challenge yourself to creatively combine the products available to you.

LIST OF PHOTOS

LIST OF ILLUSTRATIONS